# Practitioner Series

T0212023

# Springer
*London*
*Berlin*
*Heidelberg*
*New York*
*Barcelona*
*Hong Kong*
*Milan*
*Paris*
*Singapore*
*Tokyo*

## Other titles in this series:

# Åke Grönlund

With contributions from Tuomo Kauranne, Frank Hartkamp, Olov Forsgren, Huberta Kritzenberger and Lars Albinsson

# Managing Electronic Services

## A Public Sector Perspective

 Springer

Åke Grönlund
Department of Informatics, Umeå University, Sweden

Tuomo Kauranne
Arboreal Ltd., Joensuu, Finland

Frank Hartkamp
Novem BV, The Netherlands

Olov Forsgren
Department of Informatics, Umeå University, Sweden

Huberta Kritzenberger
Institute for Multimedia and Interactive Systems,
University of Luebeck, Germany

Lars Albinsson
Maestro Management AB, Stockholm, Sweden

ISSN 1439-9245

ISBN 1-85233-281-6 Springer-Verlag London Berlin Heidelberg

British Library Cataloguing in Publication Data
A catalogue record for this book is available from the British Library

Library of Congress Cataloging-in-Publication Data
Managing electronic services : a public sector perspective / Åke Grönlund ... [et al.].
    p. cm. -- (Practitioner series)
    Includes bibliographical references and index.
    ISBN 1-85233-281-6 (alk. paper)
    1. Telematics. 2. Gateways (Computer networks) 3. (Business enterprises--Computer
networks. I. Grönlund, Åke. II. Practitioner series (Springer-Verlag)
    TK5105.6. E44 2000
    352.3'8214--dc21                                                    00-026561

Typesetting: Ian Kingston Editorial Services, Nottingham
Printed and bound by the Athenæum Press Ltd, Gateshead, Tyne and Wear
34/3830-543210 Printed on acid-free paper SPIN 10759562

# Foreword

The world economy is in rapid transition from the industrial age to the "Information Society". The Information Society is causing fundamental changes, not just in the world of business, but also in the way we all access services as citizens in the future. This means that every European must become increasingly familiar with this new phenomenon surrounding us.

This development poses a challenge to the European public sector, which has played a significant role in creating the European model of an inclusive society. This inclusive model of providing basic services of general interest to every citizen, irrespective of age, ethnic origin or wealth, still enjoys wide support all over Europe.

You have in your hands one of the very first guidebooks ever produced for public organizations endeavouring to embrace electronic service delivery to the citizens. As the authors show, the biggest obstacles in keeping our European services attractive to citizens are not only in technology, but also in the many organizational, psychological and other barriers implicit in our current service delivery structures that are subject to fundamental changes.

This useful guidebook is an excellent sample of the RTD work carried out within the EU funded Telematics Applications Programme (TAP) project, paving the way to the real Citizens' Information Society.

I hope this book will help everyone in charge of developing new telematics services and applications for citizens by showing ways in which other pioneering public service providers have overcome the obstacles and succeeded in providing attractive, effective and user-friendly electronic services not only to their citizens but also to the demanding business communities.

*Commissioner for the Information Society and Enterprise*
*Erkki Liikanen*

# Series Editor's Foreword

Åke Grönlund's book is a timely contribution to the Practitioner Series. It is now *de rigueur* to have a Web site for any organization in the developed world, but the early sites were largely commercial. Commercial sites are different because the public sector does not sell products, and is largely not trying to expand its services. The public sector is interested in information, dissemination to its stakeholders and advancing the "public good". Until now there has been very little literature or support for those tasked with developing a public sector Web site. Until this book, that is.

Grönlund bases his book on the hardest of learning approaches, pioneering in the activity. He discovered, as he explains in his Preface, that what seems at first sight to be a technical problem, turns out to be a socio-economic-political problem. And the latter appears to take up 90% of the development time – Grönlund's iceberg effect. During his pioneering work, Grönlund started to identify some similarities in the problems he was addressing, and these he has structured into 12 challenges that any other developer might also have to face. These challenges become the basis for conducting the book dialogue, with a challenge being covered in each of the first 12 chapters, and with Part 1 drawing conclusions about the necessity for addressing all of the challenges.

Electronic Service Management is the label Grönlund has elected to put on his distilled expertise. The title neatly encapsulates the need of the public sector in general to manage all the services it provides, and to use technology to support this activity electronically. The advent of portals means that a city (a dominant public authority in its own area) is often in a good position to create a local digital economy around a local portal. This book tells you how to go about this.

The three chapters in Part 2 provide a more classical description of what to consider when undertaking the development of an electronic service management system for the public sector. I hope readers find, as I did, that the two parts of the book complement and compliment each other perfectly. There are many more discoveries, lessons, novelties etc. to be discovered in this book, but I shall not spoil the pleasure of uncovering them for yourself.

*Ray Paul*

# Preface

The idea of writing this book appeared after participating in several projects developing Web services in situations in which public sector organizations were involved in some part. It became ever more clear to us that managing telematic services in a city (or local government - see footnote for further explanation)[1] is a more complicated business than it is in a manufacturing company. The technical problems, typically regarded initially as the most prominent, are in fact the easiest part to deal with. Experience from all of the projects that we have participated in clearly shows that in order to become successful providers of electronic services, cities must consciously, and in an integrated manner, deal with the "iceberg syndrome". This means that several other more complicated problems are "submerged" beneath the obvious technical work required. Typically, only 10% of the problems are immediately visible, and that part is not representative. Just as you do not see the dangerous part of a real iceberg – it is wider below the surface – the technical issues that are most immediately visible to managers of electronic service projects are not those that will require the most attention. The more complicated problems of electronic service provision include issues of users' needs and behaviour, economic viability, a simultaneous need to revise the organization, and psychological and legal barriers (Fig. 1).

It is clear that there is a need to deal with these issues in a comprehensive and integrated manner. This is true in every organization, but in many ways the problems are more complicated in a city, because the products are many and very diverse, and the organization is run according to political as well as business considerations. Therefore an "Electronic Service Manager" entity, integrating knowledge about user, organizational, economic and technical issues (Fig. 2), is necessary. Depending on the local context, this publishing function may be delegated to a business, outsourced or "in-sourced" (city-owned), or organized as a cross-department committee within a city.

We have seen that electronic services projects everywhere have gone through similar problems. Projects start off as technical ventures, and insights that the other pieces of the puzzle also have to be dealt with develop slowly, if at all. Along the way, new decisions constantly have to be made, and projects move on to new paths. The changes that become necessary seem to appear as

---

1 The word "city" is used throughout the book to mean an independent local government body with responsibility for local public sector services such as schools, social services, street cleaning and local transportation.

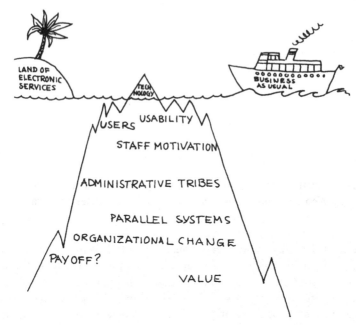

**Fig. 1** An electronic services project is like an iceberg – the technological obstacles are visible, while those related to use, users and organizational change are typically harder to detect.

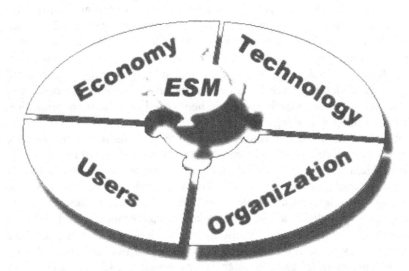

**Fig. 2** An ESM (Electronic Service Manager) is an organization that integrates the development of electronic services across multiple information and service providers, drawing on four distinct types of expertise.

surprises everywhere. This typically means that the really important issues are never dealt with, as they are only seen just as the project period is about to end.

Because of the apparent need to take a firm grip on the development of electronic services, we decided to write our experiences down in a book for others to use as a guide on the long road towards professional electronic service provision. It is a long road, no matter how well prepared you are. This book can help make it shorter and easier, because the problems to come will be more easily foreseen and ideas for solutions can be considered well in advance and in the light of experiences made by others. Even so, it is up to the skilled entrepreneur to make it happen in each city.

The book presents a 12-stage model of the road towards proficient electronic service management. We identify 12 challenges that have to be met. The stages are qualitatively different, and passing each of them requires a new focus, specific decisions and new approaches based on new insights. Without such responses, an electronic services project will soon find that it has a hard time justifying its existence. Sometimes these decisions are made without much controversy, but often they require much thought and discussion, and the issues take a long time to be settled. In this book, we analyze the nature of the challenges and suggest experience-based ways of meeting them.

We have gone to some effort to write the book in an easy-to-read style. There is a recurring theme, the story of what happens as the imaginary city of Tapville[2] makes its way from launching its first home page to becoming a proficient Electronic Service Manager (an organization skilfully managing a great number of electronic services from several providers). The theme is interleaved with analyses of the major events along the road. The purpose of writing in a "soap" style is to make it possible to reveal interesting discussions without jeopardizing people's privacy. The soaps are all true stories, but they have been camouflaged so as to provide anonymity for the people who have helped us in providing the kind of inside view of events that give valuable insights to others engaging in the same kind of projects. For the same reasons, in the cases included the cities appear under pseudonyms.

The book can thus be read at two levels: by following the *soap thread*, the reader will encounter the difficulties appearing and solutions applied along the road on a personal level. Scenes and situations from the reader's own city will be recognized, and people will be able to identify with the characters of the soap. By following the *analysis thread*, the problems encountered will be seen in the light of experiences from different cities as well as that of scientific knowledge concerning the problems pertinent to electronic service management, such as human–computer interaction, Web site usability, and evaluation of the economics of information systems.

## Who Should Read this Book?

The book is primarily targeted towards practitioners, politicians and decision makers in cities or other government bodies, with a local or regional basis, who want to develop electronic services or to improve existing systems. We expect

---

2   The name Tapville refers to the TAP, the EU Telematic Applications Programme within the fourth framework programme, during which much of the experience that makes up the empirical basis of, and the inspiration for, this book was gained.

that the most central target audience for the book is middle managers in local administration, such as heads of IT, PR and economics, deputy mayors in charge of similar matters, and project managers in related fields. In addition, consultants doing business with the above would be well advised to read it.

Electronic services are not new; they abound. This is particularly true on the Internet, which is now emerging as the most prominent medium for electronic services in Europe. There exist many experiences from commercial use of the medium. Many of those experiences are general and also apply to cities. There are, however, special requirements for public sector services that make a case for focusing on cities. Examples include the following:

- The public sector must provide a basic set of services to *all* citizens, which means that they have to be provided on a non-commercial basis; cities are often producers of such services, and even if others are producers, services will have to be paid for by tax money.
- Cities are diverse organizations; much more so than manufacturing companies. Products range from road construction and building regulation to schools and social services. Therefore the process of becoming a professional electronic service provider is quite different.
- Cities are often the focus of local culture. This means that services may have to be designed in line with, or adjustable to, local standards.
- Cities, perhaps especially so in rural areas, play a role in promoting local (small) business. This means that commercial ESMs may prove inappropriate for many reasons: they allow only exclusive rights, they carry high costs, and they have a global focus only and lack local/regional legitimacy.

These arguments have different weights in different countries, but cities play a central role in the public sector everywhere in Western society, being the largest governmental unit, and the one that is closest to the citizens, both in geographical terms and in terms of community. Cities, as large providers of services and as the most important government entity in most people's lives, are called upon to develop working standards of how information technology is to be used. This means that electronic service management must be considered as an important building block of the city of tomorrow.

# Acknowledgements

A number of people have contributed to this book by taking the time to discuss applications and what happened during the conception, planning, development and implementation of Web information systems and an electronic service infrastructure in their organization, and to comment on draft versions of this book. In particular, we want to mention the following:

Robert deBeukelaer (Informatik Centrum Antwerp), Michel Betuing and Alain Filloux (City of Nice), Uwe Schmalfeldt, Christa Standecker and Helmut Buescher (City of Nuremberg), Frank van Vliet (PIR, Rotterdam City Development Corporation), Sapfo Kloura and Nicolas Tsamopoulos (Municipality of Amaroussion), Hans Forster and Torsten Grötz (Municipality of Vienna), Emmanuel Richert (City of Strasburg), Ton Schijvenaars (Cap Gemini Inc.), Kurt Meulemans (City of Antwerp), Ludwig Hitzenberger (University of Regensburg), Carl-Öije Segerlund (Swedish National Institute for Distance Education (SSVH), Härnösand), Jerker Sjögren (City of Stockholm and Telia Inc.), Jan Olovsson (City of Umeå), Leif Rydén (Kista District Administration, Stockholm), Monica Berneström and Per Jundin (City of Stockholm), Hans Lindgren (IT Blekinge), Madeleine Siösteen-Thiel (Swedish Board of Technical and Regional Development), Tuula Piirainen (City of Joensuu), Kari Alvila (City of Joensuu), and Olli Kurppa (PKO).

The drawings were made by Ragnhild Blomdahl of Kreti&Pleti HB, Sollentuna, Sweden.

Thank you!

# Contents

# Introduction

During the past few years, many cities have followed companies in setting up "home pages" on the Internet. The number of cities currently on the Web is hard to determine, because it changes so rapidly that any figure would be out of date by the time it was published. Just to give a hint, in September 1998, "over a thousand towns and cities in the US have home pages on the Web" (Tsagarousianou *et al.*, 1998, p. 1). In Sweden, in October 1998, the figure was 289 (SUNET, 1998) – and that is the total number of cities in Sweden. They are all on the Web, even the smallest ones with only 4000–5000 inhabitants.

Already many of these home pages have developed into complete services, and many more cities plan to develop, or are in the process of developing, their Web pages into such service systems.

## Electronic Services Are Here to Stay

The idea of providing information and services electronically is not new. Teletext has been available via the cable TV system for many years in many countries, although the French Minitel is the most prominent example. However, it is the popular use of the Internet since the mid-1990s that have raised the significance of electronic services to an all-time high level. Both business and government are now present on the Web. Cities that have started to develop services on the Web have, however, experienced some problems. Rapid changes in technology have made it hard to determine what the most viable technical solutions are, which in many cases has led to repeated and profound change, disturbing production processes and confusing or annoying staff. Uncertainty about the pace of penetration of Internet use in the home has made estimates of the return on investment a matter of guesswork. Conversely, a surprisingly rapid increase in use has often turned what was at first a small technology project into a major organizational one. In many cities, projects have led to detailed discussions about what the business of a city really is, what services it should provide and how. Relations with citizens as well as with businesses are being reconsidered.

The book deals with the whole spectrum of issues pertaining to electronic services: usability, usefulness, organization, business opportunities, economic assessment and technology.

The book will help cities enter the Communication Age by providing advice and experience about how to make good use of the electronic medium, focusing particularly on the public sector environment. It suggests good examples of how to reorganize city departments, re-engineer procedures, make city processes more efficient and cost-effective, and – most importantly – provide better services.

## Cities Are Diverse Organizations, Which Makes the Road to Electronic Services Complicated

It is typically much more difficult for a city to provide services electronically than for a company. A city is the hub of many processes: it regulates land use and citizen behaviour, it runs businesses such as housing companies and power companies, it is a political organization managing public debates, it is often an important player in local culture by sponsoring or owning cultural arenas like municipal libraries and museums, and so on. Its products are diverse and often complex, and its services involve not only economic considerations, but also many other things, such as legal regulation and democratic aspects of citizen influence, equality, universal access and so on. Often the "services" are mandatory and experienced as trouble rather than a service.

Although cities have different obligations and mandates in different countries, everywhere they are at the centre of many activities of very different character.

This book focuses on electronic communication between cities and citizens: service design, service delivery, service use and responses to services. How can good services be provided? What is the proper design of electronic services? What makes people use them and how are they used now? How can cities provide for democratic interaction at the same time as economic necessities urge more effective production flows and technology offers the tool of automation? How should users' requirements and wishes best be met? And how can cities use these new ways of organizing the information and communication flow between their departments and their inhabitants?

Cities, as legislators and policymakers, as service providers and as helpers for inhabitants, have always used the same communication channels as the people they are meant to serve. When print technology was first introduced, cities started printing information. When the telegraph and later the telephone were introduced, cities telegraphed and were connected to telephone networks. Today, the fax and telephone voice-menu services comprise the common denominator technology. Today, new information technology is giving cities powerful new tools, but it is not at all clear how to best make use of them.

## Electronic Services Make Sense Only When Managed Skilfully

This book suggests how cities can best make use of information and communication technologies (ICT) for electronic services and client-organization interaction. Depending on what services a city offers, the optimal choice of electronic services must ensure that processes become well integrated into everyday routines, that people become focused, and that the organization of society covers new ground. Cities provide services for different purposes: to reduce costs, implement new procedures, improve decision making, reach their citizens, educate people, make savings, enrich the quality of life, and so on.

The use of information technology by cities will only be profitable if it is done properly. It is very easy for ICT to simply add to costs and provide little benefit. The rapidly developing hardware and software possibilities, the growth of information services, the difficulties in successfully addressing users' needs, and many other factors influence the effective use of ICT. In other words, to make good use of information technology, there are a number of considerations to take into account. In most cities, the technical concerns are much more professionally addressed than are those pertaining to use and users. One contribution of this book, therefore, is that it addresses the latter kind of issues in some detail.

## The Road Is Long, But Some Are Walking Ahead

This book offers a systematic approach to developing and implementing public information systems and services. The experiences were gathered mainly from the public sector, and mainly from cities in several European countries, during different projects ranging over a period of six years, starting in 1994. During this period, the cities, especially those who were early starters, early on adopted ICT as a tool in their everyday operations.

The organizations we have studied together offer hundreds of services to their citizens and provide good material for examples to share with you. This book describes the situations that occurred and solutions that were chosen, and the considerations and discussions of how to overcome the problems and deal with the results of the actions chosen. Some general developments can be seen over the period: from information to services, from public services to public–private partnership models, from single services to portals – gateways to services – and service bundling, to name only the most prominent.

Most people have recognized these developments, but the devil is in the detail. Therefore the most important things to learn from this book are the experiences of all the hurdles that you will encounter and the stories of how people in different organizations tried to overcome them.

## Prepare for "Challenge Management"

We present a "12 challenges" model for the development of these services. At each challenge – a stage in the development – there are certain decisions that have to be made in order to make further development possible. The term "challenge" is then used to mean encountering a situation for which previous experience cannot account; hence the organization is forced to figure out new ways of action. These decisions may be taken more or less easily in different cities. Often they take an unnecessarily long time because the problems were not foreseen. For each challenge, there are several cities in which the problems have reached crisis level in that they have forced painful reorganizations and course changes to be undertaken.

In some cases, the problems have even caused Web service development to stop altogether. There are examples of cities that never got beyond the "1000 pages challenge". There are examples of cities that experienced the result of a usability test as a big shock because they had never thought about people using their system, only about how to put the information on the Web. And there are examples of cities that experienced serious internal convulsions when it turned out – or even when the very possibility was considered – that some staff would become redundant when customers start using self-service facilities.

The problems and solutions described in the book have typical symptoms, processes and structural causes which appear everywhere, albeit possibly different in the details. The candidate Electronic Service Manager must learn to be aware of the nature of the problems and of the possible ways of dealing with them. Therefore in the first part of the book we consider them one by one. We describe the nature of the problems, we analyze them, and we present some solutions. To be sure, the solutions more often than not are not straight-forward. In many cases, cities that have taken an alternative directions have also succeeded. For this reason, the solutions should be read as inspirational stories; it is an advantage to know how others have approached a problem, but the solution in each city must be tailored to the local conditions: physical, organizational, cultural and psychological.

The cities that have embarked on the journey towards electronic service management have found that more important than the unavoidable, omnipresent public discussions of hardware and software are the strategic discussions. Since it is impossible to make accurate predictions of the economic outcome of electronic services, they have to be justified in other terms. One thing we have found in our evaluations is that investment in electronic services is internally defended in strategic terms only. Therefore in each city there is a strategic/political debate going on between people with different views of the future development and of the role of the city in that development. In order to get anywhere on the road towards electronic service management you must be able to manage this debate.

In the soap part of this book, we have highlighted some of the arguments most often used by the different proponents and opponents of electronic services, much as is typically done in a soap opera. We found the soap opera to be the most appropriate form in which to detail problems and discussions. It provides an opportunity to reveal the subtleties of discussions without embarrassing people who worked very hard to find solutions to the various challenges, but who did not always manage to get things going the way they intended.

This book, then, is what you need to prepare your arguments and stay cool throughout while managing your way along the long journey towards profi-cient electronic service management. And, while perhaps not being able to avoid the challenges altogether, you will at least be able to foresee them and make precautions so as to reduce the impact.

## About the Structure of this Book

For the sake of making the book easy to read, we have structured it in a linear fashion. We present "the road to electronic service management" as though it were *one* road, the same in every case and with new challenges popping up one after another in the same shape and the same order everywhere. Of course, this is not the complete story. The challenges do not necessarily appear in the order in which we have presented them (although by and large they in fact do). It may happen that several problems appear simultaneously. Further, some of them may not be experienced as very problematic at all, but rather as just a number of things to keep in mind when you design services; the level of trouble caused by a certain challenge varies depending on the local context.

This book contains a lot of material, and covers many issues pertaining to electronic services. Although there are good reasons for reading the whole book, it is not necessary to start by reading it from the first page to the last. It makes good sense to read it in parts, and the following is a guide to how to do that. But be warned: although the need to read about a certain challenge will certainly appear most urgent once you're involved in it, our basic advice is that the best thing to do is to read about it in advance.

Part 1 contains 12 chapters, each describing one challenge. Although it is sometimes necessary to refer to previous chapters, especially the soap opera sections, each chapter gives a picture of that particular challenge independently of the other chapters. Thus it is not necessary to start from the beginning. The reader who for some reason feels a certain challenge is most interesting may well start there. Because the challenges typically appear in the same order as the chapters of the book, cities at the beginning of their work with electronic services may be most immediately interested in the early chapters, while the later chapters will become interesting as services develop. The way to go would in that case be to read the executive summary and then select the challenges that bare most immediately on the local situation.

Part 2 describes the field of electronic service management more theoretically. The reader who wants a quick guide to what to do and where to start is well advised to start by reading this part, and then to read the chapters from Part 1 as illustrations and explanations of the advice given in Part 2 as the need becomes apparent.

## Executive Summary of the 12 Challenges Model

The road towards professional electronic service management can be seen as a 12-hurdle track that every organization aiming at truly interactive and integrated (in internal systems and operations) services must run along. Those stopping at static information or interactive information only will be able to skip a few steps.

In short, the challenges are the following:

1. "Start-up... of what?" (initial motivations differ from final)
2. "Thousands of pages..." (institutionalization of production)
3. Messy appearance (graphical design, Web organization)
4. Parallel systems (how to phase out old routines)
5. Choice of future technical platform (what *is* this thing we need?)
6. Cross-departmental integration of data resources (resources often locked up)
7. Staff motivation (electronic services mean genuine changes, typically frightening, in people's jobs)
8. Poor usability (slow adaptation to usability standards)
9. Where is the payoff? (how to measure costs and benefits)
10. From monopoly to service provider (organization faces a role change)
11. Where are the users? (how to make a system useful)
12. "Administrative tribal struggles" (social groups and "their" domains)

Let us explain these in a little more detail.

## Challenge 1: Start-up... of What? Arriving at Common Goals for Electronic Services

Cities enter the Internet *en masse*, but often with unclear motives. They are there largely because others are there. Indeed, their motives do not appear altogether clear. Why should a city be present on the Web? What goals can there be for now, for the near future, and for the long term? Web systems are typically set up initially by some enthusiast(s) and funded by project money, which means they do not necessarily outlive the project. Typically, projects promise lavishly, get a lot of press, and interfere in the work of others, making not only friends but also enemies. This challenge is only met when the decision makers in a city agree on some common, realistic and reasonably well-defined goal for their Web system.

## Challenge 2: Thousands of Pages – From Project to Organization

When the city's Web project is launched, it is typically done in the form of a project. When the project is over, pages are published but there is no special budget allocated to further Web-related work. Initially, work is typically carried out as a marginal low-cost activity by students, people hired with unemployment support or other types of cheap labour. The task of maintaining all the pages quickly overwhelms the small team of active staff. As a result, a "Web-responsible" person is identified in each department and charged with the task of overseeing the accuracy of the information pertaining to that department. An additional problem is that Web technology develops and cities have to keep up (frames, JavaScript etc.) so as not to appear old-fashioned. Further, demands for information and services increase, and there appears to be a need for automation and integration with existing computer systems.

Web maintenance has to be rationally organized somehow. This chapter describes various ways to do that.

## Challenge 3: Messy Appearance – Organize the Usability Improvement Process

Typically, as systems grow large and acquire multiple information providers, the responsibility for information provision and updating is delegated. This results in the different departments all wanting to do things their way, and having, or purchasing, the skills to do so. A coordination problem arises: top management wants the organization to appear in a coherent and stylish form on the Web, following a corporate profile. A public relations agency is brought in to implement a "graphic profile". This may interfere with work already done, as well as with the different intentions of different departments.

In addition, there is more to a mess than just its appearance. Information systems do not succeed by good looks alone - usability and usefulness are more important. A nice graphic profile may do some good for usability, but it cannot conceal poor organization of the information in the underlying system or poor data quality.

## Challenge 4: Parallel Systems – Use Electronic Services Only When You Need Them

By now, the PR agency or the internal working group has made the system look nice. Content is produced efficiently, and at least some people use the services. But all the manual operations are still in place and run just as they did before. The Web system has not replaced anything. The first cost challenge then arises: "Why is there no process re-engineering? When banks introduced automated teller machines, this led to fewer customers entering their offices. The result was substantial cost savings in those offices. Why does this not happen with our City Electronic Services?".

Re-engineering does not happen automatically. The conservative forces in an organization are typically stronger than those striving for innovation. Determined measures must be taken. And even when this is done, changes take time, and often must be allowed to take time.

## Challenge 5: Choosing the Future Technical Platform – Look Back, Look Aside, Look Ahead

For the electronic services entrepreneur, there are a number of technological, or at least technology-related, choices to make in order to avoid drastic changes in the future – which database? Which Web platform? There is also the problem of integration of legacy systems. Nobody can give a definite answer to these questions – only "educated guesses". Factors to consider are the intended distribution channels (the Internet, kiosks, TV, mobile devices), legacy systems (do they have Web extensions?), the competence of city IT staff or available contractors, the desired functionality (static, dynamic, interactive, communicative?), and the cost of hardware and software (not forgetting the cost of building and maintaining the applications, which often exceeds the acquisition cost). How stable is the platform chosen and how likely is the provider to stay in business? What is the future of a particular technology: are you about to choose a technology, based on an established technology and provider, that will soon be rendered obsolete?

Discussions of the above questions cannot be left to a Web project; the city must look beyond each project. Most telematic development projects will not meet their deadlines and they will need to run for many years in order to recoup their costs. The technology chosen should allow immediate implementation, and yet be stable enough to allow ongoing operational and development work for up to five years or more to come.

## Challenge 6: Cross-Departmental Integration of Data Resources – Don't Lock Up Your Resources

Cities that have come this far are likely to have produced working services in several departments. As the services grow, it becomes clear to service producers that it would be useful to have access to some data possessed by other city departments. For instance, tourist information could be better presented by using maps. Maps can be manufactured anew, but they often already exist in the form of GIS systems, typically owned by the city planning office or the like. Also, tourist information systems might want to expand into providing booking services. Cities may have computerized booking services for sports facilities, for instance, but those are not owned by the tourist office.

There appears to be a need for cooperation, or at least ways of sharing or co-using each other's data. How can this be achieved? In practice, the answer depends a lot on what legacy systems there are, but also on how far the different departments have come towards electronic service management. Those who have come this far are likely to want to pursue their way of doing things (which is often by "old" technology, such as the 1000-page way of doing it). Those who have not progressed so far are typically more likely to try new ideas. Neither is willing to become subordinate to the other.

This problem often arises from history. In many cases, however, problems of this kind are created by departmental reforms, internal trade regulations and so on.

This challenge can only be met by different departments agreeing on common goals in the field of electronic services. This typically requires a coordination committee mediating between the different local entrepreneurs. It also requires substantial knowledge and vision in the technological field; pure mediation may well lead to old technology prevailing.

## Challenge 7: Staff Motivation – Enrol the Staff in Your Team

When true operational Web services come to be suggested, the staff involved realize that this will affect their role as service providers. Some see a significant decrease in their income. Even more people are afraid of becoming redundant. Others simply fear losing some of their authority through not being the only ones in possession of certain types of information. This challenge can only be met if a serious discussion of the professionals' role in the new, more technologically equipped, organization is undertaken with those involved.

## Challenge 8: Poor Usability – Let the Users Be Your Guide

A low level of system use may be related to the way in which systems are designed: users simply get lost, they do not realize what a system contains, they get tired of searching in a poorly organized system, and so on. While many such problems are often easily discovered by relatively simple usability tests, very few cities have, until this stage, tried this. When they do, they often receive a big shock.

At this stage (which is actually long overdue…), service providers will have to learn about their users. Who are the people that will use your electronic services? What knowledge do they have and what do they *not* have? In what situations do they use your system? What do they look for? How do they look? These are examples of the questions that a service provider needs to answer in order to be able to design services properly. For each particular service there may certainly be special conditions, but for public services in general there are a few important facts that make a difference. This chapter discusses some usability fundamentals and gives examples from several Web site tests.

## Challenge 9: Where is the Payoff? Some Benefits Come Later

Electronic services can be delivered over many different channels, but the highest hopes and expectations have undoubtedly been placed on the Internet. Business on the Internet is a much hyped phenomenon that often falls short of expectations for private and public service providers alike. "Return on investment" is mostly stated in strategic rather than monetary terms.

There are many potential reasons for failure: that there are not enough users of a given service with access to the Internet; that the users cannot find the service; that you cannot have a service that costs money on the Internet, because the whole concept teaches users to expect all Internet content to be free; and so forth.

Most potential Internet service providers find the economic assessment of their services a daunting task. The number of uncertain factors involved defies sound financial analysis. It is helpful to look at the problem first from a variety of different angles.

Internet-based services cost money to start up. Cities have to invest in hardware, time, hiring experts, updating the skills of employees, and designing software and applications. In short, cities have to invest a lot. When does it pay back? Will it pay back? What will be the return on investment and how can we estimate this?

Many different kinds of pay-off may be expected: better served citizens; strategic advantages; better market/citizen communication; corporate profile; lower costs due to more self-service; and so on. In this chapter, we discuss the ways in which different cities look upon the "payback". We also discuss economic realities of the Internet, as well as the inability of many cities to realize rationalization gains.

## Challenge 10: What is Our Role? From Monopoly to Service Provider

Many cities do not realize that they act in a competitive environment. In many countries, private companies or public–private partnerships are taking over services previously considered exclusively public sector business. The Web is likely to contribute to accelerating this process, because services from alternative providers in many such areas are easier to find.

City organizations and staff are used to working in a monopoly environment. They are not used to thinking about what users look for, how they look and so on. This chapter therefore introduces a simple model for the behaviour of users having a problem looking for a solution. Cases include cities' responses, or lack of response, to the competitive environment, as well as interior pictures of how discussions about service provision are conducted in the cities – how cities perceive their service users.

This challenge has two implications. The first is that the city finds its role. Different cities work in different contexts, and may assume different roles; not every city needs to provide every possible service. The other implication is that service quality is most important.

What should be private, public or public–private joint endeavours is a political issue, and consequently is not the concern of this book.

## Challenge 11: Where Are the Users? Users Want Your Service, Not Your System

In many cities, people ask themselves the following question about their Web systems: "There is not much use yet – when will it come?".

This chapter discusses this problem at two levels: a macro level concerning business structure, and a micro level concerning system usefulness for users.

*The macro level discussion*: Europe's media chain is missing a couple of crucial links. There needs to be an interesting mix of local content; the services must be packaged in an interesting way by a service provider; and people need to be able to access them at high speed, via the Internet. The problem in Europe is that cities are not concentrating on finding and packaging local content, one of the crucial catalysts for getting people online.

So far, there is no equivalent of a book publisher or television or film distributor for the emerging online services.

*The micro level discussion*: A system must be useful for the users. This may seem a truism, but history proves that usefulness is often not considered. Many people see it as a great accomplishment to have produced a city Web system. But what has really been achieved by that? Your Web system may be beautifully designed, interactive, fast and so on, but what *use* do the inhabitants of your city make of it? Your system competes with other media. The interactions between your city's agencies and its inhabitants have so far been managed by the use of other media. Users will go on using these media until they find that your new system is more useful to them than the other available media. This can happen in a number of ways, most of which are not automatic.

## Challenge 12: Managing Administrative Tribes – Projects Don't Fail Because of Too Many Enemies But Because of Too Few Friends

As human beings, we have only recently emerged from a tribal existence. Loyalty to your clan was the leading guarantee of human survival for thousands of years. This legacy sits deep within our subconscious, and is the source of much of the excitement, but also antagonism, at work.

One of the principal problems of modern society is the difficulty of identifying a tribe to belong to. We feel many sympathies and loyalties, and thereby identify ourselves with many different "tribes" of like-minded people. However, it is not uncommon that our various tribes end up in conflict among themselves. In such a situation, our loyalties are torn and we are forced to take sides, often against our will. Any significant perturbation in the working environment is likely to provoke a tribal challenge – and there are few other perturbations as potentially controversial as the process of replacing manual service patterns by electronic ones.

The stated goals and business practices of many professional organizations are widely disparate. As professionals, cardiologists do their best to help seriously ill people to attain an acceptable quality of life. More cardiologists should therefore imply better care for the ill. As a professional community, they try to protect the uniqueness and appreciation of their expert skills, which are both connected to the level of compensation that the community's members receive, by limiting access to the cardiology community.

Municipalities may openly wish to serve their members efficiently and well, always seeking ways of improving their service and cutting unnecessary costs. As a professional community, however, city officials do not want to rationalize away city jobs. Cities are reluctant to shed jobs because that would decrease state subsidy to the city, as well as its relative economic importance in a region. Shedding jobs might also aggravate a city's financial position by pushing former employees into the ranks of the unemployed.

In both of the above situations, members of the corresponding "professional clans" are torn between their loyalties to their explicit professional mission and to their professional community.

Introducing electronic services amounts to changing established service patterns. The professional staff influenced by such a perturbation will be divided by their tribal loyalty. If the tribal chief or council concludes that such services will do more harm than benefit to the tribal community, the electronic service will prove to be very cumbersome and awkward to use, and definitely too immature to be seriously considered for operational adoption.

# Part 1

## *The Story of the Dozen Challenges*

# 1. Challenge 1: Start-up... of What? Arriving at Common Goals for Electronic Services

*"Faster, more effective, more fun, cheaper..."*

Cities enter the Internet *en masse*, but often with unclear motives, or motives that have little to do with professional management of electronic services. They are there largely because others are there. Indeed, their motives do not appear altogether clear. Why should a city be present on the Web? What goals can there be for now, for the near future, and for the long term? Web systems are typically set up initially by some enthusiast(s) and funded by project money, which means they do not necessarily outlive the project. Typically, projects promise lavishly, get a lot of press, and interfere in the work of others, making not only friends but also enemies.

## The Symptoms

The basic symptom of this challenge is that Web projects start without a clear plan reaching beyond the immediate project period.

At some time, the development of Web Information Systems (WIS) starts. Originally (in the early Internet days of 1994–95), this happened as a small project. Today, Web development is more often part of a larger plan, albeit not always very completely designed in advance. We could have called this chapter "The zero pages problem", hinting at the often encountered problem of making anything at all happen. Or "The blind leading the blind problem", emphasizing the fact that often a general Internet popularity boom rather than well-conceived local plans guides the development. Or we could have called it "The focus problem", stressing the fact that it is really not easy for a city to make judicious plans for a WIS as a part of its overall infrastructure plans, its public relations plan, its financial plan, its plan for the schools system etc. The problem of how to start up is of course less of a problem than that of knowing what the purpose of the final product should be. Most cities – still – do not have IT strategies in which WIS can be easily integrated other than on a technical basis (which computers to buy, that databases should be SQL-compatible etc.). As for use, uncertainty is great in most places, and for good reasons. It is hard to know how WIS should be used for self-service to facilitate citizen access and make operations cheaper when there are no plans for, or experiences of, self-service. It is hard to know how WIS can be used for education when there is little experience and when teachers are not educated or experienced in using the medium.

Cities are complex organizations. They have many different tasks, reaching from simple services to complex exertion of authority, and a lot of different goals related to economics, public service, democracy etc.

In this chapter, we leave until later the wider goals and focus on what typically happens when a "Web project" starts. We show how the big questions are typically left for later, and the project often starts in an *ad hoc* way, which later makes it less than obvious how it can be integrated with other threads of development in the city.

## *Soap*: The World Wide Web Enters Tapville

It was only 7:30 on the morning of Monday 2 March 1994, but the sun was already warming Tapville as William W. Westmark, W3 to his friends, hurried along Hurdle Street. He was on his way to a meeting with the mayor and his council. It was the monthly "creativity" meeting, which the mayor held every first Monday of the month with his top managers, and to which people who claimed, or were reputed, to have good ideas were often invited. Bill was such a person. He had managed to invite himself to the meeting because he knew the manager of personnel in person, and because he himself worked in the computer department. Since computers were a totem of the time, anything that smelled of computers usually worked well as a door opener. Also, there were many red figures in the city's books, and managers tended to look desperately for new ideas (which was, by the way, one reason for at least some of the red figures. One example was the recently opened company bottling water for export, which was going to export "the cleanest water in the world" in one-litre bottles to people in major cities worldwide. It survived only six months).

At the meeting, Bill was going to introduce a new idea, which he had learned about only a month ago when he visited a friend who worked in another city, Aheadofyou. The friend, who was a computer programmer, had shown him the World Wide Web. Bill had seen images from remote cities in the USA appear on the screen within a few seconds at a single touch of a button. He had also been shown a presentation his friend had made about his town.

Bill was very excited today. Actually, he had been so for the whole month. At the very moment of his friend's presentation, he had, as though struck by a divine flash of enlightenment, realized the immense opportunities that the new technology opened up for his little city. Today he was going to present his idea to the most important people in the city. He was up early, because he wanted to go through his slides again before the meeting.

The meeting started at 9:30 with coffee. The discussions were a bit serious; people's spirits were a bit low. Unemployment had risen all over the country for a couple of years. Tapville had not suffered so much at first, but since last year, after a military training camp closed and a major supplier to a car manufacturer moved to another city because EU transportation subsidies had been renegotiated and lost, Tapville was also in big trouble. This was the starting point for W3's brilliant idea.

He started his presentation by showing some screenshots his friend had produced for him from his computer – Blacksburg, USA, the White House homepage, and the Aheadofyou demo. There was no reaction in the room. People looked at the screen, but said nothing. Finally, the mayor said, "Well, we don't have a White House to show off anyway", and everybody laughed, as they tended to do when the mayor made a joke.

"Soon every city will be on the Web", tried Bill.

"For what?" asked the mayor.

"For letting the world know they're around. For attracting new companies. For attracting tourists. For communicating with citizens. Because it is the new way of living, electronic communication", said Bill.

"We already have a brochure. We have a department for maintaining business contacts. We have a tourist office. And we have the newspapers that report from our city council meetings. And we have economic difficulties. And we have our traditional lifestyle and our quality of life. Why should we spend money on some high-tech toys for rich boys?"

Heads were nodding. Everyone knew the mayor was right – they all felt the same.

"You are not going to *spend* money. You will *get* money for doing it", said Bill.

"Oh yeah? Why would anyone give us money for playing with computers?" There was some tension in the room by now. All expected that the mayor's question would mean the final defeat of Bill's presentation to the real-world environment. Yet another invited self-appointed Tapville saviour would soon leave the room, never to return.

"Not give you money directly, but as an effect. Look here. To set up a system like this you need a computer, which we have. You need a cable connection, which the university has. You need some people to do the job. We have 11% unemployment, so that's one thing we do not lack. Now, this is how to do it: we set up a course in Web design in cooperation with the university. This will give us free access to their computer network. We then offer the course to the government unemployment office. They will then give us students, and pay us money for giving the course. They will, in fact, also thank us, because they have trouble finding proper education for the unemployed anyway. I will be the teacher, because I have learnt from my friend in Aheadofyou how to do it. So it won't cost us. The students will produce our system for free; it will be their compulsory assignment to convert our brochures, city council minutes and so on to Web format. Their pay will be their degrees, which will give them good jobs, because soon, everybody will want systems like this, and these guys will be among the first to know how to do it. When they get jobs, they will pay us more taxes than they do as unemployed.

"And what's more, soon – within a year – other cities will envy us. We can charge everyone consultation fees to go to their conferences and tell them how we did it. And we'll have a burgeoning business going: Web design. We may sell our knowledge to other cities. Build systems for them."

"By how many people can you reduce unemployment?" asked the manager of social services.

"Let me make a humble start with 25", said Bill. "That's enough for one class, and at least a few of them are bound to be good. Later, when we've got the thing rolling, we can expand. If we play our cards right, in a few years a couple of hundred will be in education instead of in the ranks of the unemployed."

The mayor smiled. Now, this guy was really something! At last someone with a creative idea about how to reduce unemployment. The other people saw that the mayor smiled, so they too smiled. They realized Bill had won, and they thought, "Why didn't *I* come up with this idea?".

"Shoot", said the mayor. "What are you waiting for?"

It took only one semester, four months, to set up the first Tapville Web system, and during the second semester it grew to comprise 2850 HTML pages. Most of the city's information material, tourist maps and so on were now on show on the Web. Bill showed the system to his friend in Aheadofyou, who sighed with envy. He still only had his prototype, having been unable to talk his city management into sponsoring the idea. When he heard about how Bill had done it, he immediately hired him for a one-day conference, during which he would help him persuade his mayor, supported by the success of Tapville.

The conference was a success. The mayor in Aheadofyou was impressed and immediately hired Bill's friend to set up a similar course in his town. People from several other cities also came forward and invited Bill to come to their city and repeat the presentation. Bill was happy and filled his agenda with dates and names of cities to visit.

That summer, Bill left his Tapville employment for a career as an independent consultant in the "cities on the Web" trade. He not only doubled his income; he also became famous in the whole country. Newspapers interviewed him. He became part of a government committee, named the "IT commission", which was set up to promote the use of "IT", as the Internet was called colloquially.

By autumn that same year, there was no Web design education in Tapville. There was no one to replace Bill as a teacher. The university volunteered to provide one, but this would cost the city, and, as the mayor said: "Why? We already have a system. And the government has made this huge new investment in education for the unemployed. They give us money for educating 500 people a year through the existing course systems at colleges and the university, which is all we can manage anyway".

So the Tapville Web system was left on its own on the server. It worked well technically, and it looked nice, but as details in the real world changed little by little, it became increasingly obsolete. The first thing that happened was that no one answered the emails to "webmaster", which could be sent by clicking on the underlined words "mail to webmaster", written in 9 point type at the bottom of each page. The emails went to the former address of William W. Westmark, and were returned a couple of hours later with the automatic message:

> Warning! Could not send mail for four hours.....Either there is no user by that name, or the server cannot be contacted. This is a warning message only, I'll keep trying until the message is five days old.

The five days would expire without the message being delivered, and soon people stopped sending email.

Within one year, 60 of the country's 288 cities were on the Web, due in large part to the tireless touring and lecturing of IT consultant William W. Westmark. Within another year, the figure had risen to 200.

By that time, at a creativity meeting with his top managers, the new mayor in Tapville, Mr Dew Voteforme, was expressing concerns: "Why don't we have a modern Web system like all the other cities of this country have? Ours looks old-fashioned, it doesn't even have frames. And look at the picture of the mayor – it's not even me, it's the old one!" The mayor appointed a task force "to do something about the problem".

This turned out to be a tactically successful political move. The city's dailies immediately caught on, especially the *Tapville Gazette*, which had supported Mr Voteforme in the election campaign; "Rapid actions will put Tapville back in the IT lead" and "Voteforme takes a firm grip on the IT issue in his first week in office" were some of the *Gazette* headlines.

## Why Be on the Web at All?

As we noticed in the soap, it was only the existence of an entrepreneur that made things happen in Tapville. In real life, this is most often also the case. Most electronic services projects have started with a single person pursuing an idea. Take a look at the following case from Seaside City.

In Seaside City, a lot of experience had been gained in offering teletext- and videotex-based services since 1990. With the focus on Internet technology and the new graphical possibilities of the World Wide Web, several initiatives started in the country. The best-known initiative was the digital city of CanalTown. This initiative used the metaphor of a city to explain to its users how to find and use services. Because most of the national journalists live in the centre of CanalTown, much of this initiative was reported in the daily newspapers.

One day in October 1994 a journalist asked the Seaside City project leader of the teletext and videotex services if Seaside City would also start a digital city[1] initiative. At that time there were no plans to start another project using Internet technology, but during the conversation with the journalist, the project leader got a "creative flash" and envisioned very clearly both a positive societal influence and the economic perspectives. Therefore, his answer to the journalist's question was a straight "yes" without any hesitation. "Yes", the project leader said to the journalist, "we plan to open our digital city a few weeks from now".

The same day this interview was broadcast on the regional Seaside Radio, and the news was picked up by the national NOS teletext, Seaside Dagblad (Regional Newspaper), and in the Volkskrant (National Newspaper) the next day. The same morning a meeting with almost all the project personnel was held to brainstorm about this Digital Seaside. At first a digital city was created within the videotex environment offering all already existing services within the format of the digital cities metaphor.

There was envy and protest from CanalTown: one is not allowed to call something a "digital city" unless it is built on Internet technology.

A few months later the project leader started an Internet project. In a similar way, a metaphor was used: MediaPort Seaside, a digital harbour for the Seaside City region. It started with a meeting with many different organizations: small Internet-based companies, the regional daily newspaper, the Seaside City university, many cultural organizations (malls, museums), and several city employees. A structure (interface) was created and HTML pages were written, using city information available from printed sources. Also, existing videotex-based (database-oriented) services were converted to HTML format. Citizens, as "harbour workers", could make their own "container" (homepage).

---

1  The concept of the Digital City was first used in Amsterdam's Web. A characteristic of this project, which was later copied in numerous cities, was the metaphor of a city used for the World Wide Web. Information and services within the digital city were structured like a city map with streets, cafés, and squares (for example the banking square and the library square). Discussion groups are named "cafés" or the "subway". One important characteristic of a digital city is that citizens get free access to it; no subscription fee has to be paid to enter a digital city.

It is amazing what an entrepreneur can achieve. This one had a special position which gave him the opportunity to act rapidly. But his actions were not anchored in the city, as typically they are not initially. This means that the city enters the Web with no clear course.

The unclear role of the Web in a municipal context is witnessed by many. IT projects tend to have a technical focus rather than a user perspective[2]. Top city managers tend to stay away from IT[3]. One reason seems to be that IT projects often take a long time to realize, and gaining political support for projects that cross over into the next election period may prove hard[4].

As a consequence of the lack of goals, it is hard to focus and provide a good system with regard to content as well as presentation. A typical Web project starts off with the Chief Information Officer (CIO) in the organization publishing the company brochure on the Web. He does that himself with technical support from someone. In the early days (which in Internet time means 1994 or 1995), this would typically be a consultant or a project group rustled up from a local university media education programme or from a programme for the unemployed. Today, the technical support will typically come from the computer department, which has by now in most places acquired at least basic Web competence. (Increasingly, however, small companies run by people, usually just out of, or even still in, school, have started to provide very cheap competition.)

Once this is done, the debate about the purpose of the Web system starts (until this stage, only the CIO has given it a thought). Why should we be on the Web? The CIO, who in the organizations that have come this far is typically a Web enthusiast, comes up with a number of reasons. These reasons typically point in a number of

---

2  Goldkuhl *et al.* (1998) found in studies of the debate, as well as from their own projects, that projects often have a technical focus rather than a focus on use (such as focusing on the number of computers per school rather than how to use them to promote pedagogical purposes), and that strategies are unclear: "You often get a feeling that the local politicians build the net just to show they keep up with the technical development" (GP 1997-02-17, quoted by Goldkuhl *et al.*, 1998, p. 69). They also found, regarding general IT use in cities, that projects are not systematically integrated in an overall IT plan for the City. In several project studies on IT use, they found that "process thinking with regard to client-focused actions [is lacking]", "A comprehensive view of activities and IT design [is lacking]", and "Evaluation and systems stewardship [are lacking]".

3  Winnberg (1995) found that politicians and senior decision makers in the administrative field often stay away from IT, and that responsibility is delegated to project managers: "In other areas like the City Council, the specialised committees, or the administrative managers, people were fairly passive (when asking about goals etc.). The politicians referred the business to the administrative managers, and those referred to the project leader. The arguments were that the task actually was given to him, and that it required a kind of competence they themselves were lacking" (p. 9).

4  Fletcher and Otis Foy (1994) found that politicians are not so eager to take initiatives to implement new technology. The explanations given are that IT projects are often costly and and take a long time to realize. The political management in a city may change from one election period to another, and gaining political support for projects that cross over into the next period may prove hard (da Villa and Panizzolo, 1996; Fletcher and Otis Foy, 1994; Caudle *et al.*, 1991).

directions, are not always compatible and require organizational change in some way, at least in the longer run. Either this requires the CIO to increase his office with a number of people doing Web publishing, or it requires the business departments to do so. Alternatively, it requires outsourcing of these activities. In short, at this point it becomes clear to several people in the organization that the Web system will cost money if they go along with the CIO's suggestions. So they start to think "Why should we?".

Why should a city be present on the Web? What goals does a city have for now, the near future and for the long term? Entering the Web may feel like a big step forward – and is certainly often advertised as such – but, as we shall see as we go on, it's just a starting point.

The most often heard reason to be present on the Web is just being present on the Web: "One should not miss the train". It is clear that today many are there because others are. But beyond that, there are a number of potential reasons for a city to be present on the Web. Some of the commonly mentioned reasons are:

- It may be good for the city's image. Using new methods to inform the public and communicate with it makes the city appear modern.
- It may provide an opportunity to start using new methods to inform the public and communicate with it.
- It may attract investment by providing easily accessible information to companies situated elsewhere.
- It may improve the city's services to its citizens.
- It may make internal work more efficient by making it easier to share resources and information.
- Citizens may help themselves to services, as they do with automated teller machines and Internet banks.
- Democracy may be improved by making it easy to distribute information and solicit citizen feedback.

Most of the reasons, however, are often those that appeal only to the change agent, the entrepreneur. As we saw in the soap, what really sold the Web to the mayor's crew was not the thing itself, but the fact that it provided a possible solution to another problem – unemployment (which was in fact the only problem they saw. All the things Bill first mentioned were not conceived as problems at all). Cities always have other problems than the Web, and they tend to act reactively rather than proactively. Therefore there is a need for an entrepreneur who knows how to bundle things to make them appetising. As we saw, there are several risks with that trick. First, the business becomes very dependent on the entrepreneur. Second, unholy alliances are always dangerous. Once there is another solution to the problem (unemployment), decision-makers may go for that solution, especially if it, as in the soap, presents a more powerful and/or more traditional solution, and – not least important – if the entrepreneur is not there to defend the idea. In fact, often when the original entrepreneur is gone there is nobody around who *can* pursue the project.

To promote computer use in the compulsory schools of Sweden, two "pilots" in each school were educated as early as the early 1980s (one from natural sciences, one in social sciences). They were supposed to lead the way into the information society by helping other teachers in the schools to use the computers, finding suitable software, and developing ideas on how to use the computers in pedagogically sound ways. The idea was to have one "technical" pilot, with a background in mathematics and natural sciences, and one "use" pilot, with a social sciences background. In most cases, the "technical" pilot showed most interest and ambition. One major reason for that was that at the time, there were not many application areas that applied to the social sciences. "Use" was typically programming, and the social science teachers correctly saw no point in spending politics classes on that.

Among those who participated and showed interest in computers and their use, many left, often shortly after the courses, and certainly before they had had time to implement computer use at their schools in a way that would survive their resignation. They left for the computer industry to make educational software, to serve as consultants in client contacts, and to write user-friendly manuals, or for the universities to teach in computer science or informatics etc., and thus computer use never took off in most schools. And in those where it did, the whole activity was extremely dependent on a single person, who was the "Mr Computer" (yes, typically a male) of the school.

(Use finally did take off, but that was more that ten years later. The takeoff was fired by the advent of the Internet and not by the education and implementation programme of the 1980s.)

After a city has decided to enter the Web, the questions arise of what to do with it, how to do it and what is needed in order to get the job done. (Yes, it is true, it most often happens afterwards, even today. In most cities, there is an entrepreneur who manages to set a system up, and it is only afterwards that serious discussions about use start.)

It is certainly hard to make informed decisions when dealing with a new medium, which is not yet mature, neither technologically nor in terms of use. It becomes even harder when it seems this new medium will spread faster than previous new communication media did.

When dealing with the Web, special problems arise. The medium is inherently interactive and passive. "Interactive" means everyone connected is a potential sender. "Passive" means that, unlike newspapers and radio and TV programs, "homepages" do not come to users – they have to find them. There are, of course also active parts of Internet, like the email systems by which messages can be "pushed" to people. Except for information that users have specifically subscribed to receive, this technique is usually not preferred. Therefore, the information provider should expect the users to be *searching* for information. This means that users must be active and knowledgeable. We shall return to the problem of knowledge and user activity in Challenge 8, stopping at the municipal side of things for now.

Many cities are not used to looking at their contacts with citizens in this way. They are more used to pushing information at them by means of brochures etc. This means that the functions are looked at from the city's point of view rather than from a citizen's point of view: "We have this information, how can we *reach out* to everyone with it?" or "How can we make this distribution cheaper?". Even if functions are considered from a user perspective (which would mean instead asking, "What do people need in certain situations?"), there are many different groups of users, all expecting different things from their city. So what is the system supposed to be?

- Is a Web site put up to inform citizens, so that people will make fewer telephone calls to the city's employees? (This is the "business process re-engineering approach", one typical result of which is the "call centre".)
- Is it a "community" system, set up to support communication, to arrive at a (local) society where there is a warm and vivid relationship between citizens and city representatives, such as mayors, city council members and managers in the

administration? (This is the "cyberspace" approach, promoting cyberspace as a new, more human, world to live in. See Rheingold (1994) for a personal and philosophical perspective, and Johanson and Mascanzoni (1996) for a survey from a government perspective.)

- Is it set up to attract investments from industrial partners abroad by giving a view of the perspective of setting up a business within the city borders?
- Is it set up for tourist purposes, focusing on bringing more tourists to the city by presenting local sights, a calendar of events, lists of restaurants and hotels, including booking services and so on?
- Is it set up for business purposes, which in the case of a city would typically mean self-service for the citizens and enterprises.

Making decisions on what to strive for and what not to attempt is not that easy when empirical evidence of what works is almost totally lacking. Of course, any number of consultants will line up to tell you what to do, but the also have no real experience of *use*; they typically know the technology and not much more.

One might argue that it is better to wait until the Internet with all its possibilities has matured, to let others make the mistakes that beginners always make, and wait for the moment when a clear picture is there to tell you which road leads to success and which does not. For a number of reasons, here we advise not waiting at all! Entering the Web is not the hardest part of the job. As will be discussed in Part 2, it is the coherence between technology, organization, social issues, communication, marketing, business process (re-) engineering and economics which will make Web use worthwhile. The way in which the tuning of all these interrelated fields should be done is situation-dependent and can only be experienced through local practice. Therefore, it is good to make an early start (well, today is not really early...). In each city, experiences must be gained about how to make use of the technology. Good advice can be given, but experience shows that success and failure lie not in putting this or that service on the Web or using this or that JavaScript. Success lies in the integration of usability issues, organizational design issues, proper technology use, and conscious cost–benefit analysis. It is also about awareness; as we saw in the soap, it takes time before Web issues are taken seriously. There is no one from outside to tell people to do so, and insight grows slowly from within, but only after you have started to tinker with the system.

After entering the Web, a city gets reactions from city employees, from customers and from citizens. Those reactions enable the city to get a better understanding of the medium and how to use it – if someone seriously tries to do so. Typically, counting page accesses is the only follow-up that is done. What you count is then your own staff and employees in other cities taking a look around how others' systems look. We will get back to the problem of following up system use in Challenge 8, but for now our advice is to solicit feedback. Be active. Create focus groups or other arrangements by which you can get a feel for people's reactions to your system.

The first difficulty is how to get this thing going at all, and since this story is, in the end, about people, we will look at the first difficulty from the perspective of the person responsible for managing the Web. This person was, in the early days (1994), called the Webmaster. Because this person was typically very technology oriented and users tended to have *information* problems, there was a mismatch. Users wrote emails to ask "Where can I find information about childcare?", whereas the Webmaster expected to be answering questions like "How do I install a plugin to make the mayor talk to me from his Web page?".

Today, therefore, many organizations have introduced another title, Infomaster. The Infomaster is sometimes the same person as the Webmaster, but most often there is a need for another person, since the tasks of both technical management and – in particular – information management have grown.

The Infomaster realizes that the city has a lot of information that can be of interest to distribute to citizens via this new channel. From the Infomaster's point of view, the information owners do not appear very interested, or they do not have the knowledge to put the information on the Web. There is a need to design a starter kit to get things going.

There are a number of strategies for such a starter kit. Let's have a closer look at some of them.

## Problem-Resolving Strategies

### The Do-it-Yourselfer

When an organization wants to enter the Web, this often means that *somebody* in the organization takes on the role of Web entrepreneurship. Often it is not (at least for the organizations who entered early on) a major effort from the organization – it is a small project.

This person goes hunting for information to put on the Web. He or she is responsible for the Web site and wants to fill it with information. So the goal is to have a few Web pages from each department. The Web pages often contain information about the department: how many people there are, the main sub-departments, the goal for the department, who the chairperson of the department is and so on. Often, there are already one or more brochures containing this information.

If the Infomaster is lucky, information can also be obtained on where to find the department and telephone numbers. Sometimes, but not very often, some fragments of information that might be found that are of interest to citizens, such as events, what services are available, how they work, what they cost etc.

The working metaphor governing this work is "We are just transforming the old brochures into electronic format. The most important thing is to tell people that the Web is the simplest thing, it is just electronic paper". In line with this kind of thinking, the Infomaster is also happy to see that all new word processing programs behave as typewriters for the Web. So in the future everybody in the organization is going to write information directly for the Web.

There are some inherent properties of this strategy that make it lead into a dead end, as the following case shows.

At IglooVille University, the CIO started off with this strategy in 1994. He had his son, aged 16, construct the HTML pages using the university's brochure and some other material, including the timetable of the local bus lines. A Web presence was quickly established, but many departments did not even know they were on the Web. Also, the material deteriorated very quickly. For example, after a few months, the bus company serving the university area changed its timetable and the university rector retired. In the real world, that is. Not on the Web.

It would be easy to fill the whole book with examples of organizations ending up in this situation. We will stop at just one more.

The official presentation of the Internet site "city5.de" took place at a press conference in the summer of 1995. The politicians and managers were very proud of being able to present the city as keeping up with new technology.

The project was born when two or three people interested in computers and the Internet started, together with the help of a Web bureau to design the first HTML pages and learn the necessary technical skills. With a good marketing of their ideas, they managed to find funding. They pretended that they were producing HTML pages without any extra costs, and restricted their publishing work to printed material that was already available electronically, e.g. brochures, calendar of events etc.

Their products gave the impression that existing printed material was reusable in another medium without any adaptation other than the addition of HTML tags. The people worked on it in parallel with their normal work. By working in this way, no special budget had to be allocated to Web-related work.

The marketing strategy promised benefit for all, and therefore the project workers got official support to go on developing the Web presentation of the city and marketing city events over the Internet. In the following period, they made ever more use of multimedia techniques, with attractions like live cameras and sound files. With the engagement of a few people the city's Internet office was born, initially working with only three employees.

As the office went on producing in this way, encouraging city departments to hand over material in order to transfer it to HTML format and publish it over the Internet, the number of pages grew rapidly and became more and more unmanageable.

The do-it-yourself approach obviously cannot last for too long, if for no other reason than that of overload. Just how long the Web editors can keep up depends on the size of their initial funding and the available resources.

There is another risk with this way of working, and that is the working metaphor. The Web is *not* just electronic paper. It is a different medium, requiring other ways of communicating. It needs media expertise. Therefore a city working with the "electronic brochure" metaphor will eventually either have to redefine its system or stop at the brochure level.

## The Wheeler-Dealer

Doing it yourself, in-house, proves expensive when the system grows. A creative strategy may be to use training programs for the unemployed to get staff for free, or at least very cheaply.

The city of Coolmore took this approach when, as one of the very first cities in the country to do so, it started up its Web system in 1994. A number of unemployed youngsters were employed, paid mostly through the unemployment system, taught the basics of HTML coding, and set off to publish quite detailed information about the city. The system rapidly grew to what, for the time, was a considerable volume, and was well up to the current state of the Internet art. It turned out to be the most acclaimed municipal Web site in the country at that time, and the project leader toured the country to show off the results.

After some time, the project ended. The youngsters left for jobs in the emerging Web business. The city was left with a system designed for early Web browsers (Netscape version 1), and a huge number of HTML pages. This did not mean that the effort had been wasted, but it did mean that a new start had to be made.

Today, the creative Infomaster does not necessarily have to look to the ranks of the unemployed. There are, at least in countries where Web use is substantial, a growing number of low-cost consultancies that build Web systems very cheaply. These companies are small (often one or two people) and run by young people just out of (or even still in) school. They make not only Web pages, but also program pages for interaction by means of CGI scripts, Java, JavaScripts and so on. Tools now exist to make entering information on the pages a task for the regular staff after very little training.

One problem with this approach, then, is continuity. Whether you exploit the unemployment subsidy regulations or make use of short-lived low-cost consultancies, you end up needing some way of maintaining a steady course in system design (to preserve a recognizable appearance) and a steady level of information maintenance (to keep up with the continual changes in the real world).

## The Empire Builder

Some Infomasters initially envision a system that is simultaneously too big for their own department, too undefined for outsourcing, and too political to put their own jobs on the line for. These people go for the imperial role. They typically start by designing a small but nice-looking Web system for their own department only (and this is the first important point). They then show their system to the business departments, and explain to them the use that the *Infomaster* is going to make of it. Not *others*, just theselves. Being good salespeople, they often manage to make people think that they also need such a system for their departments.

Because the Infomaster realizes not only the possibilities but also the problems, he or she goes along with the other departments' ideas (after all, it was the Infomaster's idea from the beginning), but says that each department must produce its own information. The Infomaster's own role will be that of maintaining conformity in appearance and common standards for quality. The beauty of this solution is that the other departments pay, while the Infomaster rises to the position of being able to have many things done in his or her way. The Infomaster plants the seed, others grow the crop, and the Infomaster then harvests what is to be harvested and escapes responsibility for the seed that never grows. Having started early, the Infomaster's ideas about how to organize information, and even about technical solutions, will prevail, because the departments will go to him or her for advice (because, for the sake of the company profile, they have to).

## Combining Multiple Strategies

The three strategies described here can also appear as stages in the development of a single organization. There are examples of organizations who have initially taken the do-it-yourself approach, then switched to the wheeler-dealer style simply to be able to keep going, and finally end up having to go for the imperial approach.

Because of the relatively rapid development of both Internet technology and Internet use during the past few years, it is natural that organizations' goals have changed over time. There has been genuine uncertainty regarding how far and at what pace the new medium would spread. Let us take a look at the development in HandyVille since 1992.

In 1992, very few people had heard of the Internet. It was certainly not a high priority in cities. When HandyVille built its metropolitan fibre network, called MetNet (for Metropolitan Area Network), the goal was to optimize telephone use within the city. In 1993, HandyVille was honoured with the title of Cultural Capital City of Europe. Then MetNet was built. At that time, there were no plans for electronic services. In 1994, HandyVille MetNet was operational, a fibre optic network using ATM (Asynchronous Transfer Mode) technology. At the time, it was a world first. However, although the network was there no electronic services were available. So the problem arose, what services should be offered?

A pilot project was started in 1994, "HandyVille, an Intelligent City". The idea was to install a "building control system": control of electricity, central heating, tracking people coming into and leaving buildings, etc. Several applications were realized:

1. As a first step, because of an accident with the level of chlorine in one of the swimming pools, the quality of the swimming water was measured in the swimming pools. The temperature, the level of chlorine and the level of acidity were measured. The data was transferred to the city lab where it was visualized and interpreted. If necessary, the data could be adjusted remotely. A system to control – permanently and automatically – the quality and temperature of the water in eight municipal swimming pools was produced. Today, the system continuously provides the laboratory responsible for controlling water quality with all the necessary data from the municipal swimming pools, so that it is warned immediately of any incidents.

2. The application PACS (Picture Archiving and Communication System) allowed doctors in different hospitals to jointly examine scans. The data from a scan taken in one hospital could be sent to another hospital, where a team of specialists would make the diagnosis. This was a first step towards complete tele-diagnosis. All eight HandyVille hospitals, managed by the Public Centre for Social Welfare, were already linked to MetNet. Since February 1995, medical images, scanned in at one hospital, have been transmitted to the specialists in the centralized nuclear medicine department in another hospital for further interpretation by specialized personnel in order to establish the final medical diagnosis.

3. Telephone switchboards of the administrative departments are connected to MetNet. Today, 30 locations, connecting most of the departments, offer the public a single point of contact: one telephone number to reach any of the 5 000 telephones of the municipal departments. At the same time these municipal departments make considerable savings as internal calls between their premises are now free. Telephone calls and fax transmissions between different departments have been simplified.

4. Regular videoconferences between the district's headquarters are used for managerial reasons. Between the IT department's training centre and training rooms for employees in four other locations in the city, videoconferencing is used for educational motives: "teleclasses" are organized in the morning and "tele-assistance" in the afternoon. This distance learning project, called SMART, also includes the production of interactive courseware: the objective is to put these training programs on a server on MetNet, in reach of every employee and eventually of all citizens at home.

This story illustrates a typical development: the network was initiated as a technical solution that solved an economic problem – the telephone costs. Only once the network was in place were applications discussed. The first applications were for the control of technical systems. The idea of using the network for services to citizens only appeared later. This was quite natural, because at that time there were very few households connected, so there was no customer base.

There was, however, also a parallel track of development, which eventually met MetNet project. This was the decentralization of the political system.

Driven by its vision, the City Council in 1992 made an important decision: "Reduce telecommunication costs within HandyVille and offer high-quality services to the citizens by building a high performance network for the city administration."

The municipal government agreement for 1995–2000 added two important goals: "inner municipal decentralization and the refinement of local democracy". This was spelled out to mean:

● Decentralization and expansion of the municipal structure

- Accessibility and openness
- Provision of comprehensible information
- Providing optimal and adequate opportunities for participation
- Providing the best possible service
- Revaluation of the municipal council
- Maintaining an open and friendly atmosphere in the municipal council

The existence of a metropolitan fibre network infrastructure, in combination with the general boom in Internet popularity all over the Western world, made the city see new opportunities to achieve these goals. In a strategic paper of 1997 the Deputy Mayor said:

> By inner municipal decentralization and improvement of the communication, HandyVille wants to bridge the legendary gap between citizen and local government, by bringing the government closer to the community.
> By strictly applying the principle of subsidiarity and by giving decision-making power to (more) local politicians, we will be able to address local needs more effectively and adequately.
> Administrative services should be available on the spot, and equipped with the necessary tools so that they are online and can address the citizens' needs effectively and provide service without delay.

In 1994, the situation was similar all over the world. Many cities and countries had invested in networks, the Internet was facing commercialization, and worldwide, companies (and to some extent governments) were thinking about what content to provide. After all, there were at the time very few users of Internet, so services could not be expected to be immediately profitable. But starting in 1994, things began to change. The Internet became widely known, and use increased rapidly, although from a very low level. Visionaries saw the emergence of a new popular medium. Many cities, countries and indeed the European Union (EU) jumped on the bandwagon. Says a project leader, in the electronic services trade ("telematics" in the official EU speak of the time), of HandyVille:

> At that time, the EU program area of Telecities started up. The project Infosond was started, and HandyVille in cooperation with eight other cities started to discuss services and service delivery with the perspective of a more comprehensive and structured approach.
> Talks with city employees started and Infosond ideas were discussed with directors within the city. The initial reaction was mixed: some liked the idea and got enthusiastic, others didn't like it.
> In 1994, a new mission for HandyVille was formulated: "City on the move". Some didn't want to move at all. Investigations started to determine what non-electronic services were offered to the citizens and which of those could be offered electronically in the future.
> Infosond gave a push, but more important was the introduction of the "Digital Metropolis HandyVille" (DMH), the central Internet site of HandyVille run by the city's IT department.
> The DMH was the tool to promote these ideas. Via DMH, the HandyVille citizen can reach the city council, has free email and chat facilities, and has free access to all the city services available on the DMH.
> By 1998, more than 19 000 virtual inhabitants were living in this DMH, taking advantage of this new virtual community (most of the 19 000 having their own homepages).
> The DMH has proved that the "virtual community" becomes more and more mature. Already the fourth version of DMH is operational. It is no longer a simple Web site, but a real communication channel between citizens and local government. The DMH is also a tool for making citizens familiar with the Internet. The DMH is the first step in the introduction of a complete "electronic counter".
> The DMH is the showcase of the HandyVille electronic city as of now. The DMH was initiated by the city at a separate unit. It was not until much later that information provision was integrated into the daily operations of the city departments.
> From the beginning the DMH was updated and enriched with new services and information not by city employees but by DMH personnel. City services were not involved, as they were not interested. This was

mostly because at the time there were no good tools for easy maintenance of Web pages, such as FrontPage or DreamWeaver.

The city, as well as the IT department (which ran the DMH as well as the applications on MetNet), were not at the time convinced about having a structural approach. There were no update tools, no maintenance tools and no rules for publications. The basic idea was to let it grow from beneath. The idea was to get the enthusiastic people on board and let them influence the rest. At the time, it was not clear to anyone what the opportunities were for such a new communication tool, so it seemed that a cautious bottom-up approach was the most suitable.

By 1998, most of the traditional applications and services for the local administration, the Public Centre of Social Welfare, and the harbour were available. These applications and services represented about 50 000 transactions per day.

We can see that HandyVille has come from a pioneer stage to a gradually more organized situation where work is distributed. At first, staff from DMH produced the Web pages. The DMH was updated and enriched with new services and information not by city employees but by DMH personnel, because the time was not yet ripe to have the primary service producers do it. When DMH started, people from the IT department put the first information online, and then started to search for information providers (departments) in the city.

For the volunteers, in the beginning there were no tools available to put their information online. Today, tools such as FrontPage are used. Information can be maintained via well-structured templates, and new departments are trained in their use before they start.

By 1998, enthusiasm had spread from DMH out to at least some city departments. Some civil servants had become very enthusiastic, and some were even ahead of the IT department's speed, although others were way behind.

To reach this stage had taken four years. HandyVille would probably never have got there at all had it not been for a few important factors:

- Continuous *political support* from the very beginning (recall the Deputy Mayor).

- A *system champion*: the formation of a group at the IT department that took care of the DMH with great enthusiasm. DMH provided the necessary momentum at an early stage of development.

- *Endurance:* the continuous effort by the IT department to motivate city departments to continue along the road to electronic services. This effort has been considerably supported by EU projects.

- Some *early visible evidence of success*: there was a relatively rapid increase in users of the DMH (by 1998 there were around 20 000 "inhabitants"). Although it is not at all clear how this can be explained as a success in the context of the Deputy Mayor's political statement, the very fact that many people used the system regularly was seen as a great success.

- Other applications (than services to the citizens) that could help *motivate the investment*: the use of the network for telephony and for control of technical equipment, such as the swimming pools.

All these factors are probably necessary. One might expect that today the time for enthusiasm to spread through the ranks would be shorter, but there is no evidence for this. On the contrary: there is little evidence that public services to the citizens can rapidly be made profitable, and, as we shall see in the following chapters, there are several processes that work to counteract effective electronic service management in the public sector.

Because cities are political organizations, political support is in the long run perhaps the most important factor. Political support does not necessarily mean direct support from a politician. It may well mean support by city policy, which may be granted by administrative managers. But of course this kind of support will need some foundation in politics. However, long-term political support is a rare bird, perhaps especially so when it comes from a lower level. Says an experienced EU project leader in the city of RelaxenBurg:

> For projects which are planned for a longer duration than one year, the contact person may change, general strategies may change after elections in the city, political advisors may be replaced, and technical equipment in the administration and many other factors influence the outcome of a project.
>
> To start a European project you often need the support and the OK from the chief of your department. You have to explain what the profit is for the city administration, the clients of which are mostly employees in other departments. Target groups in European projects are often citizens and SMEs.
>
> But how can you measure the satisfaction of citizens? And then explain the outcome to your chief of department?

How indeed? The problem becomes even harder when you consider that EU projects typically run for 1–3 years, after which considerable progress towards better services to citizens must be proved to have taken place. Recall the HandyVille example above, where we saw that it took four years to get only as far as having some city departments provide their information and services themselves, and where there are still only 20 000 users in a city of more than half a million, most of whom use the Web for private purposes rather than contacts with the city authorities. Do we have a failure?

The answer is: not necessarily. Citizen satisfaction is hard to measure, and even if you measure it, your knowledge is volatile. Just think of how easily satisfaction with political leaders changes. No, the problem is that city departments are typically not proficient in measuring their own performance. It is very hard to say something will be "better" or "more effective" when you don't even know the efficiency, or lack thereof, of the activities you already undertake. In Challenge 9, we will discuss models for the evaluation of electronic services.


## Lessons From the Start-Up Challenge

So far in this chapter we have outlined the "start-up challenge". We have presented some strategically different solutions – centralize, decentralize, decentralize-and-control – and we have shown that both goals and organizational solutions may have to change over time. We have used the HandyVille case to illustrate our point that it takes a number of things to ensure a successful Web presence.

Each of the three strategies described here may work well in particular situations. In HandyVille, it seems that the distributed solution was simply not feasible at an early stage. As the amount of information grew, it became necessary, and as the interest among City departments increased, it became possible.

Whatever strategy is chosen, there is one thing that will typically happen. After a relatively short time, thousands of HTML pages are generated (not quite as many in the do-it-yourself case as in the other two). The Infomaster is happy at first, because the growth of his or her department, empire or product, is visible to everybody. This period of joy is short, though. It is not long before the Infomaster realizes that the next challenge, the "Thousands of pages..." challenge, has arrived.

What can we learn from this challenge? Let us go back to Tapville and see how they approached the problem the second time around.

## *Soap*: The Web Settles in Tapville

The mayor's task force "to do something with our Web problem", or "ToDoS"[5], as it was unwittingly nicknamed by the Spanish-born clerk at the CIO office, was led by the CIO of Tapville, Ms Dwit Myway. An experienced administrator, a former CEO, and an expert in internal politics, she realized from the outset that an enduring solution was needed. But what was enduring in this field and what was not? Technology was changing rapidly, and so were the organizational approaches needed.

She realized that not being a Web wizard herself she needed a reliable partner. There was not much Web wisdom to be found within the city departments, so she hired a consultancy, SolveIT Inc., which specialized in the organizational use of IT but had now begun to see the possibilities of the Web. First, the consultants and Ms Myway had long talks about the possibilities of the Web and the current situation in Tapville. Then they set up a design team made up of key staff in the key department, and continued the discussions in that group. After a couple of weeks, they came up with the following solution:

- *Delegation of work*: the Web system as a whole was the responsibility of the CIO and her staff. They would supply work and responsibilities. It was decided that there should be one "Infomaster" in five business departments (those five where some Web enthusiasm was currently found). This person should be responsible for collecting, presenting and updating information on the Web. He or she should also be the contact for customers emailing that department to ask questions.

- *Coherence and endorsement*: the CIO's department was to be responsible for the Web system as a whole. It was to provide general city information and advise the local Infomasters on matters of style in both writing and graphics, areas in which the department had considerable expertise, gained from producing external information for press, radio and TV, as well as in the regular staff magazine.

- *Education*: the local Infomasters were, as an introduction, given a crash course in the anatomy of the Web, in the use of a selected HTML editor, and in company information policy. The course was financed by project money (there was a national drive for "IT education" at the time).

- *Technical support*: to support the local Infomasters, the computer department was ordered to acquire Web competence.

---

5   "Todos" in Spanish means "everything".

There was some talk about the contents of the Tapville Web. The consultants claimed that it could be used for communication and services, not only for information. But Ms Myway was in the information business, and claimed no competence in services or "handling complaints", as she rephrased "communication". Neither did she have any desire to enter uncertain territory (after all, this task force was appointed to *settle* things, not to attempt new explorations; Billy Westmark did that, and look what happened). So, sticking to her trade, the Web systems were set up to inform citizens about the city's whereabouts and to lecture them on their own rights and duties (mostly the duties). There was no one to question the solution. It was built on firm ground, both organizationally and technically. It was bound to work.

The course went well. The Infomasters were happy, having been assigned a new and challenging task, and having been presented in the city's staff magazine as "the spearheads of the future". They set off to work with great enthusiasm and devotion. Some of the old system's content was used, but the new editors, having been taught how to present information, found that they had to reshape it quite a lot. Not only did the content need updating, but they also wanted to adapt the system to local conditions; thus each department's policy, logo and so on, were negotiated internally in every department and used in the design of the Web pages. Very soon, in less than a year, the Web could count 2975 pages from Tapville alone. In fact, if you searched for Tapville at AltaVista at that time, you got more than 5000 hits. Not only were all the city's own pages marked with the name, but also most other cities in the country had links to Tapville to show their own politicians a really nice site, in the hope of making them envious and and willing to spend more on their own Web site.

But some of the Infomasters were not satisfied with that. They became great Web fans. They started to learn CGI scripting, and started to make the Tapville Web interactive. They made questionnaires asking the Tapvillers for their opinion on this and that. They produced reports on the results and presented them to their superiors. Sometimes they even presented the results on the Web, something the local press was quick to observe.

# Analysis of the Tapville Solution

Tapville, having defined the problem as "lagging behind our competitors", took a firm grip of the situation. They defined the Web system as an information channel and, in line with that definition, assigned responsibility for the system to the Chief Information Officer. While solving the problem that they saw (an obsolete system), this solution led to several problems:

- Having assigned several enthusiastic Web editors, the seed for an insatiable appetite for growth of the system – as well as the domain of the CIO – was planted without knowing whether or not there was an actual market demand for so much information. This meant that the time until the work overload would show was prolonged, compared with the "do-it-yourself" Webmaster solution. At first, this seems good. But when the problem finally pops up (and it will) it will be so much bigger.

- The city organization was still unprepared to exploit the interactivity of the medium, following the general trend on the Internet. This means that changing the system from information to services and/or communication would need yet another reorganization.

- By assigning the publishing work to the Information Office, a double-work situation was cast in concrete. Information was not published directly from the source, but was redesigned and retyped by the Web editors. While this might be a good solution for maintaining the city's standards and profile, it introduced extra work and delay in information production.

There is also a problem with the Tapville definition of the system as an *information* system. While this might well be appropriate, the Infomasters had other ambitions, or at least they grew to have them. Had Tapville stopped at, say, the tourist department, providing only tourist information in order to market the city to attract tourists and to make it easier for them to find their way, this might have worked. It would have meant a definitional limitation to the system. But because Tapville invited all departments, eventually, to use the Web, it planted more far-reaching ambitions in the city. Different departments have different activities, and thus different needs. They also have their own way of solving things, and claim, relying on their expertise in a certain field, that they are the only ones who know how to run things in this field.

# Conclusions From the Start-up Challenge in Summary

As discussed above, the following are prerequisites for successful implementation of electronic services:

- Continuous political support to avoid costly and discouraging disruption in a development which is tricky enough in itself.
- A project champion, providing enthusiasm and creativity.
- Endurance. Services typically do not pay back, or get used by "everybody" immediately.
- Some early visible evidence of success.
- At least some applications (often other than services to the citizens) that can help motivate the investment.

These are general factors. The mundane organization of work must eventually – the sooner the better, but often impossible at a very early stage – be based on the following principles:

- Delegation of work among providers and "publisher".
- Coherence of production system and techn cal support.
- Endorsement by at least the most important actors.
- Education.

# 2. Challenge 2: Thousands of Pages – From Project to Organization

When the city's Web project is launched, it is typically done in the form of a project. When the project is over, pages are published but there is no special budget allocated to further Web-related work. This means that expansion is limited in terms of size, technical renewal and sophistication. Initially, work is typically carried out as a marginal low-cost activity by students, people hired with unemployment support or other types of cheap labour. The task of maintaining all the pages quickly overwhelms the small team of active staff and the system degenerates, causing complaints and requiring new types of solution, because the current one can only be stretched so far. As a result, a "Web-responsible" person is identified in each department and charged with the task of overseeing the accuracy of the information pertaining to that department. An additional problem is the Web technology develops, and cities have to keep up (frames, JavaScript, XML, meta-tags etc.) so as not to appear old-fashioned. Further, demands for information and services increase, and there appears to be a need for automation and integration with existing computer systems.

Web maintenance will have to be rationally organized somehow. Let us start by taking a look at how things went in Tapville.

## *Soap*: The Tapville Web Grows Out of Hand

For a while, there was calm and happiness in Tapville. The Infomasters kept up their good spirits and produced new Web pages *en masse*. There was only one problem.

Some Infomasters had received complaints from the staff in their department about the Web pages. The complaints were that the information was not accurate. Most often it was a little out of date. Staff complained that they were getting angry calls from citizens who, for instance, had received an invoice for €250 for one month of childcare, while the information on the Web said the maximum fee was €230.

"We have to spend a lot of time explaining to our clients that it is *we* who have the correct information, not the Web. And for some reason they tend not to believe us", said a clerk at the social services office. "Our information changes rapidly these days – changed fees, changed subsidy rates, closed day-care centres, new ones opened, and so on all the time. And the Information Department does not keep up. The Web is the worst problem, because people have the feeling that it should have the most up-to-date information. You know, that's what they say about the Web – 'always the latest information'. Well, I say that's only true so long as someone puts it there."

Sometimes, the information was plain wrong. As one middle manager at the school department said: "It is impossible to make the Infomaster realize that a 'headmaster' is not the manager of a school district, but just of a single school. In fact, in the bigger schools, there is more than one of them. When the Infomaster went to school the school district manager was titled headmaster, but now the title is 'School District Chief Executive Officer (SDC)'. This changed last year, when the district map was redrawn and the districts were reorganized. Fifteen districts were converted into six. The former District Managers, who used to be called headmasters, were re-titled School District Chief Executive Officers, and the former School Managers – or principal teachers, as they used to be called – managing a single school, were renamed headmasters. It's as simple as that, but the Infomaster doesn't seem to get it. So on the Web SDCs are called headmasters and headmasters are called School Managers. They even call education facilitators 'teachers'."

The Infomasters also got emails from citizens and tourists that they did not know what to do with. A typical example would be the following, which occurred one day at the tourist office.

A tourist, having read the city's online list of hotels, and having found the "ask the Infomaster" link at the bottom of the page, sent a message asking to book a double room at the Ambassador Hotel for 4–6 June. The email arrived at a time when the Infomaster had two days off. When he arrived at work on 5 June the tourist had already visited the office only to find that there was no hotel room waiting for him. After a heated discussion, the Tourist Office staff booked him into another hotel, which was not so central was and considerably less comfortable. The man left saying, "Why do you have a Web system at all when what you say there is not true anyway?".

At the weekly staff meeting, the story had reached the Tourist Office manager, Ms Yow Guide, who brought the problem up for discussion.

"Why wasn't the information on the Web correct?", she asked.

"It *was* correct, all right", said the Infomaster. "But I can't help people coming to me with problems which should not be on my desk. Booking hotels is the work of the booking service. *My* job is to collect information and publish it in brochures, the calendar of events and on the Web."

"But we can't answer emails we don't get", said one of the booking officers.

"And I can't stay here over weekends and during my vacation to see if there is email for anyone else", replied the Infomaster.

"So why don't you put all our email addresses on the Web, so that people can contact *us* for bookings, *you* for new information for the brochures, and so on?"

"Look, this Web is killing me anyway", said the Infomaster. "It's taking more and more of my time. Everyone wants ever more information on it, and I'm supposed to answer questions for the whole department 24 hours a day, seven days a week. And not only that – the information keeps changing all the time. Do you mean I should change the Web pages every time there is a stand-in at the desk for the weekend? If you want me to do all that, I need more resources for the Web work, that's for sure. I already have problems keeping up with all the changes."

Ms Guide realized she had a problem – several, in fact. Internal procedures had proved inappropriate because the Web was not integrated with them. The Web itself suddenly appeared like a baby cuckoo, eating ever more and threatening to throw out the other fledglings. On top of all this, the union representative came forward claiming that the Infomasters in all departments were facing a burnout problem: "There are so many demands from everywhere, both customers and staff. And the technology keeps changing all the time – new tools keep popping up every month. You have to check them out in order to keep up with your trade. Something must be done about the Infomasters' work situation".

There was only one simple solution in sight. The Tourist Office was paid a very small amount per year from the Information Department budget for managing the Web (this was what the CIO, Ms Myway, had to pay for implementing the "permanent" Web solution last year). So the first thing Ms Guide did was to go to Ms Myway asking for an increase in that subsidy.

"Look", said Ms Myway firmly. "The system is an *information* system, not a booking service. My department is in the business of informing people. I pay you for doing part of *my* work. If you want *services* on the Web you have to pay for it yourself."

"But people want more and more information on the Web these days", said Ms Guide. "Even if we forget the bookings, there are problems with keeping all the information updated."

"Then rationalize the way you do it", said Ms Myway. "Organize work more effectively. Bee Pee Are![1] Or apply for EU funding or something. Find sponsorship, perhaps. You're a manager, it's your job to make it work. My budget has no slack, so I can't help you even if I wanted to. And besides, if I did, I would soon have everybody running here begging."

Ms Guide was clearly getting nowhere. What to do now? She tried to bring the problem to the attention of the mayor, but he said the same thing as Ms Myway: "We have delegated a budget and some tasks to you. You manage it".

One day, Ms Guide got some unexpected help. One thing that the Information Department had put on the Web was the names, pictures, and email addresses of every politician in the City Council.

---

1    BPR – Business Process Reengineering; a radical change in production operations.

One day, the leading Tapville daily newspaper tried an experiment. It sent an email to each of the politicians (all 46 of them), asking a simple question, the goal being not the answer in itself, but to see if they read their email. Only one, a member of the Liberal party, answered. The results were presented on the first page under the headline "Politicians haven't yet realized the Web is here". The article scored some easy points by joking about politicians lagging behind "ordinary people, most of whom are already on the Web", and went on to criticise the Information Department for putting useless information and services on the Web. The mayor of course read the article and summoned Ms Myway to a meeting.

"Why do you put things like that on the Web without asking those involved if they use the email system?", he asked.

"Listen, Dew. The City Council has decided that political information should be on the Web", replied Ms Myway (who had no lack of self-esteem and was never prepared to be subordinate to her boss). "So I asked the Computer Department for their email addresses and put them there. I inform. Others should manage their part of the business."

"However", she continued, "we do have a real problem here. Many departments have expanded their part of the Web far beyond simply providing information. They provide services of different kinds on the Web. I can't feed that sort of thing on my budget, and judging from the increasing amount of complaints about obsolete information, faulty information, lack of responses and so on, they can't either."

"So what can we do?", asked the mayor, who had great faith in Ms Myway. After all, she was the one who sorted out the previous Web challenge.

"I've talked to SolveIT about the problem. They say we must automate – integrate the Web with existing systems, such as databases, so as to get rid of the double-typing we do now."

"Can you do that?", asked the mayor hopefully. "Set up a new Web challenge task force to automate?"

"I don't believe in automation", she answered. "Publishing is a work of art. You need to know your audience, be able to handle the language, handle graphics, handle layout. You need journalists and graphic designers. Extracting data from a database is not the same thing. That's work for the computer department."

## What Did Actually Happen in Tapville?

The much-celebrated "permanent" solution in Tapville has come to a halt, it seems – not just because the amount of work has grown, but also because the Web publishing management is no longer a champion of the development that seems necessary. The CIO wants to publish journalistic-style information. She is not in the business of automating business processes. She seems to have done a good job so far, but this is not far enough. As the Web grows, there is clearly a need to redesign the procedures to cope. Also, as the Web develops technically, more technical expertise is needed, as is more investment in effective technical solutions. The Web cannot stay in the hands of people who think in terms of brochures and magazines. The problem initially appears to be an economic one (staff overload), but soon reveals itself to be organizational.

What can be done in this situation? This depends a lot on the organization of the city. What *should* be done is to maintain the coordinating role of somebody with knowledge about how to inform, while starting the work on automation in cooperation with the computer department or some external consultant, the technical expertise of which is obviously needed in this situation. But Tapville was not yet ready for that. Let's go back to Tapville and the meeting between the mayor and Ms Myway.

## *Soap*: Tapville Settles for a "Market" Solution

"OK then, Dwit", said the mayor. "I'll leave the automation project to market forces. This means that you'll withdraw your distributed publishing system and stick to what you did before. Each city department will have to manage its own Web system, and they can purchase the services of the computer department whenever they need to. That suits me fine – decentralization is my thing anyway. This internal 'buy-and-sell' system of ours works fine in other areas, so let's run it on this one, too."

There were some complaints when the Information Office announced that it was to withdraw its subsidies for Web publishing to the other departments. In fact, it proved to be impossible. The practical solution became that the departments kept their subsidy in return for a promise to produce a limited amount of general information about their department on the Web. But this job was no longer considered interesting by "the spearheads of the future". They wanted to *develop* things, be creative and innovative. This led to the task of updating the general Web information being devalued and typically being delegated to the departments' secretaries to take care of in between other tasks.

Following the organizational change, Web development projects appeared in many City departments. Often, projects were initiated by the former Infomaster who had moved on to new challenges. They hired new consultants, not only from the computer department, and achieved new things:

- The Tourist Office installed a middleware package to connect its events database with the Web. Tourists could now search from a Web page on dates, types of events, artists, and so on to find answers to questions such as "What's on Today in Tapville?", "When will the Rolling Stones come here?" and "What guided tours of the city are running on 16 May?" It was a very nice application, and it saved the department the tedious work of retyping information from the database into the Web pages. As a bonus, the number of typing errors was reduced because text was typed only once. Also, which was seen as the greatest advantage by the users, events were automatically deleted as soon as they had taken place. By the earlier procedures, the calendar of events was created every Monday, which meant events that taking place on Monday night would be on the list until next Monday afternoon.

  One problem that appeared was that the application ran properly only on some browsers. The consultant company that built it, TapGates Inc., specialized in building middleware for Microsoft products and PCs, so those users who used a Netscape browser on a Macintosh had difficulties viewing the Web pages. In fact, all they could see were a few characters in the top left corner of the page.

- The Information Office produced a search engine covering the whole geographic area of the city. The purpose was to make it easier to find information without knowing exactly in which department it was produced. Private sites were also included, provided they met certain quality criteria, which were defined and properly decided upon.

- The Information Office also produced a magazine-like monthly publication on the Web. It had lots of graphics and contained edited content ranging from city facts to columns and a picture of "The Tapviller of the Month".
- At the Mayor's Office, the staff were now regularly publishing the City Council Minutes on the Web. They did so by moving their word processor files to a special folder, "the Archive", which was accessed by a system constructed in-house which tagged the text into HTML format and published it on the Web.

By now, several consultancies were engaged in the Web system. The Tourist Office had hired TapGates to create middleware and The Information Office had engaged the public relations company ReachOut, which specialized in Web graphics. And the Computer Department had built, with the help of LightFlow Inc., a local consultancy specializing in workflow systems, a proprietary system for converting word processor files to HTML.

At that point, a new problem was introduced. The Computer Department, overwhelmed by the number of requests from various city departments for help in building this and that Web or middleware application, brought things to a halt.

"We need to sort things out here", said Mr Mehrwisser (or more exactly "Dr Dr I. A. M. Mehrwisser", as his business card read), head of "IT", which was the new name of the Computer Department. "We cannot have everyone reinventing the wheel. We need common solutions. Let's build an Intranet on which each department is responsible for providing information within its domain, and let all departments use everything on it. First, we need to maintain some in-house competence, which means we have to focus – we can't use *every* technology available. Second, we have too many consultants already. They all build different things and in different ways. Let's choose *one*, the one that best matches our criteria."

These principles were easy to sell. Setting up common criteria and, toughest, choosing only one consultant from among the lot proved harder. Not only were selection criteria such that none of the eligible consultants could meet them all – graphic expertise, database expertise, middleware expertise, size of the company (for durability) – it also turned out that different departments had very clear (and very disparate) opinions about the different consultants.

To make things even worse, the city had general agreements with some of the major consultants, granting them contracts which paid them a certain amount per year. Buying too much from other consultants would mean not buying work to the value of the contracted sum, which would leave the city paying for nothing.

As things eventually turned out (which, by the way, took eight months), the contract for the Intranet, worth almost €1 million, landed with ReachOut, the public-relations-turned-into-Web-design firm. This was met with some surprise within Tapville, because the company was very small. There were serious worries in the Purchasing Department about handing a million euro contract to a company that had a turnover of no more than two million euros, especially in such a volatile business as Web design. Some competitors, such as LightFlow Inc., were openly upset, because they claimed ReachOut lacked the competence most badly needed, in middleware and databases. The bigger consultants rested calmly, relying on their annual contracts.

The reasons for the choice of ReachOut, as the story was later told in the Tapville corridors, were that because of their successful work with the Web magazine and their similar professional backgrounds (PR rather then computers) they had good relations with Ms Myway, who, in turn, had the mayor's ear. Ears, in fact.

# Problem-Solving Strategies

When entering a phase in which the Web system seems to grow out of hand unless strictly organized, various solutions may be attempted. The basic choice is between two directions: one of centralization and one of decentralization (by which is *not* meant delegation, but true independence). Both have their advantages and their shortcomings. Let us look at a couple of real-world examples.

## The Centralized Approach

The city of OreVille adopted a centralized solution in 1996, at a relatively early stage of its Web development. It decided that it was reasonable to assume that the Web was here to stay, and tried to look far ahead to see what would be needed ten years on. It settled for a workflow system (a document management system) in which every document produced in the city was marked with several labels, such as date of expiry and level of public access. Documents were then automatically published and accessible according to the marking; free internal documents were published on the Intranet, free public ones on the Internet, and documents that for some reason pertained to only a few people were accessible only by those particular users.

Moreover, the city stated that in some years' time, given the existence of this system, more and more people would use it and help themselves to information. This would mean that the jobs of many staff in the information business (front-line personnel) would disappear or change. Therefore, internal discussions about the future roles of these people were started.

This solution must be considered radical for its time. Not only did it contain a technical solution, but the seed of an organizational solution was also planted. As we shall see later in this book, the staff's role will at some point be critical for further development. In OreVille, this was foreseen, which is likely to reduce frictions (although at the time of writing we have yet to see the final results from OreVille).

As for the technical solution, it may prove unnecessarily expensive for OreVille. It started at an early stage, when no system matching its needs was commercially available. For that reason, the city developed one of its own. While this might have been necessary to get things rolling, there is little doubt that waiting a year or so would have meant being in the position of being able to choose systems from a number of software vendors. The city's choice of action might therefore mean that a legacy burden has been introduced in terms of the technology. On the other hand, the increased organizational preparedness is likely to make any forthcoming technical conversion easy to implement in the organization.

To achieve a uniform city-wide effort towards a future goal that is largely defined by what technology makes possible, a centralized approach is probably necessary. Not only is such a goal mainly dependent on a visionary champion to see it through, in a situation where technology is rapidly developing, you can be certain that if you bring four such visionaries into the same room they will come up with four different visions. In the case of OreVille, for instance, the technical solution was not given. Left to city departments, it is likely that several different technical solutions would have been chosen.

## The Decentralized Approach

In many cities, centralization is not possible beyond a particular point, at least at certain points in time.

In 1995, the City Council of Stockwerp decided to divide the city into 24 districts. The stated reason was local democracy. The city, it was said, is too big. People feel isolated from their political representatives in City Hall. Therefore, local city councils were created in each of the 24 districts. Some political decisions were delegated, but the main effort was to provide service locally. In each district, one or more "Citizen Offices" was set up. This office was to provide local information and services, but also locally adapted information and services originating from other sources.

The Citizen Offices were given some room to manoeuvre, but it was also decided that information should be provided in a uniform way at all offices. Also, in every office the citizen should be able to find information about other districts.

This borough reform meant two things from the point of view of providing services. First, a number of local entrepreneurs with ambitions (social, technical, political, business and local) appeared. Second, the need for a coordinating committee to mediate between the different local entrepreneurs became apparent. At first, though, this did not happen.

Political reasons are not the only motives for a decentralized solution. The very size of a city may call for decentralization. Other reasons might be local independence for historical or practical reasons (such as the situation in which districts are very different).

As we saw in the soap, Tapville settled for this solution. We also saw that although it led to a flowering of creativity, it also created diverse technical solutions and manners of working.

## The Decentralize-and-Coordinate Approach

The decentralized approach, as we saw above, may be necessary for particular reasons. It is, however, likely to cause problems in other ways.

In 1997 it became apparent that the local districts of Stockwerp were taking different directions regarding their Web use. Some districts, like SiliVille, with its many business in the IT trade (SiliVille is the 'Silicon Valley' of Stockwerp), kept a relatively high profile, also developing external services aimed directly at citizens. At the other end of the spectrum, some maintained that personal service at the desk, possibly aided by an internal system, was the only way to go.

The activities of local entrepreneurs, set free by the borough reform, meant that the common approach, the "Stockwerp style", was at risk. The reform had not intended just to decentralize, but also to maintain the city as a unit; all of the Citizen Offices were supposed to be able to inform people about every other district. To work in practice, this called for a common profile. This meant that a coordinating committee was needed to mediate between the different local entrepreneurs and to disseminate best practises. Such a committee was set up in 1997. This did not, however, happen by itself, as the result of everyday operations. The crystallising factor was an EU project in the Telematics programme, which had among its goals the creation of a uniform navigation system from the citizens' point of view. This uniform system appeared to require information providers across the city to provide information in a common way, and to have a common understanding of citizens' requirements.

The coordination committee was set up, with some pain, in 1997. There turned out to be problems of three distinct kinds. First, among the local champions there were different opinions about what the citizens really needed. There was also some envy, because some districts were clearly ahead of others in terms of the sophistication of their Web systems (very few had one at all at that time). Third, there was an abundance of consultants involved. The Information Office had hired a consultant to design the "City Web", which was to be the entrance to Stockwerp and the "main menu" on top of the district ones. This consultancy had originally been in the public relations business, but had moved into Web design (as many such companies did at that time). But when it came to coordinating the Web system, there were other consultants involved. There was one to which the computer department had outsourced the maintenance of the city's servers. There was another which had built a "comprehensive information concept", called Service

Centre 2000, for one city district, and wanted to propagate it across the city. Both of them also claimed to have service development concepts. Because issues of design, organization and the adaptation of basic existing computer system were involved, there was a need for cooperation between the consultants. This turned out to be difficult, since all of them had aspirations to handle everything, and because the risk of having too many cooks was apparent. As the city's IT manager put it: "We need to find invoiceable interfaces among the consultants."

# Lessons From the Tapville Solution

The choice between the three types of solution described above is not easy. Quite obviously, there is always a need for both delegation of work and coordination. But the decision on which way to go typically cannot be decided freely. There are traditions, such as in Tapville, or there are changes of direction caused by political decisions, such as in the Stockwerp case.

This is a point where external influence may mean a lot. In Stockwerp, the EU project made a significant difference (which was very hard-earned). In Tapville, there was no such influence, which, as we shall see later, meant future trouble. Generally speaking, there is a need for benchmarking at this point. What directions have others taken, and what have they learned?

In Tapville, the solution was decided very quickly: the CIO rejected the mayor's offer and retreated to the only other solution she knew – enforcing the city's policy of decentralized decision making on IT matters as well.

The solution carried with it some problems that, as we shall see later, fed at least two more challenges. First, the hiring of ReachOut meant that difficult technical problems were placed in the hands of a company which had its core expertise in another field. Second, it would turn out later the real problems with the Intranets had not been foreseen. Those problems were not primarily technical; they were about defining information items and customer needs, and in particular about matching the two. As the head of IT put it later "It would probably have made more sense to hire a librarian for the definition part. They know how to categorize terms". But at that time, no one in Tapville realized this.

Therefore Tapville soon ran into two more challenges. The first was the "messy appearance challenge", which stemmed primarily from the fact that terms were not defined well enough to make the system efficiently searchable by users, and the second was the "cross-organizational integration of data resources challenge", because the organizational social climate was not prepared to pave the way for the large-scale integration of resources that became necessary to feed the Intranet. This was mainly because the ordinary consultants, who were already working city-wide, were not those who were hired for Intranet construction. Therefore the Intranet mockup was built in isolation. Its builders did not have ears in every city department. And apparently the companies that *did* have these contacts did not in fact promote the Intranet solution under construction (some would even say that this wording is an understatement).

# Appearance – Organize the Usability Improvement Process

Typically, as systems grow large and acquire multiple information providers, the responsibility for information provision and updating is delegated. This results in the different departments all wanting to do things their way, and having, or purchasing, the skill to do so. A coordination problem arises: top management wants the organization to appear in a coherent and stylish form on the Web, following a "corporate profile". A public relations agency is brought in to implement a graphic profile programme. This may interfere with work already done, as well as with the different intentions of different departments.

In addition, there is more to a mess than just its appearance. Information systems do not succeed by good looks alone - usability and usefulness are more important. A nice graphic profile may do some good for usability, but it cannot conceal poor organization of the information in the underlying system or poor data quality.

The most immediately apparent symptom of this challenge is that the Web system does not have a uniform design across departments/suppliers. Occasionally, another symptom may show: this happens when someone tests the system for usability (a rare occurrence, unfortunately). In the case of Web systems, such tests often give designers unpleasant surprises.

# *Soap*: Tapville Goes for Styling

When we left Tapville in the previous chapter, all was fine again. The PR company had been assigned to the Intranet job. All departments worked hard to find good solutions for the integration of the Web in their businesses.

One sunny day in April 1997, there was a huge fair in town. There was a special IT feature, and Tapville representatives from the departments that were most prominently visible on the Web were giving presentations. The Tourist Office, the Information Office, the School Department and the Childcare Department were present. Each department's Web site was presented in an upbeat fashion by an enthusiastic Web Development Project Leader. They all had colourful overhead slides showing Web pages with many pictures, logos, and designed backgrounds and buttons (because of the risk of unexpected communication failures, the systems were not accessed online during presentations).

The presentations were applauded. Everyone who was anyone in Tapville was there. There was a lot of talk during the coffee break that followed. The mayor, Mr Voteforme, and the CIO, Ms Myway, bumped into each other. They were soon joined by Kay Twelfve, project leader for the Tapville School Web, accompanied by Celine Freinet, a teacher who had actually produced the School Web pages just demonstrated.

"This is all very fine," said the mayor. "I mean, so many people working so hard to produce all this information on the Web. That's really nice. But look at the pages. They all look so different. Backgrounds are red, blue, white, green, any colour. The same for the buttons. The city logo is rarely there at all. It should be on every page. After all, people must realize this is the Tapville Web. How can they, unless there's some sign to show them? The schools' pages are the worst, I think. Are they done by the pupils? Seems there are too many cooks involved. Can't you introduce some order to this, Dwit?"

"Well," said Ms Myway, who was considerably more aware of the minefield they were about to enter than the mayor, "you can't do both things, you know, Dew. If you go for decentralization, you can't come back to tell everyone exactly how to do things."

"It's all about creativity and communication." Ms Twelfve entered the discussion. "Web design is a creative process. People must *engage* in the process. They must be able to let loose their creativity, and give their personal touch to the design. This is how you make people *listen*. After all, the Web is about people *communicating*. The reader must feel 'Hey, this guy is *talking* to me. He is trying to *tell me* something'. You don't achieve this by introducing standards or by hiring a PR firm to communicate for you!"

The mayor was somewhat stunned by this explosion. But there was more to come as Ms Freinet raised her voice:

"We run a school, not a factory. Our children must be allowed to participate in the creation of our society. They can only do that by hands-on working. You learn more by active doing than by passive reading. By producing the School Web, they learn how the school works. They learn how the medium works. They learn how society works, because they also include the neighbourhood in the Web: shops, the church, City Offices. They also learn about other schools in other cities and other countries, because they too are on the Web. The Web is a pedagogical tool for our pupils, not a PR medium for the city."

"The Web is for the city as well," said the mayor unwisely. "Can't we have one public Web for the city, and an internal one where your classes can work. After all, we must make a professional impression on those who visit our Web."

"It's so typical!", exclaimed Ms Freinet, her voice considerably louder and shriller this time. "You want to make our work invisible:'Let the little boys and girls play, but not so loud that it disturbs the grown-ups'. This is the future generation you are talking about! They want to be seen and heard. And we, the teachers, are actually professionals! We don't 'play with children', we support their socialization by pedagogically proven methods. Do you know that teachers have at least four years of university education, many much more? How many courses did you take? And besides, there is a practical problem: how will we be able to communicate with other schools if we're fenced in?"

The mayor sighed. He had not studied at university at all. He had a background as a union leader. He used to boast about being a manual worker, but in fact he laid bricks only for two years before, at the age of 21, he got his first ombudsman job in the National Building Workers Trade Union, Department 114, Tapville North. Because there was no one to take over, he stayed at that job. Because the labour party had been in the majority in Tapville for many years, and there were constant vacancies for political jobs, he had soon been asked to assume political posts. He was a natural-born speaker, and had good support in the large builders' trade union. He also found that he liked the role of a politician, so he soon found himself on the fast track to high-level Tapville politics.

He despised scholars: "so many words about everything, but never any really practical advice on how to do things. And never wanting to share responsibilities when things go wrong". Now he was up against another of these self-appointed know-alls who had read one or two books too many but didn't know much about the real world. The mayor sighed very quietly. He made a mental note to himself: "Remember to call Jim". ("Jim" was James More, head of the Tapville School Department.)

He was saved by the bell. The coffee break was over, and people reassembled in the auditorium.

## Analysis – What About Appearance?

What we saw at the Tapville conference was a conflict between the interests of appearance and corporate profile, expressed by the mayor, and the interests of professionals to promote their business interests. We also noted that the existence of projects creates certain special project interests, above all expressed by the School Web project leader, Ms Twelfve. Web projects in particular have, over the past few years, typically created very strong feelings, promoted by the general wave of great promises of new technology and by the conviction carried by project leaders feeling part of the "community of IT spearheads", the huge number of colleagues working in other similar projects worldwide.

The example given here is somewhat drastic, but the problem of non-uniform design is apparent in every City Web. The driving forces are not only professional interests, but also the fact that companies are invited to join many City Webs. It is typically not possible to enforce style guidelines are on external organizations; each company wants its own logo and has its own style guide – if not formally, at least in the form of preferences and ways of doing things. While this is natural, the problem with a non-uniform appearance is in fact not just one of appearance. It also creates problems for users searching the Web. If the screen layout and interaction methods changes with every mouse click, the result is cognitive overload. This means that users have to spend a lot of time getting an overview of each screen and understanding its design. Too much of that is tiring and results in users not being able to find what they are looking for. Consider the following episode from tests of the Stockwerp Web site.

> In 1997 the main Stockwerp Web site, 'Stockwerp.se', contained a search facility that searched not only the city's own pages, but also quality approved sites provided by organizations and businesses in the Stockwerp area, such as hotels, cinemas and government agencies. The purpose was to provide users with a single entrance to a complete view of Stockwerp's Web resources.
>
> During usability tests of the Stockwerp Web site, carried out at the request of an international cooperative project that had usability as a key item, this facility was tested. User tasks included searches for information provided by different providers. It became clear that users had problems when, as a result of a keyword search or of clicking on a link, they entered a page that was organized in a considerably different way than the one they just left. They had to spend time searching for items, they didn't easily understand where to click, and they sometimes didn't see the answers provided or understand that this was the answer. They also had problems finding out what keywords to type in the search field, due to unclear organization of the information and uncertainty about terminology. This was apparent from observations, and users also commented on it during the interviews that followed.

From a usability standpoint, it is strongly advisable to make sites that are related in some way look uniform. Often, as in the Stockwerp case, this is impossible to enforce. However, it may be possible to negotiate at least a similar appearance. Usability arguments can make a difference here. No one wants their site to be hard to use. One problem, of course, is deciding which sites actually do belong together. Regional proximity is not the only factor: sites may belong to a branch of a company which has a strong case for coherent corporate appearance. There are ways to deal with such things, such as opening corporate sites in new frames while keeping the original frame with the search engine on the screen.

Once one tries to make a whole of sites from different organizations, there is no simple solution to the problem of similar appearance. The usability argument says that it is usually preferable to try, but not to do so blindly. A uniform appearance is one tool for helping users use the sites, but it is not the only one. As we shall see later (in the chapter on the "Poor usability challenge"), many other factors influence usability. So before making enemies by enforcing strict design regulations, do a usability test and see what happens. Is the diverse page design really a major problem in your case? If not, act carefully on that point and use your resources on other things: simplifying the terminology and making it uniform, improving search facilities, or dealing with other typical Web site problems.

In some cases, it is clear that strict regulations on design *should not* be enforced from the start. This is for at least two reasons:

1.  Technology keeps developing, which means that rigid rules may hamper the appropriate use of more modern, and more functional, tools.

2.  User enthusiasm for the Web should not be underestimated as a driving force. Without it, it may prove impossible to produce a Web worth having. Therefore it may well prove tactically effective to allow some disparity, especially when it does not hurt. Consider the following example.

> EDUDIST is a school in SomeCity, specializing in distance tuition for adults at college level. The students come from all over the country, and traditionally gather at SomeCity several times during a course. During 1996, government travel subsidies were cut, making studies more expensive for the students and leaving

the school with student recruitment problems. The school then decided to start using the Web to reduce the amount of travelling on part of the students.

From the start, there was some discussion about appearance. The IT manager proposed the development of a school standard, whereas the teachers claimed that tuition in English is very different from tuition in Mathematics, and Web design had to be done from the point of view of the pedagogical ideas applied in each subject. The latter course had to be taken, because the teachers' ambitions were strong, concerning both their interest in Web development and their promotion of their own way of working.

Work went very well. Within a year, the different subject groups developed ambitious Webs, including texts, tutorials, interactive tests, communication facilities and links to other relevant Web sites. In at least one case, the textbooks were completely replaced by electronic material. A usability test performed after the first year of development showed that the overall design was very disparate, but within each subject the appearance was relatively homogeneous. Because the typical student studies only one subject at the time, the variety of solutions did not appear to be a problem for the students.

From the school's point of view, there may still be a problem. It seems to be uneconomic in the long run to let each Web page producer spend a lot of time on design issues. Teachers may come and go, and with each new teacher come new ideas. While the abandonment of the centralization effort seems to have been wise for the first step – making things happen in the first place – there is no doubt that a discussion about uniformity will have to be resumed. Although the reference to pedagogical styles will probably always be an element in those discussions, results from usability studies and cross-disciplinary fertilizing of ideas are likely to make a good case for reshaping the courses in a more uniform fashion with regard to features that are not related to discipline-specific pedagogic issues, such as screen layout, colouring, toolbars, etc. EDUDIST again:

After the first year, the IT manager wanted to have independent evaluators assess the "Web courses" produced by the different groups of teachers. The evaluators pointed to the disparate design as one point of concern. They also gave some advice on other design issues, both from the point of view of usability guidelines and from experience of the use of similar systems. The result was positive: the IT manager got a case for resuming the discussions about converging design styles. This time it was easier to make the teachers see the point of common standards, or at least guidelines. It seemed the tests had given them some new ideas, as well as a common language – that of usability. This meant that discussions could continue less hampered by references to personal pedagogical styles and more focused on usability and use issues.

Independent evaluation often serves as a tool for resolving internal discussions. And there is often a need for that. First, Web design is still a new thing. It is often done in the form of a project, and project leaders tend to see the Webs as their babies. This often creates a climate that makes Web criticism a touchy matter. Second, "corporate profile" is something that does not always sit well everywhere in the organization. Enforcing it too strongly may also mean biting one's own tail, because technology changes and best practice in Web design is likely to keep changing for some time. Introducing user aspects is much less conflict-prone. There is no one to deny the appropriateness of doing so; after all, the Web is there to be used by someone. Independent assessment, particularly tests with users from the target population, often proves to be a good way of introducing the customers' viewpoint. As a result, there is a good chance to have discussions that are less coloured by personal preferences and self-esteem, and which focus more analytically on use, usability and usefulness. Such discussions are necessary. Evaluations can tell you what *not* to do and suggest ways of doing things better, but there is no single way of doing things well, and exactly how things are done must ultimately match local styles and preferences. Evaluations should not be ignored; they should just not be allowed to dominate the discussions.

Of course, the decision about "appearance" may not be a discussion of appearance at all. It may conceal a power struggle, and it may affect the ways in which different departments do business.

One year after the start of the MediaPort Seaside Internet initiative, several city departments started to build their own Web sites. The Port Authority, for example built a database-driven Web site, offering information and service to harbour-related target groups. Also, the Department for City Development created their own Web site, aiming for new international investors. The Department of Housing started an Internet service with newly built houses for citizens. At this point, the city's Central Department tried to centralize everything. It wanted to become the primary information department. The Central Department for Infrastructure, physically situated next door to the Information Department smelled a good opportunity to regain power. This was not well received by the chief information officers of the local departments. They wanted to implement their own strategies, using their own styles, focusing on their own target groups, just as things are done in paper-based publications. "Why should communication be organized differently just because another technique is used?", they asked.

Finally, a new project leader was appointed for a new project: Seaside Telematics City, which was an attempt to embed all the existing and new services and ideas in a new environment, the central city square. In order to manage this in a 'live and let live' manner, a strategy in between centralization and decentralization was chosen. We are eagerly awaiting the outcome of this. And we expect to report it in the revised version of this book, due some time around 2003 :-)

After the initial publishing on the Internet initiated by a (sub)department or several (sub)departments, a need for coordination appears which is not necessarily related to the management of a city (centralized or not). Citizens looking for city information are not interested in the source of the information – they are interested in finding the information or service they are looking for. To enable this some form of coordination is needed.

## *Soap*: Tapville Nobility Learns About Usability

Back at the Tapville Web conference, things got worse after the coffee break.

The first post-coffee presentation was given by the Tapville IT strategist, Ig Ternetskij, who reported on system use. There were diagrams showing the number of hits on the major pages. The main page was requested 20 000 times per month, a figure that was increasing. There were thousands of pages, so figures were not reported for all of them. But the strategist could present some blockbusters. One was the Tourist Office's database of events. The other was the fire brigade's "emergency" page. The fire brigade had a highly automated workflow system. Every time there was a fire alarm, this was entered into the system – automatically if it was an automatic alarm, or by the person who answered the phone if it was a manual alarm. The fire brigade had an Intranet, and the alarm immediately produced a Web page that appeared on monitors all over the fire department (interrupting TV programs in the coffee room, for instance). At one point, some wise-guy in the Computer Department got the idea of putting the alarm page on the city's external Web, and it immediately became a great success. It was noted that as soon as the emergency vehicles' sirens sounded, people rushed to their computers and logged on to the city Web to see where the fire was.

There had been some internal discussion about the appropriateness of this. Teachers complained that pupils left their schoolwork to check what was happening on the computer. Some even left school to see the fire. The firefighters complained about an increasing number of spectators, sometimes rendering their work more difficult. But Mr Ternetskij did not bring this discussion up at the seminar.

After the presentation there was time for some questions.

"Who are the people visiting your Web", someone asked.

"As you all know, the log files record *computers* requesting files by their IP numbers, not people", answered Mr Ternetskij. "For reasons of privacy, this is good. You don't want Big Brother watching every step you take, do you?"

"No, but I want to know if this system is used by *everybody*. Isn't it the case that this is just a rich boys' toy?" persisted the inquisitor.

"Not at all. We know there is a lot of use in the schools, for instance. It's not only the rich who go to school".

"But is the system of any *use* to people", asked a woman in the audience. "Knowing where the fire is is not a major problem for anyone except the Fire Brigade. Does the system help people to solving any real everyday problems?"

"We have a lot of information from all city departments", answered Mr Ternetskij. "Political information, information about day care centres. Commercial information. Events. Education. Our Web covers most activities in the city, although the information is not yet complete in all areas. But there are a lot of people working on that."

"But how many people actually visit those pages", returned the first inquirer.

"I don't have the exact figures, but there are hits on those pages as well."

"But aren't a lot of hits not citizens but people working in other cities checking out other city Webs?"

"As I said, we can't see who is requesting pages."

"But you can see if the hit is from a computer in Tapville or somewhere else."

"True, but if we get a hit from, say, Aheadofyou, who are we to tell whether it's a Tapviller checking his home town pages from a distance or a Web designer from Aheadofyou shopping around for design inspiration? And besides, I for one think it's good that cities learn from each other."

"So you don't know the extent to which Tapvillers visit the city Web?"

"As I said, given the way technology works, and complying with the laws on privacy, we can't know who visits our Web. And we shouldn't know."

The discussion was a bit unpleasant. It left the feeling that the Web could be questioned. But as the hits were many and increasing, the general feeling was that Web use was growing and would continue to grow, thus increasing the reach of the system and making it more valuable for propagating city information.

The next presenter was a PhD student from Tapville University. He had, as part of an EU project, made what he called a "usability study" of the Tapville Web. This time, things really got scary.

"I am Boc Worm of Tapville University Department of Informatics", he introduced himself. "As a part of the EU project "**In**formation and **Se**rvices to the **C**itizens at **R**equest (Insect), we have done a so-called usability study of the Tapville Web. Let me first explain how such a study is done.

"People go to the city Webs for a purpose. They don't surf around, they have some problem they want solved (unless they are city Web designers who want to check out what other cities have produced on the Web). We have identified some such common problems. Then we asked a few people, ordinary citizens representing different ages, levels of education, computer experience and so on, to try to solve these tasks using the City Web. Because the Web is currently not so comprehensive – mostly superficial information, not many actual services..."

(At this point, Tapville's IT strategist was heard breathing more heavily than usual.)

"...we have made the tasks really simple. Examples are 'Find the name of the chairperson in the local city council of Agesta', 'Find out the current price of electricity', 'Find out the opening hours of Tapville Public Baths' and so on.

"When you observe people searching – we filmed them – you can easily see where in the system they go wrong. It is also most often relatively easy to understand *why*. The findings can be confirmed by subsequent interviews.

"We found that 20% of the tasks were never accomplished. People got lost. I think that's quite a lot, considering that our testers were experienced computer users (it's hard to find anyone without any experience in computer use these days, ha, ha, ha), and well educated. And the tasks were simple. They required just a few clicks, if you choose the menus to navigate.

"We found some general flaws in the design, to which we can attribute the failure to accomplish tasks. One is unclear and *inconsistent terminology*. Another is *unclear cues* – the system doesn't tell people enough about what it is doing. A third is *departmentalization* – organization of information in such a way that it requires users to know about the departmental division of labour rather than seeing it from a user task point of view. A fourth is *cognitive overload* – there is often simply too much on the screen. A fifth is that because users meet many designs, one for each department, they must almost constantly re-create their *mental model* of the system."

"What can be done about it?", asked a technician from the Computer Department.

"There's no easy answer to that", answered Mr Worm. "Usability tests reveal what is not working, but there is more than one way to make things work. There is no single best design, but there are several dos and don'ts. Implementing them can take time, though, because you have to be consistent across the whole system – sometimes even including parts you don't own yourself. My best advice is to go through your system with the results of our study in mind and see where changes can be introduced. Some changes are simple, but some require much work – streamlining the terminology, for example. Although there are ways around that, too."

"Name one", the technician kept on pushing.

"Well, you can use software that makes use of synonyms, homonyms and the like to make search tools better. I could expand on this, but I see the moderator is eager to close the session."

So he was, and so he did. The technical solution was never presented to the Tapville elite that day. (We, however, shall return to the software solution in the chapter on "Poor usability". There, we shall exemplify the concepts of conceptual overload, mental models, cues, inconsistent terminology, and departmentalization.)

After the seminars had closed for the day, the Mayor and Ms Myway met briefly before going home.

"Phew!", said the mayor. "This university guy really gave me the creeps. People can read, can't they? And if they don't bother to read our information, who are we to blame? Usability, bah! Good thing he was so boring to listen to. I'm sure not many did. *Of course* our Web is easy to use! I've tried it myself. I had no problem finding the Public Baths. I just went to the Administrations page, then to the Technical Office, then to the Sports arenas section, and there it was! Piece of cake for anyone but an academician. I don't want a mental model, anyway – I just want a nice Web."

"Still, there is something about terms", said Ms Myway, who after all was experienced in the information business and knew how confusing you could make things by using too many and too unclear words. "Maybe we should try to standardize the municipal vocabulary a bit. Perhaps we could have a Tapville dictionary on the Web. To explain what terms mean. To teach people how things work."

# Lessons From the "Messy Appearance" Challenge

As we have seen in this chapter, what originally surfaced as a problem with messy appearance turned out to be not only that, but also a problem of usability. The usability problem was shown by tests, but the poor means for monitoring use also meant that there was no one to tell whether the poor usability actually affected use. Was use in fact mostly internal, as someone suggested? Were there only a few "real" users, citizens? We don't know, because the Webmaster had no tools for finding out. At this point, we have thus seen that there are flaws in design – users in many cases actually don't find what they are looking for, and usage figures are impossible to interpret in terms of how useful the system is to users.

Usage figures from city sites show that users typically visited only once (logged by IP number). There are many pages that are visited very little (e.g. those on politics). Is that because people are not interested, or because they cannot find them, or even that they do not realize they are there? We do not know yet, and most Webmasters around the world do not.

As for the problem of monitoring use, we will return to that in the "Poor usability" chapter. As for the problem with messy appearance, there are some simple pieces of advice:

1.   What is *really* a mess can be relatively easily decided by a test against Web usability design standards (benchmarking). Do that. But remember:
2.   Technology changes. Do not define every detail. Use common visual cues, but don't define every pixel of the screen.
3.   If the system is not really a mess, but simply has a diverse appearance, do a usability test with real users to see to what extent the diverse appearance is a major problem for them. Other candidates are inconsistent terminology, cognitive overload, poor organization of information, wrong information in relation to user problems, and so on. Spend your resources first on the problems that cause the worst problems for the users.
4.   Organize the usability improvement process. Again, because Web use will change, allow the process to be flexible. Producer enthusiasm is important, and it rests on the feeling of being able to create something; *do not define everything* beforehand.

We can see that appearance is linked to usability. Usability has to do not only with appearance, but also – at the end of the day, most of all – with content. Ultimately, some kind of editorial board, central or distributed (possibly several of them for different parts of the system or different issues), must be set up to address the issues pertaining to Web appearance and content. The editorial board must keep updated on all activities of the city within the field of the Internet, as well as with best practices in the trade. The tasks of the group includes the following:

1.   Deciding what "corporate profile"/attitude to take towards the clients you want, and specifying this at a guiding, but not too creativity-restricting, level of detail.
2.   Deciding on standards and guidelines for content, again at a reasonable level of detail.

3. Deciding on update frequency, when necessary, and other quality-of-service matters.

4. Making evaluations of the use of services and *using them* to improve quality.

5. Keeping informed about the new possibilities of the Internet in order to implement them within the city.

6. Trying to understand users' requirements, demands and wishes, not just as a reaction to direct complaints, but for the purpose of spotting what directions use is likely to take at some time in the future.

7. Encouraging local Web champions who want to try to experiment with more advanced systems or new kinds of services.

8. Propagating the results of such experiments within the organization.

These tasks cannot be settled once and for all. Not only does technology change, so do users and use habits. As systems become more useful, contain more and better information, and become better known, more users will come. Also the general dissemination of technology in society will contribute. According to Table 3.1, the telephone needed almost ten times as long as the Internet to reach 50 million users. In early 1997, 15% of the Swedish population used the Internet, including 22% of those aged 16–35 (Österman and Timander, 1997). Today, there are reports that Sweden, as well as the rest of Scandinavia and the USA, have over 40% Internet penetration in the home[1], while some countries in southern Europe have only around 4%. All of the figures are rising, but at different rates in different countries, in different regions within a country, and among different user groups. Users will become more experienced and more demanding. There will be an increasing number of good sites around, and your site is competing. If your local online bookstore has a poor site, people will buy books from stores elsewhere. There will be competition in more areas. Although some government business will always be local, the Internet makes it easier for people to see what other cities provide for their inhabitants and require similar services in their home towns.

The list of tasks for the editorial board makes it clear that simply hiring a PR firm to fix the appearance of the site will not do the trick. They can give you some useful ideas for graphic design, but a librarian is likely to do a better job of organizing the terminology. One of the things currently on the agenda in government is how to use meta-tags; this seems like a simple idea for organizing the Web, but the headache, of

**Table 3.1** Time to reach 50 million users for some technologies (adapted from Holst *et al.* (1999, p. 242))

| Technology | Number of years from introduction to use by 50 million people |
| --- | --- |
| Radio | 38 |
| TV | 13 |
| Internet | 4 |

1 Öhrling Coopers & Lybrand (1998) found that in September 1998, 46 of the Swedish population aged 18–74 had Internet access at home and/or at work. Forty per cent said that they actually use it. Among those who use it in the home, 26% use it daily; among those using it at work that figure is 43%.

course, lies in how to classify the contents. In no city is the definition of terms crystal clear. Furthermore, it makes good sense to try to achieve uniform definitions of at least a basic set of terms on a national level. Some countries have taken a centralized approach to this (for instance Norway), while others, like Sweden, are currently using a bottom-up approach to chart meta-tag contents.

There is also a need for technical knowledge to understand what it is possible to do technically. For evaluations, expertise in usability is needed. Because many of the tasks of the board are not about making decisions, but instead require negotiation, political competence is also necessary.

# 4. Challenge 4: Parallel Systems – Use Electronic Services Only When You Need Them

By now, the PR agency, or the internal working group, has made the system look nice. Content is produced efficiently, and at least some people use the services. But all the manual operations are still in place and run just as they did before. The Web system has not replaced anything. The first cost challenge then arises: "Why is there no process re-engineering? When banks introduced automated teller machines, this led to fewer customers entering their offices. The result was substantial cost savings in those offices. Why does this not happen with our City Electronic Services?".

Re-engineering does not happen automatically. The conservative forces in an organization are typically stronger than those striving for innovation. Determined measures must be taken. And even when this is done, changes take time, and often must be allowed to take time.

Let us start with a case where things went well.

In Seaside City the job vacancy agency started to distribute its information electronically in the early 1990s. Initially, they did this by use of videotex terminals placed in all job agencies. Later, they also published the latest job vacancies on teletext and interactive teletext. From 1995, this information was also made available on the Internet.

The service was started for efficiency purposes. All job vacancies were stored in a paper-based file system, which had several drawbacks: it was expensive, it was hard to retrieve information from it, and information was often not up to date. At the end of the 1980s they started to publish the job vacancies in a special job newspaper, which was sent to all people looking for a job and distributed in several public places.

> With the advent of electronic publishing of job vacancies, new target groups could be reached, information was more up to date, and the quantity of printed newspapers could be reduced. They also stopped sending the newspaper to every customer – a great saving.

This is an example where the introduction of an electronic service more or less immediately led to positive effects: the Seaside City job agency not only achieved more efficient dissemination of information, but also reduced its costs. But this does not happen automatically. Let us introduce another example from the same city.

> The SME Information Office of the Seaside City corporation for city development offers information to SMEs on available SME housing. This information is available in a DataPerfect database, containing information from over 30 commercial real estate offices. In 1995 an application was built to enable SMEs to retrieve information from this database through videotex or interactive teletext. The update procedure for this application takes a couple of hours. A command starts the automatic update procedure, which makes an output file from the database, converts it to videotex structure, and then sends it by phone to the videotex server.
>
> One year later, this service also became available in a more sophisticated way through the Internet. The update procedure there is also automatic, but takes only a few minutes.
>
> Now that the Internet application is running, the staff at the information office are no longer willing to update the videotex application. Though it is still available through videotex and interactive teletext, the information is no longer up to date. The office staff do not want to keep up all those parallel systems, so they unilaterally chose which service would be updated and which would not.

In this example parallel system were kept, but one deteriorated because it was more tedious to manage and because the new one was perceived as more modern. It is, of course, not good to half keep a system – to keep it available but not at good quality.

## *Soap*: The Tapville Web Dream Team Hits Economic Reality

One rainy day in Tapville...

The Tapville Web project is going fine again. The system's corporate graphic profile has been given a comprehensive overhaul by the PR consultants, ReachOut. Everybody is happy again, and the Web looks better than ever.

Today, the Director of City Finances, Mr Calvin Culator, has attended a management information meeting and has listened to a presentation by the general Web project operations manager, Mr Web Macahan, about the project activities. A couple of staff members from other departments – social services and technical services – participating in the development project also tell about their experiences. They present Web pages, activities so far, and future plans, but Mr Culator is not happy.

"We have been tracing Web activities in the different departments", said Mr Culator. "It is not easy, because much work done on the Web is not accounted for in the Web project but is hidden. People do Web work as part of their regular activities: marketing, client contacts, report writing, minute writing, and so on. We've had to talk to people about what they do and make estimates based on that.

"Although we can't pinpoint every euro, it is evident that several person years of effort have been spent on development, but all we've got so far is a multitude of Web pages and some inoperative service prototypes. And it's not just city staff working hours. Computing equipment has had to be upgraded and external software companies have been hired to develop the prototypes."

"But the projects are EU funded", objected Mr Macahan.

"It is true that the departments have received some partial funding from a national development project, but the brunt of the financial burden, equivalent to €500 000, has simply been taken out of departmental budgets", Mr Culator hit back. "And that's without counting the hidden costs. We estimate those to be another €150 000. And this money is 0% EU funded."

"But Cal", said the Mayor, "isn't it the same in other cities?"

"I don't know", said Mr Culator. "I've talked to some people. It seems nobody has done such a thorough investigation into Web costs as we have. Seems to me the Web is a cuckoo in the nest everywhere."

"Of course it's hard to say what reasonable costs for development are", said Mr Macahan. "Services will pay back eventually, no doubt, but the road is long. Still, once you're on it, there's no way back. That would mean wasting all the investment so far. Not to mention lagging behind other cities."

"I don't know about the necessity of the system", replied Mr Culator. "But I *do* know that yesterday we had a finance meeting at which the social services department announced a deficit of €10 million, compared with their budget, and asked for permission to exceed their budget accordingly. Investment's fine if it pays back, but we also have to pay our bills in the meantime."

"And there's another problem, too", he went on. "The Letters to the Editor column in the *Gazette* is having a heated debate about the city forcing frail elderly people to go on living alone unassisted in cold houses, because of insufficient staffing at the home care division. What do we say to the papers when they ask us why we are spending money on the Web instead? And frankly: how come you have wasted half a million on something that is not usable in any activity, without ever giving any indication that you would be doing something like this in the two previous annual city budget seminars?"

"The work was never expected to drag on for so long", said the Social Services presenter. "But we have to move at the same pace as the other European cities participating in our project. And EU bureaucracy means that we have to produce so many reports. It actually takes time away from working."

"And as time went by, we realized that the project required the use of external software development", said the presenter from Technical Services. "And the company profile programme took time and cost money."

"Well, we had to enforce that", said the mayor, "because it didn't happen by itself. We have had several EU projects and each has developed its own style guide. If you guys had talked more to each other instead of flying around Europe eating expensive dinners, we would have had a more conforming system to start with. Perhaps even a profitable one."

This was clearly not a good day for the Web project team. And it was getting worse.

"Well, we have this situation", went on the Mayor. "What can we do about it? Cal?"

"We can't have everybody running around and hiring expensive consultants doing prototypes", said the Director of Finance. "We must be in control of expenditure. And we must make sure that all spending conforms with our plans. Our city goals are more important than those of EU projects. Those projects are just a means of getting money for things we want to do anyway. Project leaders must realize that."

"But we must report to the Commission on our project results!", exclaimed the Social Service project leader somewhat indignantly. "Project goals must be fulfilled! And it's not like we're playing around having fancy meals at the city's expense. Our style guide is based on scientific research, and so are our user requirements. We know what needs to be done to provide proper services. It only takes time to implement the knowledge, because knowledge and results have to be disseminated within the city. Departmentalism has to be overcome, and people need to be more open to scientific findings and the technological state of the art."

"Well", Mr Culator said with a little smile. "There's more than one way to write a report. And scientists disagree on most things, anyway."

"So, what do you say, Cal?", said the Mayor. "Every investment and consultation contract must be endorsed by you beforehand?"

"Definitely. But plans should also be checked by Iam[1] for coherence in terms of sharing of resources and matching the city's IT infrastructure. Having a check on spending is one thing, but conformance with overall IT plans and activities is also important."

"A group, then", said the Mayor. "You, Cal, and you, Iam. Plus anyone you feel is needed. Reporting to me and to Dwit whenever there is something to report. Deal?"

There was no opposition to the decision. The mayor went on to say that Cal and Iam were to promptly work out a plan suggesting measures that would ensure that the extra spending could be recouped within three years.

"Suggestions for the recovery plan within a month", the mayor said, looking more at the Web team than at Dr Mehrwisser and Mr Culator. It was clear where the mayor had placed his bets.

"So, guys", the mayor closed the meeting. "The days of wine and roses are over. Let's get Tapville back to reality."

# Analysis – Cutting Gordian Knots Looks Impressive but May Prove Unproductive

The development of electronic services to citizens is a long-term process. In the course of the work, an increasing number of staff and management become involved. Each new person and department has to be introduced to the mission of the project. And not only must they be informed about it, they must also be won over to contribute to its goals.

Much of the information to be conveyed is tacit – it cannot be easily explained in words. After initial misunderstandings, the new contributors start to appreciate how they could use the new services for the benefit of their customers, as well as easing their own daily work. Each such suggestion calls for a modification to the technical implementation of the service. Some suggestions cannot be implemented at all, and the external software company employed, or the internal city experts, must spend time thinking of possible work-arounds.

Electronic services are socially complex processes. Their development is a highly transient phenomenon that will typically take between six and eighteen months of collaboration with users and staff before going into operation. All this unforeseen complexity necessarily adds up to substantial unforeseen costs in time and money. Moreover, the issues that arise with each new service are initially mostly unique: there is no ready-made answer to any of them. The costs keep on mounting, often without any concrete, visible improvements for citizens or staff.

---

1   The reader may recall that "Iam" is Dr I. A. M. Mehrwisser, head of the Tapville IT department.

At some point, when most city departments have already been involved in these activities, the cost will be taken up at city management level, and questions raised about whether it is ever going to be possible to recoup it. In the short term – under, say, three years – this is a very hard question to answer.

Alexander the Great's cutting of the Gordian knot has become the symbol of creative executives finding simple working solutions to complex problems. While there is no question about the need and appropriateness of Calvin Culator's argument that he needs to be in charge of spending, the hard solution chosen is very debatable. It is likely to kill much Web enthusiasm and reduce the possibility of engaging in new projects. It would probably have been wiser to go for a softer solution, certainly including some element of control, but most importantly including some measure by which experiences from individual projects could be propagated across departments so as to increase project quality rather than just keeping strict budgetary control.

Let us now take a look at some strategies commonly chosen when in a situation similar to that of Tapville.

## Sweat It! – Staff Overloading as a Cost Cutting Measure

Since service staff have participated in electronic service development, they can be assumed to have done so in order to rationalise their work. In Tapville, home care staff participated in the development of Internet-based teleshopping. It had been calculated that they might save a third of their time by not having to physically shop on behalf of their elderly customers. The manager of the Social Service Department saw this as a great opportunity to demonstrate improved efficiency to the City Council. He ordered the daily norm of operational home care staff to be raised from three clients to four.

In reality, home care staff had not yet learned how to use the new service. Any time they might have saved was spent sorting out confusing situations arising from inappropriate use of the teleshopping service by inexperienced staff and service operators alike. The staff were outraged by the new order, and became hostile to developing the service any further. After six months of unsuccessful trials, and after the shopkeeper who had initially participated in service development had left, the service was shut down. This investment was never recovered.

## Serve Yourself! – Throwing the Burden Onto Users

An alternative to staff overloading is to transfer some of the workload to users by asking them to carry out for themselves some tasks that were previously carried out by staff on their behalf. This will allow staff to be made redundant, or preferably to be transferred to other tasks.

Users – citizens – are typically happy to do things by themselves under two conditions: either they save time or money by doing tasks themselves, or they get a better quality of service that would not otherwise be available at all. An example of the former would be a service, such as applying for an extension to a licence, a residence certificate or other similar task, that does not require personal presence. Filling in the necessary information on a Web form would forward the application to an appropriate official, who prints, checks and approves it, and sends the relevant document by mail.

An example of the latter benefit could be seeing information on available rental apartments or job opportunities on a Web site, without having to visit an appropriate office to view it.

> If you visit the City Library in FarawayTown on a typical afternoon, you will find that all 10 terminals available for checking the status of an individual book are occupied, while normally there are fewer than a hundred people in the library at any one time. The library system automatically checks for the presence of the volume requested in any of the other city libraries. A similar system works between all the university libraries in the country, and allows people to browse for books nationwide on the Internet. Remote loans are initiated by a librarian, however, in order to cover the legal responsibility for the fate of a book borrowed in the standard manner.

In the latter case, there is an improvement of service. Cost recovery occurs only if self-service inquiries replace telephone or visit-based ones. In the former case, staff effort is saved, but the revenue from a service fee will also be diminished. The economic impact of introducing electronic services will therefore depend on whether the service to be replaced by self-service was a profitable city activity. Typically, the fee for a self-service arrangement must be zero, or at least substantially lower than the fee for the corresponding human-mediated service. This is the primary way to attract users to transfer to self-service without causing complaints by removing the human-mediated variant altogether. Yet another argument for this is that making the self-service activity a paid-for service is somewhat complicated given the current state of the art, since it requires users to have an electronic payment capability. For the time being, this is a much rarer commodity than an Internet connection.

It is also possible to overdo the self-service aspect. A good example of this is provided by banks in Finland.

> Since the late 1970s, following a global trend, Finnish banks have introduced ATMs (automated teller machines) in increasing numbers. It is common to have farms of ATMs providing different self-service functions grouped in the entrance lobby of a bank office. Since 1996, most banks have also aggressively promoted Internet-based self-service payments and balance inquiries.
>
> The public mostly used the ATMs as cash machines until the economic crisis that hit Finnish banking in 1991 forced almost all the banks to dramatically restructure their office network and staff. The reasons for the crisis were not found in customer service, but in bad loans, but customer service was the easiest target for cost cutting.
>
> To cover their losses, the banks increased the service fees for human service, while initially offering self-service facilities for free. Moreover, they reduced staffing levels in offices to a degree that brought constant queues to branch offices, with queuing times frequently between 15 and 30 minutes.
>
> As a result, all of the impatient customers left the branch office for good. In the 1980s, a bank office in Finland was a fashionably furnished, clean and efficient place to visit, with busy customers negotiating their business with officials in a somewhat opulent atmosphere. In the 1990s, the remaining offices have moved to cheaper locations, and the floor is filled with dozens of chairs, where retired and unemployed people patiently sit, chatting among themselves while waiting to be served. Professionals and young people are nowhere to be seen.

Not only has the bank branch office fundamentally changed its image, online banking is just about to begin. Once customers lose the habit of meeting the people serving them face-to-face, they become permanently mobile, hunting for bargains in service fees, loans and mortgages alike. Banks in Finland are doing good business again, but they may not know the final consequences of the transition they have initiated.

Without really intending to, the large Finnish banks have shifted the target of their personal customer services from high-income clients to low-income ones. The emerging market niche for personal services to busy high-income customers, unwilling to spend hours queuing to be served, was quickly spotted by a number of new entrants to the banking scene. Many new banks offering personal service to an exclusive clientele have quickly gained market share in Finland. Moreover, they couple loans and personal investment advice to their standard services. Such a coupling has proved highly profitable compared with the ever-decreasing profitability of basic personal banking services to low-income clients.

## Making Web Services Pay Back Themselves

After a settling period, the Internet team and the Task Force in Tapville will realize that producing services for citizens in the Information Society is a subtler task than simple automation for self-service. The real goal must be to integrate Internet-based service components into the total service process in such a way that they improve the service and save time and labour, all at the same time.

In such a process, there are some key principles to follow.

### Select A Popular Service

It is not useful to automate a service that needed only a few dozen times a year. There is no way of recovering the development costs if the service in its current form does not demand a lot of work, no matter how suitable it might otherwise be. This may seem self-evident, but when it comes to public sector electronic services there is much talk about providing services to "weak groups", be they elderly, handicapped or whatever (without much discussion of what "weakness" means). While these groups should not be excluded, electronic services only make sense if there are people interested in using them. Elderly people, for example, often already have services arranged in a manner that works well for them. They don't need to save time, for instance, which is one of the common arguments for electronic services. So in many cases they are not likely to become users of electronic services just because they are elderly. There may be other reasons, of course, for them (or someone on their behalf) to be interested, such as when home care staff do shopping for their clients. Find out those reasons before implementing a service. Don't let political correctness obscure reason.

*Give users a genuine improvement of service.* If the electronic version of a service does not save users any effort, they will not use it, as this simple example shows.

Soul City wanted to provide applications for day care placements over the Internet. A system was built whereby information about all day-care centres was provided, prices and available places could be checked, and applications could be filled in and returned online.

Nobody used the service. Analysis revealed that people who are new to the childcare system (those who are about to register their first child) need to discuss a number of things with the administration officer. It is not just about choosing a site. Most people want the nearest one to where they live and will choose that one if they can. Because most centres are government-owned, the teaching and fees are the same everywhere and staff may rotate among sites. Distance from home is often the only difference between them.

But often that centre is already crowded, so parents have to go for the second-best choice. In that situation, they want to discuss the possibility of getting a place that is sufficiently nearby, or of obtaining alternative forms of care (such as in-family care), and so on. So they call an officer to ask. Once the discussion is finished, they can order a form there and then. It does not make much sense to hang up, log on to the Internet and fill in a form. There is typically also not much of a hurry – a day or so doesn't matter; people tend to apply months in advance because there is at least a three-month waiting period. In fact, a premature choice may reduce the chances of getting a service at all. If one chooses a service for which there is a long queue, one may end up receiving a day-care place so far away that it is useless in practice, instead of a (slightly less preferred but considerably more useful) family service nearby.

Another group of users includes people who want to register their second or third child. In that case, there is a guaranteed place at the same day-care centre as the other child(ren). So this group is not in much of a hurry either. The Internet system provides no added value.

To give some examples of the benefits of clearly improving the quality of a service, let us look again into the world of books.

Amazon.com, the well-known Internet supplier of books and music, is quickly gaining market share in international book sales. This is at the expense of specialist book stores in towns and small cities. The hook Amazon catches its customers on is two-pronged. Firstly, it has a selection of millions of different volumes, unmatched by any physical book store on earth. Secondly, since it has no shops to maintain, it can undersell any bookshop, particularly on low-volume titles. Amazon wins simply because it offers a better service to an important customer segment: knowledgeable, selective readers.

As a consequence, in Faraway Town, and simultaneously in six other small cities and towns in Finland, one of the two specialist book stores in the city was sold to its competitor in 1997. In this decision, the two decisive factors were adverse demographic developments and the impact of Amazon in a country with high Internet penetration.

Another case of clearly improved service, again from the world of books, was discussed earlier; where the Finnish libraries clearly improved their service by adopting city-wide and nationwide electronic search systems, which ensure that a book can be easily borrowed if it resides in any library using the common information system.

### Use Telematics to Eliminate Simple, Tedious Service Processes

It is very easy to be over-optimistic about the degree of automation brought about by an electronic service. Most services, simple though they may seem, are simple only for intelligent humans communicating with intelligent human clients. Many obvious human functions, such as calling a client for clarification about an application, are not within the scope of a machine's capabilities. Choose services for electronic implementation where a person currently merely investigates documents, fills in a form, makes rule-based calculations etc. – not ones where it is necessary to communicate with other people.

Call centres are nice intermediaries between manual and fully automated services. They process simple queries in a very efficient manner, with agents sharing their working hours between many different types of request. Call centres should not be used to handle complex inquiries that require specialist knowledge and case-dependent analysis. Such requests will receive incomplete and possibly incorrect replies from non-specialist call centre personnel. But allocating simple queries to a call centre will eliminate the need to maintain physical information points in places where the volume of queries does not justify full-time occupation costs.

### Insert the Electronic Component of a Service Seamlessly Into Current Operational Practice, with Minimum Change to Established Working Patterns Unless Gains Are Apparent to the People Involved

Sometimes this principle requires stopping the service re-engineering process short of its useful scope. This happens if a technically simple improvement towards self-service would, for example, call for a complete change to a staff member's working pattern before the electronic service can be adopted at all. It is even more dubious to change a person's responsibilities. The ensuing retraining and renegotiation process in such a situation easily outweighs the expected economic benefits. It is better first just to carry out the modifications that eliminate certain processing stages, but do not eliminate staff roles in a service, as the following example shows.

> A teleshopping service was developed for FarawayTown's home care staff in Finland. In the service process, a home care staff member visiting a client phones the back office and leaves the client's shopping list in a voice mailbox. At a suitable moment, a staff member working in the back office listens to the voice mail and keys the order in on a Web form. The order form is sent out to the shop for printing, and the goods are collected and delivered on twice daily rounds to clients.

The service eliminates the need for a home care staff member to go shopping herself on behalf of the client. She can both save time, and spend some more of it with her client. A calculation of working hours shows that FarawayTown home care department saves €7 per shopping basket in working hours, after deducting the fee that the shop charges for collecting and delivering the grocery. Moreover, the city can offer the teleshopping service on its own to the many elderly clients who do not yet need full-blown home care services. Economic reasons would force most such clients to be left without any service at all at present. The teleshopping service thus simultaneously saves money, improves the service that current clients get, and allows new clients to be served with a great reduction in anticipated costs.

### Once You Have a Service That is Used, Find a Way to Make Savings

Realizing savings is often hard in a public sector environment. Often, making people redundant is no real saving because what was once salary cost reappears in the form of unemployment support. It is likely that a better way is to find work for people in new positions. Still, you must ultimately be able to prove that your investment in electronic services will pay off, one way or another. But rationalizing internal procedures in a city is a Sisyphean task. It is much easier when it comes to purchasing services.

> Stockwerp purchases press coverage services for certain employees in the city. Many people need to know what is written in the press about the city; whether events are reported correctly; what image is given of the city; and so on. In 1997, the biggest daily paper introduced an electronic search facility through which people themselves can search, by keyword, a database containing articles from four major daily papers. The archive goes back one year.
>
> This service not only increases the search facilities available (the data was not filtered by the press agency, everything was ready at hand, and search patterns could easily be reconfigured), it also made it possible to give the service to more people and it saved costs.

A city not only produces services, it also uses them, some of which are produced by the city itself. Benefits from services may come not only from reducing staff or costs, but also from expanding, increasing the service level, selling services to a wider audience, and even exporting services. Do not automatically (through tradition, political correctness etc.) exclude any of these possibilities. Shrinking is not the only way.

### Do Not Expect, or Promise, Economic Gains in the Short Term

Even if you follow our advice, you are not likely to make great economic benefits soon. The possibility of replacing manual services altogether in a public sector environment is not immediate. Even if a service becomes very successful, you will have a hard time changing the organizational structure. And because electronic services will never be used by everyone, there will always be at least some need for other delivery media. Automated teller machines have been around for a long time, and many people still never use them, for various reasons.

## Conclusions From the Parallel Systems Challenge

The list below summarizes the conclusions discussed in the previous section.

- Select a popular service. Do not let political correctness obscure reason.
- Give the users a genuine improvement in service.
- Use electronic services to eliminate simple, tedious service processes. Choose services for electronic implementation where a person currently merely investigates documents, fills in forms, makes rule-based calculations etc. – not ones where it is necessary to communicate with other people.
- Insert the electronic component of a service seamlessly into current operational practice, with minimum change to established working patterns.
- Once you have a service that is used, find a way to make savings. This may be done by decreasing in size and reducing the number of staff, but it may also be achieved by increasing your domains: by increasing the service level, by selling the service or even by exporting it.
- Do not expect, or promise, economic gains in the short term.

# Future Technical Platform – Look Back, Look Aside, Look Ahead

For the electronic services entrepreneur, there are a number of technological, or at least technology-related, choices to make in order to avoid drastic changes in the future – which database should we use? Which Web platform? There is also the problem of integration of legacy systems. Nobody can give a definite answer to these questions – only more or less educated guesses. And because more is better, there is a good argument for dwelling on the issues pertinent to technical platforms.

In electronic services, technology is strongly intertwined with social factors: accessibility by intended users and technical competence of the intended developers. In fact, the human factors are more important than the technical ones. The Internet technologies are themselves not particularly complex, but the human and organizational problems that arise from the integration of the operations of different actors that the technology lends itself to are.

Factors to consider are intended distribution channels (the Internet, kiosks, TV, mobile devices), legacy systems (do they have Web extensions?), the competence of city IT staff or available contractors, the desired functionality (static, dynamic, interactive, communicative?), and the cost of hardware and software (not forgetting the cost of building and maintaining the applications, which often exceeds the acquisition cost). How stable is the platform chosen, and how likely is the provider to stay in business? What is the future of a particular technology; are you about to choose a technology, based on an established technology and provider, that will soon be rendered obsolete?

Discussion of the above question cannot be left to a Web project: the city must look beyond each project. Most telematic development projects will not meet their deadlines and they will need to run for many years in order to recoup their costs. The technology chosen should both allow immediate implementation, and yet be stable enough to allow ongoing operational and development work for up to five years or more.

This challenge typically comes as a surprise. Most people think that setting up an electronic service system is mainly a technical challenge. Consequently, people go through lots of effort to check out the latest technology. There are, however, other aspects of how people choose technology that are more worth discussing. In the long run (sometimes not so long), as we shall see, these are also far more important than any particular technology itself. Therefore this chapter deals with the social processes around technological platforms, rather than the platforms themselves.

There is a point in each project when, for the first time, a lot of money has to be spent: buying hardware, buying software or spending money on in-house software development and maintenance. Faced with this situation, the problem is changing every week because of the extremely rapid development of Internet-based solutions. This leads to the question: why should I spend a lot of money today for something I can have for free tomorrow and will be obsolete the next day?

So project managers cannot make up their minds based on their own knowledge – most project managers are not engineers, and even for technical specialists this task is very difficult. Thus they must trust somebody. Unfortunately, there are different opinions.

## Evolution of Electronic Services

Electronic information and electronic services are often mentioned as though they are equivalent to each other. In fact, both information and services can be delivered in many different ways, ranging from simple unidirectional "broadcasting" to highly interactive communication, potentially involving clients, staff, workflow systems, databases and specially designed interaction software.

If we look at the history of Web systems, a general trend from non-interactive "pages" to interactive services can be discerned. The evolution of Web information systems often passes through the following stages:

1.  Static Web content: "pages". These are used for advertising products and announcing news.

2.  Dynamic Web contents. There will come a point when the content of a site gets too vast, too complex to overview, or changes so frequently that updating the Web becomes a problem. From this point on, content must be collected from databases, already existing or specifically designed for the new Web service, based on queries from a search engine.

3.  Interactive electronic services. Many organizations would save a lot of work if users themselves could provide input to the system. Examples include requests for product information, government forms and applications for standard items such as birth certificates.

4.  Integrated electronic service processes. When services of type 3 above become integrated in office routines in an automatic way (integration with workflow

systems, decision-making processes, databases, data warehouse systems etc.) we may speak about integrated services. A simple example would be a telephone voice menu by which you can order a birth certificate, which is printed and placed in an envelope automatically (and today typically mailed manually for security reasons – to make sure it reaches the person whose personal identification number was given, even if the request was in fact made by someone else).

A more advanced application would include a citizen applying for housing allowance from a Web system. Because the decision is made based on income and family situation, these items could be checked against the city's inhabitants database, and a decision could be delivered and filed automatically.

One should also mention at this point a technical development towards more self-adapting services, in which software agents collect information about users and adapt their work to user preferences (as explicitly stated by users or inferred from their actions). Such tools can be implemented at levels 2, 3 and 4 above.

The development cost, in both time and money, increases geometrically as you climb this ladder. This makes it tempting to delay the upgrading of services, but unfortunately (for the cautious accountant) the appetite of customers tends to grow rapidly. Because interactive services and integrated processes depend on several parties, changes in any of these create problems.

The following case (from Seaside City) concerns a real estate application directed towards SMEs where the need for technical updating became apparent less than one year after finishing the first implementation.

In 1996 an application was built showing SMEs what business premises were available. The Information Office had constructed a DataPerfect database which contained information on available premises in the Seaside City region. The information was collected from over 30 commercial real estate offices. A mirror database was constructed to make the information available on the Internet. After evaluation of the prototype involving end users, the application was further adjusted and has been in use since the end of 1997. Information workers within the information office can update the database themselves and start up the automatic routine to update the mirror database for the Internet application after every update.

In early 1998 it became clear that the city development corporation, of which the Information Office is a part, was going to change to a new database system, totally different from DataPerfect. In order to keep the mirror database operational, technical specifications had to be written down in order to have this new database give the same output as the old database. Otherwise the mirror database would have to be adjusted to conform to the technical specifications of the new database, and then the Internet application would have to be changed. No funding had been allocated to do this.

In August 1998 the new Oracle relational database became available for the SME real estate information. This database stores more detailed information than the former database. To implement this in the Internet application would require a thorough revision. Until now there had been no real wish, either from end-users or from the Information Office, to do so. Finally, it was decided to have the same output files from the new Oracle database as came from the old DataPerfect database and while doing so to leave the qualitatively better information out of the Internet application until there was real need to include it.

There are three conclusions to be drawn from this case:

1.  Technical possibilities grow quite rapidly, but the budgets to use them do not. So you are not always able to offer the latest state-of-the-art techniques within your electronic service.

2.  Do not try to keep up with technology solely because new possibilities arise. When something works as it is – that is, it actually provides value-added services

to users and works well technically – you should leave it at that. Don't go chasing new technology.

3.  Nevertheless, at some point new technology will catch up with you. It is therefore important to design your system in a way that makes it possible to add new technology whenever it appears to be feasible.

We will return to point 3 at the end of this chapter, when we will outline the functional specification of a modularized electronic service system.

## A Good Metaphor is Worth a Dozen Consultants

There is no point in trying to give detailed advice on particular software in this book: the market and technology develop far too fast for that. There are, however, a few other aspects of how people choose technology that are worth discussing. In the long run (and sometimes not so long), as we shall see, these are also far more important than any particular technology itself. Therefore this chapter deals with the social processes around technological platforms, rather than the platforms themselves.

## *Soap*: The Gun Fight at Metaphor Corral

William (Bill) W. Westmark scratched his head for the umpteenth time that afternoon. Bill, an early Web pioneer, is now the information manager of Tapville, in charge of Tapville's activities on the Web. The Web is still not a success and he is now completely out of ideas. He has talked to everybody he knows and tried nearly all their suggestions. He is tired of the entire Internet and decides to call it a day. On the way home he realizes that it is the first time that he has gone home before 7 o'clock since it all began, two years ago. He remembers the first meetings he had regarding the Web. Is it only two years ago? It seems like ages. He was excited and everybody was envious of him. He was going to lead Tapville onto the Information Superhighway, as the mayor put it.

### The New Media Industry

When he and Harrison Internet Provision Inc. (HIP) originally set up Tapville Web, they talked a lot about "this new medium" and about it as an information channel. HIP pointed out that everybody knew that a Web has to be regularly updated to be attractive. They decided that the Tapville Web should be updated once a month. Another big topic was the layout and design of the Web pages. Should they stay with old-fashioned look of Tapville's brochures, or go for a more modern "cyber" look? In the end, it became a mix: the first page was very modern, but most of the pages were more or less just the same brochures in electronic format. When Bill thinks about this process, he realizes that they only thought about the Web as an interactive magazine. They never discussed what implications followed from this magazine metaphor.

Bill now wished intensely that he had thought about this at the particular monthly meeting he had with his own staff and HIP about the Web. They had collected links to other service providers in the city and put them on a special page. This page had now grown out of proportion. It was too long to download in one piece, and it was hopeless to read. Lisa Surfalot in his group said she had seen a catalogue on a Web, which was browseable like a telephone book. HIP immediately stated that they knew how to build one. The outcome of the meeting was that HIP was to produce a prototype of a link catalogue.

## The Catalogue From Hell

HIP was mostly staffed by people from the media industry: graphics designers, copywriters etc. But there was Henry the Hacker. Henry took on the task of building a catalogue. Two months later he had built a prototype. The prototype was a database where you could store a headline, a description, keywords and the link. HIP put in a few of the sites from the old link pages for the demo. The demo at the monthly meeting was a huge success. It was really great: you could browse and sort and even search for keywords! What a difference! When asked about how difficult it would be to implement the catalogue, Henry stated that the prototype was more or less ready to run as it was. They decided to use the catalogue as the main entrance to the entire Web site. Every page was put into the catalogue.

Four months later Bill was burning the midnight oil for the fourth day in a row. He just couldn't get it. The citizens were sending angry emails about how impossible it was to find anything on the stupid Web site. It seemed the keywords put in by HIP did not match what people were looking for. His staff had started to refuse to edit the catalogue, saying that it was tedious, and that they weren't employed as typists anyway. There had been many complaints from the service providers about the catalogue being out of date. They claimed they had sent lots of changes to the descriptions which had not been put in the catalogue. What had gone wrong and why? And what should he do?

The IT manager, Nolan Farmer suggested that he should talk to Barn Administrative Data inc. (BAD), the city's main computer consulting firm.

"Them boys know how to deal with a real database", Nolan said in his characteristic way. Bill thought that there couldn't be that big a difference between a catalogue and a database, but agreed to meet BAD. What was there to lose?

The BAD people had done a bit of homework on the Tapville catalogue. They started firing questions at Bill:

- Why is the database not full-text indexed?
- What is the quality of the administrative tools?
- Why isn't the updating of the database pushed closer to the source of the data?

At first, Bill got angry at being cross-examined by a bunch of computer nerds. But little by little he started to understand what they were talking about. Full-text indexing makes every word on every page searchable. Instead of just being able to search for predefined keywords, the user can enter any word and get a list of the pages that have that word in the text. Of course! That would solve many of the complaints from people who were not able to find what they were looking for. Then there were the administrative tools that his staff were using to update the catalogue. The BAD guys said they were too difficult to use, and that the updates to the databases were far too slow. They showed a demo of another tool, and Bill realized that it would reduce the update work to a third of what it was. BAD also pointed out that if a proper security system could be added the service providers listed in the catalogue would be able to update their entries themselves. That would reduce complaints and reduce his staff's work by another third.

Bill asked BAD to prepare a proposal. It turned out they had already done so, and they had priced it extremely aggressively. The CEO of BAD wanted to get into the Web business, and was not pleased at all that Tapville had contracted HIP.

*A Database Is a Database Is a Database*

The BAD project turned out to be a bit more difficult than Bill had expected. BAD had several connections with the IT department, and issues such as IT strategy entered the agenda. What database tool should be used? Which development tool? A Tapville standard for project documentation, which Bill did not know about, suddenly popped up. The administrative overhead of BAD was much larger than in HIP's projects, and it took a full six months before the "first version" of the database was ready. After two months of testing, fixing and training, it was finally up and running.

It was when Bill's department started to fill the database with content that the real surprise came. The database system turned out to have many limitations in layout and design. And a page that was not included in the database could not be indexed or searched at all. BAD stated that Bill had accepted the record definition and that "page" is not a term used in database design. HIP raged about BAD knowing absolutely nothing about communication and Bill's staff refused to "remake all the pages they had already made". Bill himself thought the whole thing looked ugly on the screen, but he dared not say so at this point.

The database was released, after another two months of fixing and filling, with a party thrown by BAD. The whole city council was invited, and the BAD CEO, Zeke Wolff, gave a speech about a "new era of computing".

**The Final Curtain**

Naturally, there was an outcry. The general opinion was that the Tapville Web was too boring. The manager of tourism said that Tapville's hotels might as well close down if the Web was going to be no more attractive than the phone book. The only thing that Bill found surprising was that people still said they couldn't find information that he knew for certain was on the Web. That had been the reason the database was built in the first place, and why they had accepted limitations in layout and design.

**He Who Seeks Shall Find**

Sitting in his house early that evening, having gone through the last two years in his mind, Bill couldn't let go of the feeling that there was something he had left out. Somewhere along the line he had been close to a solution, but when and what? Suddenly he remembered a conference he had attended about a year ago. There was a guy talking about metaphors and the problems you run into when trying to establish new ones. He had talked about the difficulties of using old ways of doing things as metaphors for Web projects. At the time, Bill had considered it to be academic nonsense, but know he realized what the guy had been talked about. But what was the solution? And what was the man's name?

The next day he went through all his files and piles of papers. And for some reason, there it still was: the conference invitation. Dan Clearview of Transcendental Systems was the metaphor guy. He called Transcendental Systems and got hold of Dan. The conversation led to Dan agreeing to review the Tapville Web project.

# Dealing with the Metaphor Problem

If you are invited to drive a speedboat and you have never even seen a speedboat before, the owner may say: "It's just like a car: you steer with the steering wheel, go backwards or forwards using the gears. The only difference is that you don't need brakes because the water brakes for you". The car is a metaphor for the speedboat. It allows you to use the knowledge you have about cars while dealing with an unknown object. Metaphors are very powerful tools, but they also have disadvantages. You become restricted by the limitations of the metaphoric object. For instance, if you only think of the speedboat as a car, you don't realize you can sleep in it. It's also hard to derive the idea of water-skiing from the car metaphor. If you don't use any metaphors you won't have any restrictions, but it may take a long time to learn to use a new thing. It may even be dangerous.

The problems encountered by Bill in Tapville came from the improper and unconscious use of metaphors. The HIP consultants thought of the Web as a magazine and used their knowledge of printed material. Later, Lisa introduced the catalogue metaphor, which is also a printing metaphor. Last, BAD introduced the database metaphor. The problem was that while all of these metaphors are useful to a certain degree, they don't solve the problem on their own. And mixing them only makes things worse. Also, the different consultants were not aware of the limitations of the old knowledge and lacked the "new" knowledge. You could say that HIP were skilled car drivers and had read about motorboats in a magazine. But that did not make them professional motorboat captains, fit to organize a weekend trip to the islands. BAD were great diesel engine engineers, but that did not make them experts in shipping.

Dealing with this resembles the famous chicken and egg problem. Which came first, the chicken or the egg? The answer to that problem is the same answer that Bill needs. They didn't just appear: they evolved. The early Web included only "text pages" with hyperlinks. The "page" is a metaphor, of course, but it differs from a paper page in three important aspects. First, it does not necessarily look the same every time you read it. If you remove the typeface that is used from your computer, the page will look different; it may not be readable at all. Second, the size of a Web page is unlimited. It may be of any length or width. Third, any number of copies may exist at any time. But in general the paper page metaphor is appropriate. Hyperlinks are more complicated, because there is no metaphor for a hyperlink. The concept is really not applicable to non-computer areas.

Today most surfers have learnt how a Web page works and what you can do with it. Therefore a Web page has become a concept of its own. The development of the underlying technology, however, pushes the limit all the time. Images, movies and forms are often used today. Again, there are differences between the metaphoric objects and the Web correspondence. For instance, an order form may calculate the order total itself, something that the original paper form never could.

Using metaphors is important, since it allows people to use knowledge that they have already acquired, thereby making a Web site easy to use. In many cases today the users also expect more than the straightforward copying of capabilities. For instance, today a Web order form *should* calculate the totals; simply putting a "dumb" paper form on the Web would annoy many users.

So is the Tapville Web a magazine, a catalogue or a database? Well, it is all of those and much more. It might be a self-service office, a library, a switchboard, and a number of other things. The choice of metaphors and how to apply them must be made based on the intended and actual use of the Web.

From the beginning, HIP used only the magazine metaphor. That was insufficient when the list of links grew. When they took on the catalogue they stayed within the printing context, which annoyed users who had grown accustomed to the interactivity of a Web catalogue. They could not transcend the printed matter. BAD used the database metaphor fully, and lost the graphical expression that people have come to associate with the Web. They could not transcend the old computer technology.

There is no correct metaphor, and the Web has not stabilized into a thing of its own. A system may also include several different metaphors. Therefore it is important to choose carefully between possible metaphors. If the user-level metaphor is chosen, you will have to choose a technology. Various technologies can support different metaphors to different degrees. It may be difficult to change the underlying technology later, as when everything had to be typed in all over again in BAD's database. Therefore it is wise to take into account possible future developments when choosing the technology.

Tapville could have decided on the following:

- The front page and general presentation should be like a monthly magazine.
- The list of links should be a searchable catalogue.
- The presentation of each link should be like a paper brochure.

The technologies used could then have been:

- HTML pages for the first part, organized as one Web using for instance Microsoft FrontPage.
- Single HTML pages, presenting each link.
- A database built in a standard database tool that stores the links, supports full-text indexing and includes administrative tools. The administrative tools should also deal with the single page presentations.

In this way, the user could flip through the magazine part, browse and search the catalogue, and then view a catalogue item. The service providers could easily maintain their data and presentations. They would also have had the freedom to design their presentations in any way they wanted. The whole thing would have been relatively easy for Bill's staff to maintain.

Prototyping should be used when developing new parts of the Web. All kinds of users should test the prototypes, not just the staff. If conflicts with the underlying technology are discovered, both the metaphors and the technology should be reviewed. If new technologies are needed, great care should be taken to find ways of evolving the Web without forcing users to relearn or content producers to revise their content. Every claim that one metaphor or one technology deals with everything and is superior should be met with scepticism.

There is a tendency within companies working with the Web to prefer the metaphors of the industry that they originate from. For instance, people coming from the advertising industry prefer to view Web pages as brochures and claim their skills in communicating via printed matter to be the most important. People from the computing industry tend to focus on the technical integration and claim that the generality and flexibility of the technical platform is of utmost importance. The successful ones are those who manage to transcend their roots.

## *Soap*: War of Words

It all started a week ago, when Wendy, manager of the Estate Department, called. Wendy's department owns several buildings in Tapville, and lets offices to companies, and she had read about an air travel booking service that someone had put on the net. Couldn't the Estate Department's list of free office space be put on the Tapville Web, with a pre-reservation facility?

HIP first said that it was a piece of cake to "publish" the Estate Department's office space system on the net. But now everything had gone haywire.

Tapville had a Microsoft Web server, the leading software on the market. Microsoft said that its Web server could "talk" to any computer system. The Estate Deptartment's system was built on an IBM mainframe by BAD. The system was eight years old, and had not changed very much in that time. In essence, the office letting business had not changed in 15 years.

Since that morning the BAD and HIP consultants had been arguing over how to connect the Web server to the IBM mainframe. Bill had learned that the database on the mainframe was very old, and couldn't be accessed easily. Terms like hierarchical, relational, DL/1, DB2 and SQL-Server had flown across the room for hours. Now the consultants had an animated discussion over something called middleware. MQ-series, ShadowDirect and SNA-ODBC were debated. Tapville's IT manager, Nolan Farmer, had entered the discussion saying that there was "no way in hell the mainframe would be put outside the firewall", a statement causing panic in both consulting groups. Bill didn't know what any of these terms meant – well, except hell – and it didn't seem to be the right time to ask.

A week later, BAD presented an estimate for the cost of putting the office letting system on the Web. The cost would be five times Bill's yearly budget. BAD claimed that the entire system had to be rebuilt. HIP had left a memo saying that Farmer's security strategy was paranoid and that if that was altered, they could fix everything within a week or two.

## Dealing with Specialist Jargon

Every specialist group has a jargon, or special language. It enables specialists to communicate efficiently between themselves. It does, however, exclude non-experts from the conversation. In general, using jargon in conversation with non-experts is unacceptable. The consultants should either explain the terms they use or refrain from using them. If the issue discussed is of such a detailed nature that terminology and names such as those in the above story are required, the experts should sort it out themselves and prepare different proposals that explain the consequences in lay terms. Bill should not feel incompetent: it is the consultants who are incompetent. If they can't explain what they are talking about and what the consequences of different options are, they are out of their depth. Bill should not accept the situation, but ask them to leave and come back prepared. He should require both HIP and BAD to send people to the next meeting who are capable of sensible argument and clarification. If any company cannot provide such people, they should be removed from the list of possible suppliers.

## Conclusions on Metaphors

Like Bill in Tapville, you need a working metaphor for your system to give yourself and others a picture of what you are trying to build, and to help you choose between the solutions that consultants will try to sell to you.

What then would have been the metaphor for the Tapville Web? While there is no metaphor that captures the whole of the Web, you need a metaphor for what you want to do; something that captures not the technology, but your service. As we saw in the Tapville story, different metaphors could have been used for different parts of the system.

You need a working metaphor, and you need to know its limitations. It is a guide for your image of your service – nothing more and nothing less.

It is important to stay on top of your consultants. They typically sell you a solution based on their own expertise, without realizing all your problems. Use their solutions whenever they fit into your plan, but don't let them set the metaphors for you. See what happened to Bill.

There are several current metaphors in the IT area. They are all presented as "the" solution, but they all have advantages and limitations. Let us just give a brief overview.

- *Workflow analysis.* A good way to design electronic service processes, but avoid overplanning and excessive rigidity of roles.
- *Intranet/extranet.* A good user interface metaphor for both citizens and city staff, but it does not support service process design very well.
- *Computer-supported collaborative work* and *groupware.* Although administration is not really unstructured communication in the context of citizens (a situation this metaphor often alludes to), this is a very powerful metaphor for flexible collaboration within the service provision process. It also facilitates citizen participation and interaction well.
- *New media publishing.* Appropriate for city information, but less so for services. Overemphasis on visual appearance.
- *Electronic administration/electronic commerce.* Often puts excessive emphasis on IT technology, but brings good Web techniques to the forefront.
- *Virtual office.* Appropriate for city officials' generic working practices; less appropriate for individual services.
- *Virtual community.* A good metaphor for the role of citizens' while interacting with the administration: keep simple things simple, avoid unnecessary structural restrictions and facilitate rich communication.
- *Multimedia content services.* Overemphasis on integrating visual and textual information. May cause the services to become unusable.
- *Value-added services for telecommunications.* Overemphasis on the distribution channel. It does not really matter whether users access the services from a fixed or mobile device, as long as the service is usable with the bandwidths and screens available.
- *Data warehousing, database applications.* These are more relevant to information management than service processes, but databases are necessary for any dynamic

or interactive Web service, and data warehouse approaches are rapidly becoming more mature and could certainly be useful as the quantity of data becomes so vast that it becomes impossible to gain an overview of it in any other way.

These are a few of the more common current metaphors; there are others. We have simply named these to show that they have limitations and advantages, and using one of them necessarily leads people's thoughts in certain directions. Before you use any metaphor, be aware of those directions. If that is not where you want to go, do not use that metaphor. The power of a metaphor lies in that it leads many people's thoughts in the same direction. But the modern car would never have been created had not the early metaphor of "horseless carriage" been abandoned. On the other hand, vague metaphors like "Web" may be powerful at an overall level, but not necessarily in other contexts. The concept of the World Wide Web has spawned ideas of worldwide cooperation, but saying that you want to create a Web for staff interaction in your city may make people draw analogies with obscure government organization and think instead of cobwebs – hard to get an overview of and even harder to overcome. You might even get caught.

So, who should you listen to? Both external consultants and city departments tend to see city services from a predefined viewpoint that fits nicely into their own business mission. Be aware of this bias when judging different technical metaphors to adopt, but do not let such a concern delay decisions.

- Find out the basic facts about a number of relevant technical metaphors yourself.
- Try to start planning with a blank sheet of paper, with the goal of providing good service to citizens with minimal trouble from information access and storage.
- After formulating a vision, see if you can find a technical metaphor that supports that vision.
- Be prepared to use external advice more than before: rapidly changing technology forces organizations to outsource an increasing portion of their planning.

## How to Build an IT Infrastructure

Many city data processing centres and IT departments have several legacies on their shoulders. They have evolved over three decades and carry the slowly sedimenting remains of all the technical fads and fashions of the corresponding period in their operating practices and technical infrastructure. Examples of such phenomena include mainframe, minicomputer and client–server-based systems; terminals and PCs of various generations; different network structures and protocols; a myriad different operating systems; and so on.

The heaviest legacy of all, however, comes from the numerous specific applications written at a particular time for a particular function that, unfortunately, still work and cannot be mended or replaced because the people that know these applications have long since left the data processing department or the vendor that provided them. There is even a special name for such applications: kludge.

It seems that change always comes as a surprise to data processing managers. It therefore feels appropriate to present some guidelines and a case study on how to build a data processing infrastructure that is less likely to suffocate in kludge.

There is really only one key phrase that is needed: *dynamically modular design.* Modularity means that component subsystems can be replaced from time to time without affecting the other components very deeply. The challenge in modularity comes from the difficulty, if not impossibility, of defining a stable set of component subsystems that are invariant over time. Let's look at some developments.

- *Computers* have evolved since the 1970s from standalone mainframes, via minicomputers and workstations, to PCs. While technically we have seen a development from many different mainframe operating systems, through VMS and Unix dialect stages, into a Microsoft Windows-based world – and therefore a unifying tendency – simultaneously computing subsystems have multiplied. There are many different kinds of server, each specializing in an increasingly narrow task, coupled to a network of user PCs. These servers are differentiated by the application software they run, as much as mainframes in the past were differentiated by their different operating systems.

- *Applications* used to be proprietary, tailor-made for a particular mainframe. Later, many were written for standalone PCs. The most extensive recent applications follow a client–server paradigm. The most recent trend is towards Web-based environments, where all applications are accessed using an asynchronous Internet protocol. From a system maintenance standpoint, we have returned to the many mainframes era.

- *Networks* have evolved from terminal networks through proprietary minicomputer networks and Unix workstation networks into PC networks. Increasingly, the latter are now turning into Internet-compatible intranets and extranets.

- *Data organization* has evolved from simple files, through various generations of database systems (hierarchical, network, relational, object-oriented, multimodal, ...) into distributed document bases and Internet-based, openly searchable document and object collections.

If we look at the above developments, it seems hard to find anything that could have stood the test of time through all of the above developments. Yet some functions have remained intact.

- *Data storage* is a function that all computer systems and data organization methodologies support.

- *User access* has been facilitated all the way from terminals to the Internet.

- *Service operation* is also a mission-critical activity that is supported by all the stages listed above.

- *Communication* between service components has undergone a steady increase in depth and quantity from nil to CGI scripts between (almost) any applications on (almost) any computer.

Structuring the computing and communications infrastructure according to the above functions and dynamically defining the conceptual interfaces between them facilitates a more stable development process. Each of the components is under independent planning, but there will be strong timing coordination. It is always preferable to touch only one component at a time in order to minimize uncontrolled interference caused by simultaneous changes.

It is, of course, important to be aware of what is happening in the world around you. The advice can be summarized as: look ahead, look behind, look aside and look after. Now, what do we mean by that?

### Look Ahead

To make the best technological choices you should take note of the life cycle of IT-systems.

Hardware will run until it becomes too expensive or too difficult to maintain or the requirements are exceeding their capabilities. This period is currently about three to four years.

Different software packages have very different life cycles, ranging from one or two years to about eight years (not counting COBOL programs from the 1970s made fit for year 2000).

So the decision on a hardware and software platform should focus on a time measured in years, not in weeks. For that reason it is important to choose systems and tools that will stay around and be reliable for the next couple of years. The best chance of that happening may not always be to follow the current market leader but instead to rely on standards that just have settled. These standards can be *de jure* standards (like the ISO[1] standards) or *de facto* standards based on common usage with some kind of well-known agreement (RFC[2]). In dealing with the Internet, the latter are to be preferred.

More important is the usage. You can imagine every installation of a system as a particle that has a mass. If there are enough particles working together they make up a body with gravitation that attracts more particles. Moving or destroying this thing requires more energy the bigger it is. Your system will not become obsolete as long as there are enough other installations building this "mass" and it requires too much energy to destroy it.

If there is a standard in a specific topic that has just settled (and that is not changing every two weeks), act decisively to adopt this standard and avoid any non-standard exceptions. Allowing exceptions from that standard will cause big trouble the first time you have to update your system. This advice will stop you using several Internet gadgets, which are often manufacturer-dependent.

If there is no standard, or a standard has not yet settled, avoid doing expensive development work. Try to keep such parts as simple and cheap as possible, because

---

1   International Organization for Standardization

2   Request For Comments: a document in the standardization procedure for Internet technology. A proposed standard is published as an RFC and, if it reaches a sufficient amount of use and meets technical requirements it may be declared a standard by the IETF (Internet Engineering Task Force). Some technologies become *de facto* standards during the period in which their official status is RFC.

you may have to replace them rather early. Those parts should be treated as proto-types and kept in mind for the second advice.

## Look Behind

More important than the actual technical implementation of an electronic service is its internal structure and its interfaces to the world. You should not think of an electronic service system as a black box. Any electronic service will reflect your specific way of providing that service and the specific relationships between different users and different aspects of your service (e.g. different departments of the city). The technical realization is always an image of such relationships. If you keep the structural information as a blueprint of your actual electronic service you can adapt it to a new service much more easily and you can rebuild the service in a new technology once it becomes outdated. On the other hand, you should avoid coupling your service too hard to organizational relationships, as these will change.

The structural information that you need may be reflected in a relational data model, in detailed documentation of the software development, a summary of rules and an explanation of the reasons why the rules are set, a list of problems that came up and their solutions, comments from users etc. Keep this information over the system's lifetime – you will need it sooner or later.

## Look Aside

You are not the only place in the world providing an electronic service. And your city is not only running an electronic service. There are a lot of influences and dependencies. In your city, there may be rules for strategic technical platforms, and there are people actually involved in IT production.

It can be rather difficult to make electronic services fit into the technical environment that already exists in a city administration. Often services grow, and have to grow, outside of the existing IT structures. It may even at times be necessary to break some rules to get up and running in time, but you must not ignore their existence.

You cannot expect understanding, acceptance and help from IT people if you don't accept their work and their problems, mundane as they may seem. It is important to clarify where the electronic service has to conform with the city IT environment and where the freedom to act on a new task can take precedence.

The rules of an organization's IT structures are often based on experience, and frame conditions that are also useful in an electronic service project. You should use that information basis.

Obviously, it is not constructive to reinvent the wheel. So it is very useful to have a look at similar services that are already running. If you don't find something similar or useful there, be proud to be the first (but in most cases, you will find something; government generally lags behind in electronic service development).

Sometimes there are several different solutions. It may be not possible to analyze everything, but you should at least ask for the most successful. Do not hesitate to contact the providers. They will not have much time to talk to you, but on concrete questions you should get concrete answers.

## Look After

Maintaining a system does not just mean repairing it if something is broken. This is not even half of the truth in electronic services. Maintaining an electronic service requires a lot of maintenance work. Some of the work has to do with maintaining the technical solution, but most of it is about dealing with the content. You will have to take care over what your system will actually provide. Delete the obsolete information, consider and reconsider what is worth putting into the system, and ensure that this will be done frequently. This sounds very simple, but in fact it can be the hardest problem you will face. Typically, this should not be the job of the IT department, but it often is. This job requires genuine understanding of the use of information (not just the use of systems). If the IT department is charged with this job, it is most important for it to acquire such competence.

On the other hand, in the technical context there are also some tasks that are often not foreseen. It is necessary to update the systems on a regular basis, you have to deal with failures and recovery, you will find it necessary to enlarge the system for performance and capacity, and you must make sure that your system is able to interact with other systems wherever this requirement occurs. It is nice to have a lot of resources to build and maintaining interfaces, but typically you won't. *IT stewardship* is the term commonly used for this task of maintaining applications and knowing at what point (by what criteria) it is best to phase them out of production.

Nobody will care if your electronic service is ten years old and not built with the latest development tool, but is instead based on an old-fashioned database and Web server, as long as the contents of your system are useful and it works well in the changing IT environment.

Let us now look at a few cases regarding some of the different aspects mentioned above. First, a case concerning the basic infrastructure, networks and computers from the city of MiddleWhere.

In the late 1980s, the IT of the city administration was based on two mainframe computers, to which about 400 terminals were connected. The connectivity was implemented on a proprietary system consisting of two switching nodes in the centre and a single hard-wired telephone line to each terminal. Every terminal had a direct modem connection to the mainframe, as was usual at that time. The lines themselves were in the possession of the city's fire brigade as they came out of the former fire alert network. All technical equipment was rented from the mainframe vendor. As a consequence of this "closed shop" paradigm, there was no connection to the outside world.

In 1990, the idea of Local Area Networks (LANs) arose. At that point, a long-term strategic decision was made: instead of buying or renting a complete network solution from the traditional computer supplier, it was decided to engage engineers in communication and computer science to plan and implement such new technologies. As a result, a plan was made not only to concentrate on local networks within buildings but also to set up a ring of fibre optic cable connecting all the main buildings of the city administration. This seemed to be realistic, because the fire alert network was built using telephone cable going through tubes in the ground instead of simply being buried, and therefore it was possible to replace the old copper cable with a modern fibre optic cable without having to dig anything up.

The main purpose of this ring was to replace the old and expensive mainframe–terminal connections, and to be successful it was also necessary to replace the terminals themselves by PCs. A pilot project in the IT department was set up for that purpose. After some adjustments (finding a proper terminal software and so on), it was ready to be implemented.

In early 1994, the fibre optic ring went into operation, connecting more than 80% of the city's administration from the start. It was about 25 km long, with 12 nodes and a bandwidth of 100 Mbit/s (which was a lot – at that time ISDN, with 64 kbit/s bandwidth, became popular). With the maintenance done by qualified city staff, it was possible to maintain a high level of reliability, and some fears about the possibly unpredictable effects of the new technology could soon be allayed.

At one node of the ring the mainframes were attached to the network, and at other points PCs attached to local networks acted as terminals. Most of the old terminals were withdrawn in the following months to save their rental fees. The last terminals were switched off at the end of 1996. Without any additional money (in fact overall there were even savings from cutting down the rental costs), not only was the old mainframe–terminal connection replaced and modernised, but a powerful network infrastructure was established.

This fortunate development drew on a number of clever decisions made earlier, such as running the wires through tubes, which made them easy to replace.

The next case, also from MiddleWhere, concerns investment in basic infrastructure software.

Just as with the tubes of the fire brigade's alert network, some other long-term strategic decisions were made. An example is the question of the supported network protocol(s). As the ring was planned and set up it was not clear which network protocol should be used. There was the ISO-protocol for connecting PCs to mainframes and there were local networks running IPX/SPX with Novell NetWare. There were also some exotic Unix computers running an unusual protocol named TCP/IP (at that time, nobody outside the universities had heard about the Internet). Because it was not clear which of the protocols would be the future standard, the chief engineer of the network department decided that the whole network with all its components must provide any of these protocols.

To understand the importance of this decision, consider that at that time about 80% of network traffic was done with ISO protocols and about 20% with IPX/SPX. Only 1–2 percent of the network traffic was done with TCP/IP. It was thought that the ISO protocols would become the standard for the future. By late 1998 we could see that this has changed dramatically: IPX/SPX has grown to 60% but is already decreasing. ISO has disappeared completely, and most traffic is now handled by TCP/IP, the basic Internet protocol suite.

Drawing on that powerful network, which by the end of 1998 had more than 200 km of fibre optic cable and connected more than 3000 PCs and servers (including the two mainframes, which are still running), it was quite easy to set up value-added services. These include a comprehensive email system, secure connection to the Internet via a firewall, and intranet services, all available to a large number of city employees immediately they were set up.

This case shows that one should not rule out things that at an early stage may appear "academic" or otherwise peripheral, as the TCP/IP protocols were considered. In the early nineties, few outside of he academic world could foresee the growth of the Internet (and to be sure, few inside of it would have dared forecasting such an explosive growth). Yet, those who did not by default rule out the upcoming TCP/IP protocol got a head start over others at relatively little cost. It is not just about installation; early starters will by the time a certain technology becomes popular, and traffic soars, have a considerable competence advantage.

Finally, let us look at a case where services to users were maintained through several profound technology changes: the case of the European Centre for Medium-Weather Forecasts.

CMWF (the European Centre for Medium-range Weather Forecasts) is an international weather forecasting agency in Reading, UK, which has a mission-critical operational forecasting task. Every night an operational two-week weather forecast is run and communicated to more than 20 member states, each with quite different levels of computational and communications infrastructure.

ECMWF always uses the fastest available supercomputers to produce the forecasts. In addition, it must archive all the forecasts and all the weather observations since the inception of forecasting in 1979. The observations are collected from all the countries in the world over an ancient network operating via a telex protocol, supervised by another organization, the World Meteorological Organization (WMO), part of the United Nations.

In addition to forecasting, ECMWF supports 200 internal users, mostly researchers needing advanced workstations, but also administrative staff with PCs, and several hundred external users in member states.

The Computer Division is led by a Head of Department, who has some 80 staff. A special position among the staff is held by a strategic planning advisor to the Head of Department, whose mission is to follow developments in computing and communications and suggest updating strategies.

All the central computing and communications equipment, as well as data archives, reside in a computer hall whose floor plan must be carefully reorganized during every major systems update, in order to facilitate periods – typically six months long – of running two systems in parallel.

The Computing and Communications infrastructure is divided into four subsystems:

- Access networks
- Data archival
- Operational forecasting engines
- User service engines

Access networks have undergone a transition from telex and analogue terminal phone lines through frame relay-based connections to current broadband connections that include external ATM connections and a broadband Internet access line. Simultaneously, the internal networks at the weather centre have been upgraded from Cray-dependent point-to-point links, Hyperchannel and Decnet to a mixture of Ethernet, FDDI and HiPPI connections. Many Web-based access methods to products for member states have recently been adopted.

Data archival has grown from tape reels operated on an IBM mainframe and a Cray-dependent file management system from Los Alamos National Laboratories through Storagetek robots to an optical tape cassette-based completely transparent file system running on an IBM cluster server. The operational forecasting engine has grown from a single Cray-1 to a set of machines that includes a 116 processor Fujitsu distributed memory supercomputer, along with a bunch of other supercomputers by Fujitsu and SGI used for research and testing of future versions of forecast models.

Initially, all user access was made by terminal connections directly to the Cray-1 supercomputer. Since then, user access has been built through a CDC Cyber stage into a Unix workstation-based environment. The environment features numerous different servers from many manufacturers, such as HP, DEC and SGI, for various specialized tasks, including graphics, access services for external users, and user file storage. Administrative personnel use PCs that sit on the same network, after initially residing on a Novell PC network. Some member states still insist on Decnet access, which mandates hosting a number of VAXes.

Through all these changes, and despite a large number of hardware and software failures over the years, ECMWF has not lost a single forecast in 18 years. That is, the system has been able to compute a complete forecast with all the thousands of auxiliary computer jobs on dozens of different machines for every single 24 hour period of the previous 6000 such periods. During that same period, every single application code has also been replaced at least two or three times. Such an achievement is possible only with a modular IT infrastructure and a phased and coordinated update policy.

The ECMWF Computer Centre is much narrower in scope and much smaller in the number of users than any city data processing department. It is therefore clear that a consistent IT policy can more easily be followed in such an environment. However, the time criticality and complexity of its operations are comparable with many information processing activities in cities. For this reason, it serves as a good ideal to strive for in organizing city information processing infrastructure and maintenance policy.

# System Architecture and Organizational Setup

Regardless of what metaphor you choose for your ideas, one of the basic requirements of a sustainable system for electronic services is a basic technical and organizational infrastructure that is robust enough to cope with changes that will come. Technology changes rapidly, and both service requirements and organizational ambitions change, albeit typically not so rapidly.

Within the Infosond project, an organizational setup of a general electronic service system was defined to be used as a reference model (Lutze *et al.*, 1996). We shall briefly present this architecture here.

## System Architecture Principles

A system for electronic services can be described as the junction between multiple suppliers and users of information.

Factors that are important in order to provide for integration include:

- *Compatibility*: many functional elements are being developed for use in different and often already existing complex systems. These systems do not necessarily provide a common interface. Compatibility so far means the ability to easily adapt the kernel to the outside world (the complex system with specific interface requirements).

- *Reduction of functional dependencies*: the more subsystems are functionally independent the less information they share and the fewer subsystems are affected when one is removed or changed. If two subsystems are highly linked, then the stronger the communication the heavier the workload for networks and computers and the more we create a technological weakness in those parts of the subsystem which can be easily overloaded.

- *Modularity*: each component can be plugged into a higher level system without the necessity of adapting the system.

- *Non-regression*: addition of a component should not decrease global system performance.

## Actors in Electronic Services

The actors in a general electronic service system are:

- *Information and Service Provider* (ISP). An ISP is an organization with a particular link to citizens in the administrative or public domain. This organization generally has an interest in communication with people to provide information such as forms, administrative procedures and frequently asked questions. An ISP can be physically connected to the integrated city information system or not, and it might or might not have an information system.

- *Integrated City Information System* (ICIS). ICIS is an organization that includes human, software and hardware resources with the mission to design and install applications needed by the ISP and to keep the application in conformance with users' requests

- *Media operator.* This term defines the company which provides the physical access to ICIS services: (alternative) telecommunication operators and private or metropolitan networks.

- *Optional network operator* (or provider). This concept describes the possibility of contracting the services through another network service provider such as an Internet provider, online services or private networks (intranets).

## General Functions in an Electronic Service System

The functionality provided by an integrated information system must cover:

- *Editing services.* Although many organizations will want to provide "camera-ready", completely formatted, material to the service system, it is typically necessary to offer SMEs, small government organizations and associations a publishing resource allowing them to deliver multimedia information services to citizens, especially when these organizations have no internal resources to do so.

- *Ability to access legacy information systems.* It is important to provide citizens with convenient access to existing systems.

- *Delivery of public interactive services.* Several public organizations must deliver services through a common access system, which requires the ICIS to interface transparently with the different ISP information systems.

- *Value-added services.* An ICIS can economically provide value-added services that are beyond the practical possibilities of single small providers, such as a search engines, a thesaurus to facilitate searching, use evaluation, user studies etc.

Lutze *et al.* (1996) presented a general functional architecture for an electronic service system, including a list of actors (Fig. 5.1).

For an organization that is to act as the hub of an integrated city information system, it is important to establish an organizational setup that can cope with the basic requirements of electronic services:

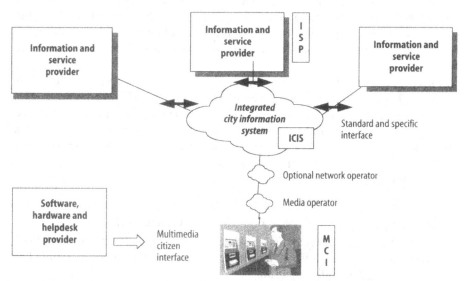

**Fig. 5.1** Actors in a general electronic service system (from Lutze *et al.*, 1996, p. 25).

- Services may be produced by different providers and in different formats.
- Services may be delivered in different media, requiring different formats.
- Input comes from users in the form of questions, which must be managed.
- To manage user navigation and staff administration, there is a need for value-added services of different kinds.
- Services change, and new value-added services will be invented. Such changes must be easy to implement.

These functions must be implemented in a modular way so that each part can survive changes occurring in other parts. There is one prerequisite for being able to do this, however, which we have mentioned but have not yet particularly emphasized. This is the existence of what Lutze named "ICIS". This is an entity strong enough to create and maintain this infrastructure, a task which requires investment in competence for upgrading the value-added services, maintenance tools, user interfaces etc.

In Part 2, we will call this entity an ESM (Electronic Service Manager) to denote that it does not necessarily have to be a city department. It may be outsourced, or it may handle services from both government and private providers.

# What Role Should Technical Concerns Play in Electronic Service Provision?

Organizational arrangements and service processes outlive all technical solutions. Therefore it is important, but too often forgotten, to give priority to service process restructuring over the choice of technology.

Technical metaphors influence the way in which electronic services can be set up. The bias emerging from a given metaphor may be both useful and harmful, so an attitude of compromise is needed. But it is definitely advisable to prepare for the overhauling of technical metaphors once every decade or so, or even more often.

It is easy to overestimate the importance of technical systems, either software or hardware. The information content is far more important, and far harder to change. It is important to be prepared for complete content conversion exercises from one technical platform to another every couple of years. The positive side of this seemingly discouraging statement is that it will make the legacy system problem much easier than retaining all the old systems.

The technical maintenance cycle is three-tiered:

1. Implement a new metaphor as a prototype.
2. Start migrating services one at a time to the new metaphor.
3. When the obvious services have been converted, the remaining ones will need constant patching to fit the metaphor. Keep doing this until a new metaphor has been chosen for implementation.

## What Degree of Technical Innovation is Appropriate for a City?

There are four pieces of advice we want to give on this point, simply and straightforwardly:

1. Cities should not normally be at the forefront of technical innovation. While many, for different reasons, try to get well ahead and use the very latest technology, the costs increase rapidly the closer you get to the newest gadgets. While it makes sense to use new tools, do not be the first to install the latest version of anything. There will be bugs. Some will never go away, but at least they will become known, as will fixes. Says Alan Dennis (1998) at the conclusion of three years of Web development:

> Don't chase new technologies.... Continually redeveloping systems to take advantage of new technologies is an irresponsible waste of resources because it comes at the expense of other systems. Information systems are developed because they add value to the organization... information systems continue to add value whether they use obsolete technology or the most advanced techniques. The only reason to redevelop systems is if new technologies offer clear business value.
>
> The Web is dominated by computer enthusiasts. They – we – love technology and the exciting things it enables us to do. Most users aren't like us. They don't like change... WIS enable users to perform work.

   Some cities are developing software in-house because no adequate market solution is available. The advice here is: be careful. Software development is a high-risk and high-cost business. Let others do it, just follow what they do and use the best. So:

2. Build upon off-the-shelf technology.

3. Be innovative in service processes rather than in technology. The expertise in a city should be how best to serve citizens. Develop that ability.

4. Define your role with respect to other players, public or private. An appropriate role for a big city is often relatively smaller than that for a small rural town, the latter often being an important economic hub in its region.


## Distribution Channels

There are many telematic distribution channels available to reach the users, and a suitable mix is needed that achieves a good compromise between accessibility, cost, the need for access and the need for technical skills from the service provider or some external agent that can be engaged.

The *Internet* is the simplest and most universal medium to use. Internet technology is becoming a very important compatibility factor between all telematic media. It is therefore clear that for most electronic services, except for purely voice communication-based ones, the Internet should be at the heart of the media palette. However, the mere existence of a Web site will not bring users to a service.

*Internet service providers* are many, and their ability to bring users to a service varies greatly. The most focused ones are the *commercial online service providers*, whose service is often subscription based. They are very consciously service publishers, and will be able to regulate the level of visibility of individual services in their range of services very efficiently. The downsides to their use are the often high costs associated with the high visibility of a service within their bouquet, as well as their preference for worldwide or national services, which relegate local services to a secondary role. This applies also to search engines that offer similar visibility options.

A *regional Intranet* has proved a successful solution for many cities and regions. A regional Intranet offers cheap or free Internet access via a regional home page to all users from a restricted phone number area. The low cost of access gathers local users to the regional homepage where local services can be successfully attached. The downside here is the cost of providing the free service, and particularly the possibly rapidly growing foreign Internet traffic fees. It is highly recommended therefore to try to negotiate a flat monthly Internet access fee for the regional intranet servers with a national or international Internet service provider.

The Internet can also be accessed via *cable* and *satellite modems*, attached to a TV outlet and branching out to a PC. Currently there is much less competition locally in satellite and cable media than in Internet service provision. Normally this means that in any given city there is only a single access provider that merits attention. This access provider must provide all its subscribers with a set-top box that acts as a modem between the TV and PC protocols. Few cable and satellite access providers yet provide uniform access to the whole Internet, but this is likely to change. Cable and satellite penetration vary greatly among countries, satellite being more prominent in the UK, for example, and cable being more common in Central Europe.

The greatest benefit of cable or satellite access is their potential for *broadband access*, facilitating live video streams to users' homes. As far as public electronic services are concerned, much can be done with narrowband connections. And even though broadband infrastructures are increasingly being built in many countries, public services must also be accessible also over slower connections for a long time. Broadband techniques vary, including techniques such as ADSL, which gives broadband access over telephone lines, making use of cable television networks and installing new fibre optic networks. It is clear that the growth of broadband connections will happen at a different pace in different countries. It would be unwise, however, to underestimate the incentives that the growth in Internet use is providing.

Medium band technologies such as *ISDN*, while on the decline in many countries, offer some advantages for use in the home and the small office. Firstly, it makes video telephony an option, and has widely adopted protocols to support it. Secondly, an ISDN phone line is intelligent enough to switch automatically between data traffic, faxes and voice telephony, so that all can proceed in parallel.

TV sets can be used to deliver electronic services via *teletext* and *videotex*. Their principal advantages are the wide access and low cost of terminal devices: standard TV sets. The downsides are related to their being text-based only, and relatively slow to browse. Also, the input from users has to be keyed in from a handset, making it a somewhat cumbersome process. However, teletext and videotex-based services have proven quite popular in many places, and are in widespread use.

*Kiosk devices* can be made very accessible when located in public places, emulating telephone boxes. Also, because their system environment can be maintained over an ISDN-based network, they are simple to maintain centrally, yet provide many advanced communication options, such as video telephony to a service agent, intelligent maps, voice commands and touch screens. Most modern kiosks are Internet-based, making it easier to tailor applications for kiosks. As a downside, the cost of setting up and maintaining a network of kiosk devices must be taken into account. Proprietary kiosk systems are to be avoided, since the separate maintenance of their content will soon become an expensive legacy. It has also proved difficult to attract external content providers to kiosks to share in their cost.

On the other hand, providing PCs for Internet access in public places, such as libraries, citizen centres, Internet cafés and even pubs, has proved a very popular compromise solution. First of all, such PCs provide equal access to the Internet to all citizens, not just those who have access at work or who can afford a home PC. Secondly, the users can choose the ways they use the Internet as they wish, unlike on a kiosk device. Thirdly, users will educate themselves voluntarily and very efficiently while using public PCs, without any necessary training initiatives by local authorities.

While useful in some places, in the long run the kiosk idea still represents a dead end street. There are several reasons for this.

*First*, when it comes to services to citizens, it is clear that the home will serve as the base for interactions with government as well as business. Already, there are many automated or semi-automated services offered via the phone or the Internet: banking (both media), forms from government (the main medium is the phone, but increasingly the Web is used), book stores (Internet) and many others. People are already used to being able to do a lot of things from home, and as services expand the interaction with them becomes increasingly complex and time-consuming. There is no way that anyone will take a file of documents with PIN codes and bank account numbers and go out into the street at 11 p.m. to do their banking business from a kiosk.

There are only one or two areas where kiosks can play a role, and in these areas only as a special kind of access point, not through the merit of containing proprietary software. One such area is tourist information. Tourists in a foreign city may make use of a kiosk to find a restaurant or print out a map. But even this information will to a large extent be collected at home via the Internet before the journey starts. After all, most people will want to book the hotel in advance. They will want to learn what to see in, say, Stockholm before they go there, so they don't have to spend valuable time on their short stay to search things, only to find out when they get home that they missed the Vasa[3]. This means that information accessible in kiosks around the city will also have to be accessible on the Internet.

The same goes for kiosks in, for example, banks, where customers can access their bank accounts to learn about balances, make transfers etc. These services are already offered on the Internet, and the terminals are only a complement to the Internet. Although these kiosks may serve a purpose, it is clear they have to be compatible with the technology used in the home.

---

3  The Vasa was a famous warship that sank in 1628 on its maiden voyage. It was salvaged in 1961, and is now contained in a separate museum. It is the only completely preserved ship in the world from that time. With the exception of the rigging, it is complete in every detail. The Vasa museum is the most popular museum in Stockholm in terms of number of visitors – a "don't miss" place.

*Second*, because integration is essential both for the effective use of resources and for ease of use on the part of the customer/citizen, the use of open software is the only way to go.

*Third*, because much standard e-commerce software is becoming available very cheaply, in the long run the cost will be reduced, as very little in-house development and consultancy time will have to be employed.

*Fourth*, because this standard software will be commonly used, familiarity with the applications and standardized ways of user interaction will be achieved without effort.

As for the quality of the necessary administrative tools, clearly Internet technology is currently lagging behind kiosks. This is bound to change, however, as application areas expand – a process which is already happening.

Telephones are still the preferred user devices for most users of telematic services. *Call centres* can perform a lot of duties for citizen users, especially when supported by Internet access. They can be used to provide telephone users with the same access to Internet services as PC users have. Moreover, because end user access is mediated by trained agents in call centres and is not carried out by the untrained users themselves, fewer problems occur in accessing databases and the often intricate information presented.

In the near future, call centre agents will be able to pass on data along with the call, allowing end users with PCs to have their requests processed by knowledgeable people and receive the answer on their computer. If the volume of calls is sufficient, a city can set up its own call centre. At lower volumes, it is easy to outsource call centre activities, since, just like Internet services, they are location independent.

In addition to facilitating universal voice access, *mobile data services* are growing at an impressive rate. Firstly, all mobile traffic is digital to begin with. Secondly, there is an upgrade path available for services, from the current SMS (Short Messaging System) based text services through WAP (Wireless Access Protocol) based interactive services all the way to future mobile multimedia services. These feature prominently in the next generation digital mobile telephony standard UMTS, or W-CDMA. They can already be tested today on many PDA-type devices that couple Internet access to mobile telephony. A downside in mobile services is the proprietary nature of access to them. It is currently still necessary to negotiate with both a teleoperator and a mobile phone manufacturer in order to get a WAP-based electronic service working.

*Smart cards* are at a rather similar stage of development to mobile data services at the moment. The processing and memory capacity of smart card processors is already sufficient to operate many intelligent services. They are also quickly becoming Internet compatible, supporting JavaScripts. However, access to distributing services for smart card access is very restricted at the moment, and is unlikely to become widely available in the near future. The main reason for this is the necessity of having access to a wide network of smart card updating terminals. Currently the two most prominent access point networks are the automated teller machines of banks, and the SIM cards of teleoperators in mobile phones, which are both in proprietary hands.

However, many European countries have plans to introduce smart cards for use as official ID cards for personalised access to public services, such as health care services and related payments and benefits. Such decisions will open up access to smart card distribution to public service providers, and later on to private ones as well. Simultaneously, both credit card companies and mobile phone operators have started to migrate their services to smart card platforms, opening an avenue for other service providers to join their distribution channels.

# Business Choices – Who Should Develop and Maintain Your Telematic Applications

The choice of telematic technology is linked to the question of application development and maintenance. This is an issue with technical, economic and psychological dimensions. There are basically three ways to go about the development and maintenance of telematic applications (as well as many other IT systems): management by the IT department, outsourcing and partnerships. Let us take a brief look at the three.

## The Traditional Solution: Development and Maintenance by the City IT Department

The traditional solution, development and maintenance by the city IT/EDP department includes at least the following pros and cons:

+    The IT department knows the current applications.
+    They already possess hardware and telecommunication contracts.
–    They have to hire and train new staff to master new technology, increasing the cost and development time.
–    They may lack the vision of what a new service could be.
–    They may have a vested interest in trying to stay in operational control of the new applications as well.

## The Outsourcing Solution: Bidding for Development and Operation of Electronic Services

The outsourcing solution calls for at least the following considerations:

+    It allows even large technical overhauls by changing the supplier, therefore making the city a more flexible and agile service provider.
+    There is no reliance on the city's own staff, with rapidly outdating skills and (sometimes) work motivation.
+    It allows the hiring and learning stage to be bypassed, both in time and in money.
+    It allows the operation of the city's MAN, server hotels etc. to be simultaneously outsourced.

- Most companies bidding in big outsourcing campaigns are traditional EDP companies as well, and they may have defects and biases similar to those of the city's IT department: capital investment in old software and staff oriented towards traditional application structures.
- They often do not know the business of city services, beyond the technical issues.
- The financial cost is often high and difficult to recoup, unless it is possible to downsize the staff in the city's IT department.
- Outsourcing has become a well-established business as far as LAN and MAN operation, server hosting and software environment maintenance are concerned. For these activities many competent providers exist, and in such cases outsourcing is an attractive option. This is less the case with new electronic service development, in which the human and social components are as important as the technical one.

### The Partnership Solution: Making the Most of Service Development

In electronic services partnerships, the city outsources the technical development work to a small, flexible and often local software development company, while itself assuming a significant role in the development of the user and service provider view of the new services. This is a flexible solution in which the cost of outsourcing is proportional to the degree of innovation – and therefore work – desired. It facilitates unprejudiced development of new services from scratch. This approach often results in using commodity software and hardware to implement new services. An example:

> The FarawayTown teleshopping system was set up as a public–private partnership involving PKO, a local retailer, the city of FarawayTown – their homecare staff – and Arboreal Ltd, who built the shop. The technical platform is a PC running the free Linux operating system. The teleshop is maintained on a miniSQL shareware database, written using Perl scripts (also freeware). The total cost of the hardware and software is of the order of two PCs.

A partnership solution allows the city to become an active proponent of local businesses becoming telematic by pooling public electronic services with private ones. This will boost all regional service providers, helping them to get fit for business in the Information Society. Such a solution also boosts the local and regional identity and loyalty of citizens and businesses.

## Some Recommendations

While detailed advice on which software to use is impossible to give, because of the rapid pace of technical development, there are a number of dos and don'ts that we have highlighted in this chapter:

- Use Web-compatible technologies only.
- Do not delay development for fear of the Internet – it has already proved its usability for all kinds of sensitive services. The market will solve the security and

payment-related issues in due course. Until that time, build trials upon existing solutions.

- To communicate with citizens and between city staff, push for the wide adoption of email.
- Don't go chasing new technologies! It is very easy to become overwhelmed by the rapid technical development on the Internet. However, users want services, not gadgets.
- Legacy systems – do they have Web extensions?
- What is the competence of city IT staff or of the available contractors?
- What functionality is desired (static, dynamic, interactive, communicative)?
- What is the cost of hardware and software? Don't forget the cost of building and maintaining the applications, which often exceeds the acquisition cost
- How stable is the platform chosen and how likely is the provider to stay in business?
- The opposite question to the above: are you about to choose a technology based on an established technology and provider that will soon be rendered obsolete?
- Most electronic services development projects will not meet their deadlines and they will need to run for many years in order to recoup their costs. The technology chosen should allow immediate implementation, and yet be stable enough to allow ongoing operational and development work for up to five years or more.

# Departmental Integration of Data Resources – Don't Lock up Your Resources

Cities that have come this far are likely to have produced working services in several departments. As the services grow, it becomes clear to service producers that it would be useful to have access to some data possessed by other city departments. For instance, tourist information could be better presented by using maps. Maps can be manufactured anew, but they often already exist in the form of GIS systems, typically owned by the city planning office or the like. Also, tourist information systems might want to expand into providing booking services. Cities may have computerized booking services for sports facilities, for instance, but those are not owned by the tourist office.

There appears to be a need for cooperation. How can this be achieved? In practice, the answer depends a lot on what legacy systems there are, but also on how far the different departments have come towards electronic service management. Those who have come this far are likely to want to pursue their way of doing things (which is often by "old" technology, such as the 1000-page way of doing it). Those who have not progressed so far are typically more likely to try new ideas. Neither is willing to become subordinate to the other.

This problem often arises from history. In many cases, however, problems of this kind are created by departmental reforms, internal trade regulations and so on.

Integration always entails a need for new organizational structures, and in practice this is a hot spot for innovations and negotiations. Steering groups, editorial boards and project coordination teams are invented to cope, but also to avoid fundamental organizational change. There is much at stake; in the worst case conflicts may reach deadlock, stalling not only innovation but also operations. Integration today often proves more complicated than ever because of the current trend towards breaking up organizations into more or less independent units.

In this chapter, we will go a little deeper into these problems and possible solutions. It should also be said that many of the problems and situations described here are similar to problems described in textbooks on organizational change; they are not novelties appearing with the Internet.

The chapter has two parts, which are interrelated but start from different angles. The first part is about general organizational matters. The second part is about information quality, striving for which has organizational implications, and the lack of which often has organizational reasons. The latter part starts with the section "Data Integration and Data Quality".

## *Soap*: Clashing Conquistadors

In Tapville, there was an active engineer working in the Engineering Department who had become seriously bored. Deep in his heart, he had a secret ambition to become a famous artist and a dream to be celebrated as a hero. His current work appeared to provide neither the prospect of fame nor the opportunity to be creative.

Then, all of a sudden, he started hearing about the World Wide Web, and of ways that cities could and should present themselves on it. Our Artistic Engineer started to learn HTML and produced some Web pages. The results looked good to his eyes. Since he only had an Internet connection at his office, he started spending more and more of his working hours, and not just evening hours, on producing Web pages. He chose to start producing Web pages for the city, in order to justify his activities to colleagues and to his boss.

Our Artistic Engineer was enthralled by the prospect of getting his city onto the Internet, and was able to get a lot of high-level people, and the leading local newspaper, to back him up. He worked very hard, and eventually got several thousand Web pages made to chart the newly found El Dorado of the Internet. The local press was awash with news of the conquest, and our Engineer finally achieved fame.

Meanwhile, in another corner of the vast administrative matrix of Tapville, in the Services Department for the Disabled and Elderly, a strong-willed city Clerk with a Conscience felt that his clients had a problem. There must be an easier way to find public help than going through a myriad offices just to find out what one ought to do to get a social benefit, he thought. Legislation and administration long ago ceased to address the needs of the citizens. Instead, they have started to evolve according to their own internal laws. Many well-educated adults get lost while trying to find the right offices to contact and the right forms to fill in order to get a benefit, let alone the elderly who really need such services.

Our Clerk with a Conscience started to assemble notes that linked services and forms together, to be used by various groups of people who needed to quickly locate the necessary activities and contacts to get a benefit. He started publishing this as an edited newsletter, a contact list that was regularly updated. The newsletter was seen as a great help to people in need of getting a benefit. It was also used by city officials to help their clients. The newsletter received wide public acclaim for achieving its goal. The Clerk finally received some well-deserved gratitude for his Sisyphean efforts.

Our Clerk now spends most of his time calling people and editing his huge database of links. His work would be greatly helped by the Internet, where his various contacts could maintain their information themselves. He has been thinking of this possibility for some time, but because of his age and the fact that updating the information keeps him very busy, he has not found the time to learn enough HTML to start converting his system over to HTML himself. He has spent quite some time thinking about how his newsletter should look like on the Web, though.

At this point, it occurs to the Artistic Engineer that the contact list for the disabled and elderly would be a nice thing to have on the Tapville Web pages. After his initial effort, the Engineer has grown fond of a new, sleek Web design style, and he keeps revising his pages to look more hip. The city of Tapville now portrays a quite flashy image on its Web pages. So he wishes to have a well-known highly acclaimed city service, such as the contact list, to complement the modern image of Tapville.

The Engineer contacts the Clerk and sets up a meeting, seeing an opportunity for mutual complementary help: good electronic content for the Tapville Web pages, and good Web skills to get a nice application onto the Web. The meeting proceeds in a somewhat suspicious atmosphere, however. The Clerk keeps asking whether he should give out his huge collection of links, a very valuable asset, to the local newspaper to make money from, without the city or the people in need getting any of this money.

The meeting ends inconclusively. Subsequently, the Clerk makes a sour remark about the Artistic Engineer's endeavours in a TV interview, accusing him of building a picture of the city as a private business empire. He even hints at the unscrupulous profiteering of some city officials while in public office. The Engineer is outraged and promptly denounces the claims of the Clerk in an article. He accuses the Clerk of being a recalcitrant city official that does not see that his work will soon be rendered obsolete by the direct presence of all his contacts on the Internet. A spectacular public fight ensues, and the citizens hear more about Tapville on the Internet than ever before.

Simultaneously, the Business Services Department of the Tapville city administration enters a provincial development project on Internet services to citizens. They quickly agree with the city Public Relations office on a systematic plan to start putting city services on the Web. These departments jointly carry out some studies that point to a functional Web design style that builds upon a hierarchy of questions that citizens most often pose. A well-designed and functional Web site ensues after two years of hard work.

At this point, the question emerges of how to integrate the two Tapville Web sites and the contact list. Although the Artistic Engineer has by this time left the city administration he still possesses the clout to decide on the fate of his Web site through his previous department head. He refuses to change the structure and the design of his site to conform to the new functional layout. Meanwhile, the Clerk with a Conscience keeps complaining about his need for a Web assistant. He is promised one, should he agree to conform to the functional Web design. For the time being, he remains resistant.

The three services are all left afloat. Without each other, they are all too limited. There is no city department to be assigned the task and the budget to maintain the city electronic services. As months go by, the stalemate grows into a management problem that forces the Mayor and the City Board to make rapid decisions on matters they are ill equipped to cope with.

## Too Many (Cocky) Cooks...

The saying is that too many cooks spoil the broth. While it is clear, as we saw for instance in Challenge 1, the start-up challenge, that champions – local heroes – are certainly needed to get things rolling, it may also be said that too many heroes make no soup at all. Typically, a local hero is needed to resolve each of the challenges discussed in this book, but – also typically – the solutions may be only partial. Therefore the local heroes who once heralded positive developments may at some point turn into obstacles, either in their own right or as a consequence of local hero wars like the one described above.

Another problem in the development of electronic services is that heroes sometimes go unrewarded from the episode because they have to line up with established actors who at some point decide they can go on by themselves. The next soap episode gives an insight into this problem.

## *Soap*: Recalcitrant Roles

In Tapville, the young and brilliant managing director of a desktop publishing company was doubling as a research assistant at Tapville University. He was originally forced into such a double role by economic concerns, but has lately enjoyed it because of the intellectual excitement his two roles provide.

He became introduced to the Web very early on at the university, but as a professional in publishing he was constantly displeased by the poor support given to graphical design by HTML. The young desktop publishing manager became overjoyed when the Portable Document Format (PDF) was introduced by Adobe. Finally there would be a layout tool that adequately matched the needs of the publishing industry.

The small desktop publishing company was doing a lot of subcontracting to the leading regional newspaper. Because of this, the young manager had good access to the elderly CEO of the newspaper. Despite his age, he was still keen on new technology. The newspaper always had the most modern printing machines in the country. Since there was a big national fair coming up in the region, the young manager suggested to the CEO that they jointly produce a trial Web version of the regional newspaper, to be displayed to the public every day all through the fair. To produce this version, PDF would be adopted.

Despite some technical problems during the fair, such as the telecommunications between the fair and the newspaper not working, so that the daily issues had to be transported on a diskette, the Web edition of the newspaper during the fair was a success. Prompted by this success, the young manager and the CEO decided to start the development of a Web edition of the regional newspaper.

Although the newspaper was doing very well economically, they were not used to investing in development projects. In order to finance such innovative development, the young manager spent a lot of time finding possible sources of development funding. He assembled a consortium consisting of the newspaper, its traditional IT supplier and his own company in a consulting role. He even managed to get the National Association of Newspapers to join in, because the project was the first of its kind for a regional newspaper. The goals of the project were ambitious, too: to establish the regional newspaper as the leading Web publisher of all kinds of regional content, even electronic services.

The IT supplier had also been active in its product development. It had developed a platform specifically designed for newspapers to produce embedded Web editions. This tool involved browser-based user interfaces not only for viewing the resulting Web paper, but also for classified advertisement management, page layout management and article and picture management.

The CEO was very impressed by the new tool. It matched exactly the needs that he thought a newspaper's Web edition would have. He thought the main user group would be expatriates from the region who wished to remain up-to-date on local developments. He eventually got a prominent client in this category, because a member of the Tapville City Board moved abroad for a year to take up a Visiting Researcher position. He declined to give up his seat on the City Board, indicating that he remained sufficiently well informed about Tapville developments through the Web newspaper. Earlier on, the City Board had already started publishing its agenda and minutes on the Web.

Given such an excellent tool for Web publishing, the CEO did not really understand what he needed a consultant for. After all, it was the newspaper that knew best about publishing. And the IT company was able to sell it their new product and give them adequate technical support. He could set up links to any electronic services he wished to associate with the Web edition of the newspaper, without asking anybody's advice. The CEO also noticed that the young manager had written a substantial order for his services in the project plan, to be financed from the project funds. To him, all this looked increasingly like a money machine for the young manager's company.

In the end, the CEO decided he would go it alone, supported on commercial terms by the traditional IT supplier only. He ceased to invite the young manager to project meetings. Puzzled by the sudden lull in the hitherto hectic project activity, the latter grew increasingly disappointed. He had been working for two years in order to set up a viable, innovative business niche on the Internet for the regional newspaper. He had received no pay whatsoever for all his efforts, not even a thank you.

As a small consolation, the National Association for Newspapers did order a state-of-the-art report from the young manager on the opportunities that Web publishing and electronic services present to regional and local newspapers.

The Web newspaper has continued with the same profile for two years now. It is still free of charge and gets some revenue from Web advertising. There is some daily interplay between the paper and electronic versions of the newspaper, but there are no new business models beyond the confines of newspaper publishing. The newspaper is not on a track leading to Electronic Service Management activity.

## Not Only in the World of Soaps

What happened in Tapville has parallels in many cities. The following case is just one of many.

In the Stockwerp suburb of SpriteVille, an information system used by the generalist staff at the Citizen Office was developed in cooperation with a consultant company. The company provided a system based on many years of experience and a service model developed by the public sector in Denmark and largely adopted in Stockwerp. The staff enthusiastically put much effort into providing information, including useful extras such as prescribed action plans in certain client situations, advice to peers on what to do in unclear situations, and lists of persons to contact. The plan was to use the information and the design of the system in the Stockwerp Intranet, so as to get a uniform information system across the city. But the consultant charged with the Intranet development said the information could not be used, and started anew. Understandably, it was not possible to engage the staff at SpriteVille in yet another exhausting development project within a year of the previous one, which they were quite happy with. After less than a year, the company had produced a prototype of the Citizen Services part of the Intranet which was deemed useless, so the company was taken off the project.

In this case, the local heroes were simply discarded without much analysis of their work, and new ones were appointed by another project, without much success. The fact that the material was quite useful – and used – at a pilot implementation of the Citizen Office concept, that in fact it was well structured, and that it was developed according to a relatively widespread and accepted model was of little importance when the new consultant entered the scene.

While it is clear that new ways of doing things must sometimes render obsolete work that has previously done, there is little evidence that this need was even analyzed on this occasion. It was rather about a chain of different consultants entering consecutively, each selling their own prefabricated solution rather than solid analysis, in much the same way as we saw in the metaphor soap in Challenge 5.

Handle your consultants. There are many of them – don't let them set your agenda for you. You will only find yourself with multiple incompatible agendas.

Treasure your users and your professionals. They are not easily replaced, and you depend on them to make service happen.

Handle your heroes with respect, but don't let them get in the way of further development.

## Whose Business is it Anyway? Lessons on the Ownership and Organization of Electronic Service Processes

Electronic services are not products or services. They are service processes. When defined in functional terms alone, they almost invariably transcend many organizational boundaries. There are many content providers,: somebody must produce the Web technology involved, there must be a teleoperator or a cable TV company involved in delivering the service to the customers, and so on.

The border-crossing activities that are needed to put good electronic services together invariably create tensions across existing organizational boundaries. Such tensions are strong enough to break a good electronic service concept. As long as the service does not possess an organizational "home", it remains prey to organizational, political or business battles. A proper organizational home for an electronic service must encompass all the relevant connections to existing organizations that are vital for the production of the service.

In this section, we discuss various ways to navigate the stormy waters of organizational strife. There is no foolproof prescription for how to get through, but the advice given here will help in many a complex situation.

As the two episodes of the Tapville soap presented above demonstrate, there are primarily two different kinds of key organizational people whose endorsement and support are needed to set up an electronic service.

- *Top managers.* Top managers identify themselves with their organization. For them, the existing hierarchical structure, well-defined and well-understood functional and business relationships, and a well-understood role for their organization, is a top priority. Top managers are generally positive towards new developments as long as they expand or consolidate their organization's current fiefdom. They become concerned if their organization appears to be in a danger of having to yield control of some part of its core competence to an outside party, even if this would promote the mission of the organization. Their motto: *Stay on top of new developments.*

- *Change agents.* Change agents are people who have initiated some new developments in their organizations – and sometimes outside them – in the past, often at considerable personal sacrifice. They feel very much like intellectual parents to their brain children, and eye jealously anybody who may be able to make a profit from what they see to be their personal intellectual offspring. Although the service or concept created by a change agent may well live on its own by now, relaxing even a small part of parental authority is bound to be a painful experience to the intellectual parent. Their motto: *The parent must have the final say.*

The two groups of key people can only be persuaded by arguments that provide a counterweight to the above key concerns. Since it is often necessary to violate the above concerns in setting up a successful electronic service – it needs to be provided by several partners jointly and integrate content from many sources – some rewards that may be used to alleviate the frustrations of top managers and change agents are the following:

- *Positive publicity.* Allow the organizations and their managers, or the original innovative services and their inventors, to be the stars of the new service as well. In the eyes of the public, this also reinforces their ownership of the new electronic service, although operational control may reside with a new organization.
- *A joint venture.* Set up a joint venture together with the key participating organizations and individuals that makes all strategic decisions on the new service. Such a joint venture may equally well be a management board within the city or a new business venture in the case of a private service.
- *Script attractive roles for partners.* The least that a successful electronic service manager should do is to think through the roles of all the key organizations he needs in the new electronic service concept. He should write them out as well, in order to have persuasive arguments to present to sceptical partners, seen through their own eyes.
- *Bring along a prominent partner.* Bring a strong partner to the consortium that the current partners would gladly align themselves with. Most people and organizations like to be seen in famous company, and electronic services consortia are no exception.

We shall now take up the Tapville story again, to get an example of bringing reluctant partners together.

## *Soap:* Tangling With Tourism Networks

The Tapville tourism services scene is in turmoil. The city management is dissatisfied with the performance of the city tourism information agency. Despite substantial recent spending on promotion activities, the tourism services providers and hotels in the city are not receiving any more visitors than before. A decision is taken to privatize the agency. The ticket sales activities are taken over by a tourism shop entrepreneur whose company also sells group travel services. The activities are to move to a newly opened prominent museum building in the town square.

The Tapville Web project has been working with the tourism agency for a year to set up an Internet-based ticket booking office. Some of the staff have migrated with the activities to the privatized ticket sales company and the project has lost its home base. The entrepreneur is sceptical of the Internet, never having used it himself, and just wants a working ticket sales application without any ill-defined extensions to "the virtual world". The Web project had worked for a long time to couple Internet ticket sales with a regional Internet-based reservation system, in order to create a complete new regional online tourism promotion and booking service.

Simultaneously, the prominent multimedia services that will portray the new museum building on the Internet is being hotly contested between a regional and a national teleoperator. The former insists that regionally prominent institutions should advertise regional businesses, while the national teleoperator does not accept any joint efforts with its competitor. The latter operator can offer abundant nationwide publicity to promote tourism to the museum, and to Tapville in general.

Facing this complex decision problem, the Web project manager lays out a conceptual map in which he charts a business niche for all the players, as follows:

- He offers to take on the responsibility for the installation of a standard ticket sales software package for the tourism shop entrepreneur if the latter agrees to collaborate on the Internet package too. He promises to add a function to the Internet package that allows for the rapid creation of proposal letters for group travel, based on information accessible from the regional Internet booking service.

- He proposes that the national teleoperator be accepted to provide the telecommunications to the museum, providing at its own expense broadband telecommunication connections between the museum and the premises where the tourism service servers are hosted. This will allow large-scale simultaneous access to both ticket sales and booking services, along with the museum's multimedia services.

- He approaches the National Tourism Agency to take on the Tapville tourism services platform as a pilot service for their national online tourism services project. This will allow them to complement regional tourism content in the service with online ticket reservations to popular national events, such as rock concerts and sports events that many Tapville citizens also attend. The National Tourism Agency is a welcome partner for any organization in the region.

- As compensation to the regional teleoperator, he volunteers to set up a research project and apply for funding from European sources with them to develop an online community environment that would attract local people to use the Internet more, thereby generating revenue for the local teleoperator. This environment will feature both regional and national tourism services, including popular national events that will certainly get people to use the environment.

Equipped with such a plan, the Web project manager sets out on his hopeful mission to reconcile and rebuild the threatened online tourism services project. He is somewhat concerned because of the complexity and abstract nature of the benefits to the various partners in the scheme. It will be hard work to persuade them all and this will cause delays in the implementation. Without such a complex scheme he would not be able to please all the partners, however, and he will need the support of all them, either now or later on.

# Cross-Departmental Cooperation Strategies and Possibilities

There is one major lesson to be learned from the last episode: be there. Meet often with your partners. Reinforce their belief in your common vision. Show your own commitment to the common cause by spending time with them. If you are not there to hold the flock together, natural divergence or organizational ties will pull the partners apart. Electronic services projects are an exercise in persuasive communication more than anything else.

This last requirement is a hard one, despite its apparent simplicity. It is very difficult to say how much presence is required to keep a wary bunch of partners together when they are uncertain of their faith in the common vision, suspicious of one another and of you, and unsure of whether even a successful final outcome of the project will do them any good. The amount of time and management that must be spent on such a role in a project is substantial, and this requirement puts an implicit limit on how many simultaneous electronic services development projects a single person can run, no matter how skilful, committed or energetic that person is.

When one sets out to improve services to customers or citizens, it is likely that data resources from different departments will have to be integrated. While there are obvious gains to be made, there are often also unexpected improvements that may follow. Or they may not. Supporting professionals by non-compulsory systems is a sensitive matter. Unless there are gains to be made by the individuals using the system, the potential advantages will never be realized. This case from Suburbia illustrates this.

In early 1998, Suburbia established, within the framework of an EU Telematics project, an application aimed at improving the service to the citizens at the "Citizen Office" established three years earlier. Originally, operations were based on handwritten forms. The new application introduced the electronic media of email, attachments and Web documents. The purpose was to provide better services, for instance by making email requests from citizens possible and by monitoring replies, shorter response times *and* better follow-up of internal procedures by means of some control functions, such as tracking pending works and monitoring workload and response times. The service thus had a clear citizen focus: the motivation was to provide better services in a way that was immediately visible to citizens.

The system was first implemented in a semi-automated way. It was integrated with the Citizen Office, which was also a kind of call centre; All requests passed first through the front office, where there were always two people working: one with technical expertise, and one with administrative knowledge. Simple questions would be answered immediately by the front-office staff. If they were unable to answer a question satisfactorily, the question was passed on to back-office experts (by email, personal contact, or phone). The answer was then delivered back to the front officer, who delivered it to the citizen.

This method of working was somewhat ineffective. It certainly improved response time for simple requests (those that the front-office personnel could answer) and simplicity of access. But the indirect way of answering the more complicated questions meant that there was a risk of the answer being distorted because the messenger, the front officer, did not understand it properly or could not explain it properly. Because of this, there was also a risk of follow-up requests caused by an incomplete or unintelligible answer, which would have to pass along the same route.

In fact, a typical answer to a complicated request was a request for a personal appointment: "come and see me in my office".

While there was some scepticism at the outset, back-office staff soon found out that the system could actually bring advantages to their work situation. At first, they tended not to answer the citizen directly by email. It was considered too time-consuming to write down a complete answer. Hence the tendency to

scribble some sentences on a piece of paper and hope that the front officers, who had considerable knowledge about city operations, could interpret the (often incomplete) answer.

After some time, it was found that by taking the time to answer thoroughly in writing, the need to call
on people for personal appointments was drastically reduced. By the summer of 1998, more than 30% of
the requests were dealt with without the need for a personal meeting.

## Designed and Opportunistic Advantages

The Suburbia case shows how advantages from redesigning operations may come in
two ways: by design or as the result of new opportunities.

The designed change was that the front office took care of the simpler questions,
thus reducing the response time for those, and provided a one-stop shop for all
questions, thus facilitating access for citizens. The computer system was implemented to speed up interactions, and so it did.

But it also did something else. It made the back-office staff realize that they could
improve their own work situation by working in a different manner. Instead of
postponing a complete answer to a second interaction, a personal meeting, they
found that by being proactive – answering more completely on the first occasion –
they could reduce the number of time-consuming personal appointments.

The system also meant that information had to be shared. Because detailed
answers were given in writing, knowledge was transferred to the front office. There,
answers could be reused, thus reducing the number of occasions when back-office
experts had to be consulted.

In fact, there were other advantages. The new system made it possible to plan jobs
in a way that reduced travelling – jobs could be pooled so that several could be dealt
with in a single trip.

The common denominator for the latter type of advantage is that they were not
actually designed but occurred as people realized they could do things differently
and gain something themselves from doing so. While people may pay lip service to
the idea of better services, it is more likely that they will in fact produce better
services when there is also something in it for themselves. Advantages like these
might have been hoped for by the system designers, but they cannot easily be
dictated. It is only when people realize the advantages that they will start to change
their procedures.

In a service organization, much of the quality of the service is left with the
individual professional. It is therefore important to design systems in such a way that
they can get some advantages out of it for themselves.

Clearly, however, the satisfaction of the professionals, managers and change agents
is not the only thing to aim for. Although it is a necessary condition for providing
good services, it is not sufficient. Given freedom, people and organizations tend to
build empires, which most often means not only running things as usual but also
includes weaving consolidation and/or expansion plans. In the following we shall
pay some attention to the systems aspect of things.

In summary:

- Involve top management – no real change will occur without them on your side.
- Make sure the change agents don't go unrewarded.

- Get the professionals on your side – make sure there is something in it for them.
- Give the professionals new and challenging tasks, not just more work.

## Data Integration and Data Quality

Different people use different names for the same things. Services involve professional languages and colloquial languages. Databases have different definitions of terms. Integration of professional cultures, different user communities and different databases calls for translation between them, or the subservience of one database or culture to another. At the technical level, databases can be replaced or data dictionaries can be created to translate between existing systems, which are left as they are. This is simple compared with the task of integrating the different languages of different cultures. In total decentralization everybody is allowed to use the local language, and in total centralization everybody is forced to use the centrally decided language. Both sides have pros and cons, and the solutions adopted are closely related to the history and culture of the actual area. Using the proper terms may seem trivial, but is not, and failure can cause severe problems. As the following soap shows, problems might not even be detected.

## *Soap*: Whoops Arnold, We Had You Fooled

Arnold was seriously considering moving to Tapville. Arnold is an exemplar of the new generation who use the Web as an integral part of their lives. Arnold tells us that in some cases he enjoys surfing into a city as much as paying a physical visit. Arnold currently has an opportunity to move to either of his two favourite cities, Tapville and Nextville, and he has to make a decision. As part of the decision process, he visits the Tapville and Nextville sites several times. During those Web visits, he has discovered many good things and opportunities in both of his favourite cities. Finally, his choice is Nextville.

Arnold moves to Nextville. He thinks life is fine, and he is sure he made the right decision. Meanwhile, back in Tapville, one of the more ambitious politicians has raised the question of why so few young families have moved into Tapville in the last year compared with previous years. A questionnaire is sent out to all families that have been asking for information about Tapville. Arnold is among those surveyed, and because Tapville is one of his favourite cities he gives honest and detailed answers.

"The main reason for not moving to Tapville", he says, "is that according to the information on the Web there are so few childcare opportunities, especially in the Sillycon Valley area, which I had in mind to move to."

The analysis of the answers makes it clear that many families give poor childcare as one reason for not moving to Tapville. Because of this result, the answers are analyzed more closely and Arnold's answer is the trigger for a new investigation.

The strange thing is that in fact the Sillycon Valley area has a very ambitious childcare programme, renowned far beyond the Tapville city limits (but unfortunately only in pedagogical circles). From the very beginning, children play with languages and logic according to the most modern educational findings. There are also many experiments with integration between older and younger children. A six-year-old, for example, can be a mentor to a four-year-old. Because of this new approach, the professionals are no longer called nurses but teachers. They also have better salaries than their colleagues in other places. An aspect of this development is also that all childcare units are now labelled "beginning schools", and on the Web they can be found as part of the school system. That is why Arnold found so few childcare places in Tapville: he couldn't figure out the search terms.

One result of the investigation was that a serious data integration problem was found in Tapville. Different names for the same things and different meanings for the same terms are found in abundance around the city. The problem has been observed but nobody really knows what to do about it. When the investigating team realized the problem, they suggested a change back to the old childcare name, but that caused a burst of protest from the personnel involved.

## Organization and Information Structure Are Connected

The Arnold story shows the close (often too close) connections between organization and information structure. People use different terms for the same thing in different places (even if the childcare system in Sillycon Valley was radical, it was still about taking care of children). Now, what happens if you delegate organization and information responsibilities? Look at an example from Stockwerp.

> In 1995, the City Council of Stockwerp decided to divide the city into 24 districts. The stated reason was local democracy. The city, it was said, was too big. People did not have much affinity with their political representatives in City Hall. Therefore, local city councils were created in each of the 24 districts. Some political decisions were delegated, but the main effort was to provide service locally. In each district, one or more "Citizen Offices" was set up. These offices were to provide local information and services, but also locally adapted information and services originating from other sources.
>
> The Citizen Offices were given some room to manoeuvre, but it was also decided that information should be provided in a uniform way in all offices. Also, in every office, the citizen should be able to find information about other districts.

From the point of view of providing services, this borough reform meant two things. First, a number of local entrepreneurs with ambitions (social and technical as well as political and business) appeared. Second, the need for a coordination committee mediating between the different local entrepreneurs became apparent.

When services are to be offered at any service point in the city, there is a need for a common approach in many areas: information items must be defined in a way that makes them compatible, and there must be a user interface that accommodates many different data sources in a uniform way, etc. This does not happen automatically.

> Stockwerp provides information about pre-schools (for children at the age of five or six, the year before they go to the regular school).
>
> This service is found as Children, Youth and Leisure activities in the district of SiliVille, as Children and Youth in MariaVille, and as Childcare in SpriteVille.
>
> From the point of view of the computer department this is really a mess because it is very difficult to get a clear view of all the pre-schools in Stockwerp. The Arnold case is more than likely to be repeated.

Solutions can be found in different ways:

The approach in RelaxenBurg is to solve this challenge by giving an Infomaster all the power and responsibility to decide what key words should be used. The Infomaster is in charge of the list of keywords that can be used. The Infomaster also advises people how to use these keywords as an important part of the Handbook on Web publishing.

The RelaxenBurg solution will work as long as the Infomaster has a good grasp of all possible terms. But is this really true? The Infomaster may be in the position to dictate what terms the city staff use, but is it possible to tell the people on the street what to call things? Aren't people much too inventive in finding new names for things? These rhetorical questions have already been answered, implicitly, with "no" and "yes" respectively. At the expense of RelaxenBurg, we can provide another case for our thesis that dictionaries that translate from professional to colloquial languages are the only enduring solution.

In RelaxenBurg, a lot of energy was put into the design of a system for helping commuters plan local travel. With this system, it should be easy to select your location, your destination and your arrival time. By using that information, together with the different timetables for public transport, the system should be able to offer a good suggested travel route, by train, tram, or subway.

The interface was tested with pilot users. The users managed to navigate well in the system, but the problem was that they often used other names for the stops than the official names in the timetables. For instance, when a user asked for Opern (the Opera), there was no hit because the official name of the station was Opernplatz (Opera Square). A number of similar examples made the potentially very useful system not so useful at all. Users did not like having to spend time guessing the official name of a bus stop or subway station. In fact, the response from users was so negative that the system faced closure.

As a tentative solution, the system was integrated with a database containing the names of all public transportation stations and a street database, so the stop could be connected to the names of the stops, nearby streets and buildings. Unofficial names were also included.

Preliminary tests after the change showed that the usability of the system had increased and optimism spread again among the responsible managers.

# From *Ad Hoc* to Competence Development

As we can see from the cases above and the Tapville story, there are situations where there is a great need to mediate between different actors, organizational entities and languages. Often it is a question of how much action space and power local departments should be given in relation to the central decision makers. We say this only with reference to the technical problems of getting things as right as possible, although there is certainly also a power dimension to it.

RelaxenBurg chose a centralist strategy, giving an Infomaster the role of concept and term manager. As the two RelaxenBurg cases show, this strategy must be combined with an element of delegation in order to take properly into account the colloquial/local use of language. Simply using the official names of the stations was not enough. Other names used by different groups of users had to be included.

In SiliVille this tricky question of data integration has been further developed along the lines of the following solution.

Each service provider has been given the opportunity to describe the service at four different complementary levels; (1) the commonly used local name; (2) a summary of the service, including the people involved and the location, contact information and venues; (3) a free area for text, pictures and links to electronic services, and finally (4) the most important keywords to be used for the service provided.

The result is a database covering service providers. The database is complemented with a search engine developed to include a list of synonyms, developed from a dictionary and from findings based on use, and stopwords (words ignored) making it possible to search for free text using all the different names of the service. An editor is responsible for keeping the synonym dictionary up to date (in the event of new nicknames appearing, for instance).

In summary, the providers try to describe their service in order to make it easy for citizens to use it. At the same time, an editor has control over all possible variations in the names for a service.

In the SiliVille solution, the editor is charged with balancing the pressure from the centralist desire to use just one language – which would certainly make things easier to administer – and the users' colloquial languages, which increases usability. In this way, SiliVille is trying to manage the two basic problems of centralization and decentralization. Total centralization can never work in a complex environment, because complete adherence to rules cannot be achieved. Too much decentralization, on the other hand, may mean a loss of quality. Certainly, key terms must mean the same across a city, and often across a country. Colloquial language often does not make the correct distinctions necessary from a legal point of view. And so on. It is important to distinguish between the terms used for searching and the terms used for execution. The SiliVille navigation system is designed to facilitate searching, leading users to the right service starting from different, or unclear, perceptions of where to look and what to name the thing that they are looking for. The underlying production system might or might not change its use of terms, but this is a different matter.

The importance of this balancing function increases as the Web service expands to include private services as well as central government-financed public services.

The SiliVille application integrates private business as well as sport clubs and voluntary service sector organizations into the system. So a lot of local businesses have joined the site and more are joining every day. This means that if you are a visitor at the SiliVille Web site and write "I would like to go to a party", you will receive an answer that includes both private restaurants and public places where parties can be arranged. There is also a good chance that you will get some hits for places where it is possible to buy presents and flowers.

One may well ask why a city should bother with businesses in its Web system. Our answer, based on experiences with many projects, is that the role of a city in an electronic service system can vary a lot. As a general rule (to which there are certainly exceptions), a small city in a sparsely populated region will assume a more prominent role than a big city or a small city in the neighbourhood of one or more bigger cities. In a small rural town, an important role of a city is often to help local small business survive. This typically includes the goals of purchasing locally when possible, supporting joint marketing initiatives etc. It may also include the role of being a hub for electronic services, providing or co-funding servers, advertisements, technical support, education and so on. In a bigger city, there will typically be other organizations large enough to do this.

## Web Integrators – a Critical Resource

We have seen above that integration does not happen by itself. If you want to achieve integrated electronic services, someone has to do the work of mediating and negotiating between the different actors involved. As in any successful negotiation, it is not just a matter of finding out the relationships and responsibilities between organizational entities, it is also a creative process of inventing new structures and new methods of cooperation. It is also the process of getting people involved in the implementation of these new structures. All of the cases and Tapville stories (which are all disguised real-world cases) indicate that "embryonic" incremental attempts to create such a body of organizational competence are more promising than the grand plan approach. While there is certainly a need for a grand plan to see beyond each individual challenge along the road, it must be carefully implemented by means of tenderly nourished embryonic services.

The case below, from Stockwerp, shows something of the embryo development process: some steps in the creation of a Web service integration system.

> Initially, there were projects. One of those projects was a bit more imperialistic than the others. It attempted to take a common approach to Web services for the whole city. This project, an effort to create a "navigator" – including several tools to help users find and access all electronic services – realized there was a need for a broad steering committee with a strong mandate.
>
> At the next stage of development the level of ambition was raised to also include coordination of some other ongoing citizen-oriented IT projects in the city. The first meetings showed that there was a real need to share information among the different projects. It was also clear that some projects looked similar, and therefore coordination groups with a narrower scope were established. One example was the group coordinating three projects; the development of the next-generation electronic tourist guide, the electronic guide for cultural events during 1998, when Stockwerp was the cultural capital of Europe, and the Navigator project.
>
> Drawing on experiences from the first year, it was decided that the steering committee had to be permanently included in the organization. Eventually, the following three parallel steering committees were established:
>
> ● The council for IT-supported activities. This council, chaired by the IT manager, was very much an initiative from the IT department to create a forum for discussions about future computer applications.
> ● The council for integrated Web services ("the Web Council"), chaired by the information manager.
> ● The council for market-oriented IT activities, chaired by the manager of city land and business development. The council is responsible for large external IT projects, such as the Bangemann Challenge.

The experiences from the Navigator project clearly pointed to the need for a central city Web service steering/coordination committee (in fact the word "Web" might well be excluded – more about that in Challenge 10). This body must assume responsibility for matching citizens' needs and the services provided, as well as the coordination of and integration between different projects and systems. Further, such a committee must also support initiatives for new services and continuously evaluate the need for and reactions to existing services.

Even if the majority of people can agree on the need for such a committee, it takes skill and ambition to get it implemented in a city. The reason, of course, is that it is a new creature trying to find space in an old structure.

From the standpoint of the actors within the old structure it is impossible to say whether this new steering committee should belong to the IT department, the Social Services department, the Information department or the External Affairs department. The question of representation in the Web council is also tricky. The Navigator project experience shows that it is important to have the right mix of people in the steering council, representing both the most innovative departments and those most important from a historical perspective. Furthermore, the council must be small enough to be able to work but big enough to be representative of the service-providing parts of the organization. But perhaps more important is the personal chemistry – the group must work well together. Groups like this always run the risk of becoming just another arena for departmental, or even personal, chauvinism.

Representation is important because most questions contain elements of position statements and negotiations. But there is also an element of organizational learning that takes place in connection with the Web council meetings. The following case is an example.

> The Stockwerp council for integrated Web services was trying to coordinate the proceedings of the Culture Capital '98 project (CC98) and a project developing the next generation of the city's tourist information systems.
>
> The project organization of CC98 soon realized that one important access point for visitors could be electronic services. They developed a data model and an interactive interface including all, as they saw it, of the relevant aspects of the cultural events of the year. In parallel with the activities of CC98, the department responsible for tourist information had an operational system for event information. In addition, the idea was to further develop this system in cooperation with a EU project, which had as one of its purposes to expand the use of kiosks as an access point to electronic services.
>
> Since the situation seemed to lead to the wheel being invented twice, or even three times, the question of why all three of these projects could not cooperate to develop one common solution was raised in the council. The underlying assumption was that cooperation would give a better solution for less money.
>
> After several meetings involving the two project groups and the management of the existing tourist information service, the picture became a bit more complicated. The department responsible for tourist information had, over the years learned that a simple data model was needed to continually obtain complete and relevant information from the event providers. From their point of view, the CC98 data model was far too complicated. The CC98 could understand this argument, but they were in a different position. They had far fewer events than the tourist department. The project was also running for a limited period. In that context, they calculated that with a central office to update information, it would be possible to use a more complex data model. With such a model, they could also develop more interactive services compared with the tourist department.

This case shows that data integration is a complex matter that needs competence to be handled successfully. While there was no technical integration in this particular situation, the case demonstrates that a "Web council" can serve as a forum for learning and competence development.

# Economic Gains?

So far, we have spent a lot of time on different kinds of problem, the solutions to which brought increased usability and thus long-term (but not necessarily short-term) economic gains. We now present two cases where a substantial return on investment was obtained very quickly, despite considerable costs and technical complexity. This is a case involving the use of maps in GIS systems.

> In RelaxenBurg, online access to a technical GIS system of the city is provided not only to other city departments, but also to all construction companies invited to submit bids to pave roads, lay underground cables or set up construction sites that will block traffic for a time. Such companies can check the GIS system directly to see the nature of the road surface at the proposed site, the presence of pedestrian crossings and parking lots, or any existing cables or plumbing. This allows them to plan beforehand the temporary measures needed to complete the proposed works and to assign definite costs to them.
>
> As an example, the cost of re-paving a road will depend heavily on the surfacing material used, since the constructor is required to restore the former status of the surroundings completely. The first result of online GIS access is more accurate bids, but the real savings emerge from the uncontroversial nature of contracts

assigned on the basis of such bids. Since the constructors have access to the system, they are also expected to use it and cannot afterwards refer to unforeseen expenses while restoring the environment.

In this case, economic gains could be realized quite quickly. In the next case, the gain was the ability to actually be able to produce a service that will not bring profit directly to the electronic service provider, but to the providers of the services to which access has been facilitated through the existence of the system.

Another use for GIS data is in tourism. In the emerging Finnish tourism service Matkain, maps are used to connect tourism activities to routes through the country. You will be able to make requests for motels and other kinds of accommodation, sights, petrol stations, and so on, along any given route, or in any area. The maps are produced on the fly from the GIS database of the National Geographic Survey. Symbolic information is attached from databases supplied by other organizations, who collect and update such information in each area, such as the National Board of Forestry for national parks or regional tourism agencies for accommodation available in the region. The service would be substantially downgraded without the contribution of external service providers. On the other hand, it would be impossible for a tourism service provider to produce the complex GIS systems needed to couple maps to symbolic information, for reasons of both expertise and ownership.

In the case of GIS systems, the technical complexity and the ensuing costs, as well as the ownership of the basic maps on which the systems are built, typically entail a central approach. There is also often a need for considerable interaction with users to make maps simple enough to use. GIS maps are very rich in information, and considerable simplifications are necessary in most situations to make maps easy to read (focusing only on the use context at hand), appear legibly on the screen and on printouts, and so on.

## Conclusions

This challenge can only be met by different departments agreeing on sufficiently common goals and means in the field of electronic services to make it possible to reuse and co-use systems created in some department. This typically requires a coordination committee mediating between the different entrepreneurs. It also requires substantial knowledge and vision in the technological field; pure mediation may well lead to old technology prevailing.

- There is often a lot to gain from integration and cross-departmental use of systems, both in direct economic terms, as the GIS case shows, and in terms of usability, as the SiliVille and RelaxenBurg integration efforts show.
- Coordinating committees ("Web councils", editorial boards etc.) are needed as arenas to handle the negotiation and learning processes involved in creating a uniform city-wide approach, not only to electronic services, but to services in general, which is the bottom line.
- The task of organizing such a coordination forum is highly skilled, since it has to develop a new structure of competence at the same time as supporting the transformation of old static IT solutions into a dynamic Web concept.
- The work of bringing cross-departmental data and legacy data onto a Web site is also genuinely complex and time-consuming. This amounts to a "data warehouse" approach, which involves issues of translating between different uses of

terminology, different professional and user cultures, and different data definitions in different databases.

- It is important to note that not all results can be planned. It is important to provide place in which the creativity of the people involved can find space to act. This will lead to unexpected things happening, but it is important to maintain momentum in the development.

- In order to make this work effectively, there is a strong need for the involvement of top management. Direct involvement is good, but even more important is that coordination groups should actually have a strong mandate.

- The need for information, education and discussions around this new development cannot be underestimated. This task could be called vision management.

- Externally funded projects can be an important trigger for the development of the necessary integration competence (as the Navigator project did in triggering the formation of coordination committees), because they typically bring in demands for user requirements and enforce cooperation.

- They may, on the other hand, also lead you astray if they are seen just as extra income and not as a tool for development. Such a view will lead to cities wanting to do the least possible, which often means relying on dinosaur technology and thus both failing to integrate different data sources and making the delivery process more problematic.

# 7. Challenge 7: Staff Motivation – Enrol the Staff in Your Team

When true operational Web services come to be suggested, the staff involved realize that this will affect their role as service providers. Some see a significant decrease in their income. Even more people are afraid of becoming redundant. Others simply fear losing some of their authority through not being the only ones in possession of certain types of information. This challenge can only be met if a serious discussion of the professionals' role in the new, more technologically equipped, organization is undertaken with those involved.

## *Soap*: Tapville Enthusiasts Try to Improve Citizen Services

In Tapville, there had since long been complaints in the press about the hardships citizens that had to endure when trying to use public services. A major complaint was that the city organization was so complex that it took an expert to find out which department housed a particular service. Once the address was found, short telephone hours made attempts at contact arduous. During the short hours the phones were open, they were typically busy.

In this situation, someone came up with the idea of a "Citizen Office". These offices should have long opening hours, providing citizens with immediate help in standard matters and navigation help in more complicated ones. They should help to find a way through the labyrinth of the Tapville city administration complex.

The offices were set up and were greeted with acclaim by the Tapville press. The subsequent two years saw a huge increase in customer visits, and independent evaluation showed that citizens were quite content with the new service. The number of staff trebled during the first two years of operation.

In the third year the Internet arrived. The offices were endowed with email, as were all the other city departments. Use was not great at first, but there were some enthusiasts. One was Canay Helpju, manager of the Tapville Citizen Offices. He realized that the email system could speed up citizen services considerably.

His idea was simple. He had measured response times at the Citizen Offices and had come to some very clear conclusions. For the simple matters, those that could be answered immediately by the generalist office staff, response was quick. There was almost no waiting time at the office, and phone queues were rare, probably because of the generous opening hours. It was different with the "difficult" questions – those that had to be passed to the back office for an answer. In these situations, the front-office staff faced almost the same problems as the citizens had done before. Even though in most cases they knew which person was the expert on a particular subject, they had to spend much time on the phone trying to find people. And when they did, the right people were often not able to answer immediately. They were often out of their offices, answering their mobiles while on their way between meetings, and often not even able to make a note. So they had to be called upon once more for a reminder. Answers were also often incomplete. That is, the answer seemed to be correct and complete, but when the front officer delivered it to the citizen who had asked the question, it often turned out that there were follow-up questions. Because these typically asked for even more details, the expert had to be called upon again. Together this meant that the average response time for "complicated" questions was long. With a range from one day to infinity (yes, there were questions that were never answered), the average was ten days.

This situation bothered Mr Helpju. Why, he thought, could we not use email for this procedure? Sending email would mean the people at the other end could not forget the question: it would look them in the face as soon as they looked at their computers. And delivering an answer in writing would probably mean a more exact answer. At least the front officer would not risk mishearing or forgetting parts of it. So not only would the response time be shortened, but the quality of answers would increase. And as a third benefit, Mr Helpju would be able to increase his staff's expertise. By saving questions and answers they would be able to reuse them. As things were now, some of the complicated answers were remembered – those to questions that were asked relatively frequently. For the less frequent questions, details were forgotten as time passed, and eventually when a question recurred there was no one who dared answer it without consultation because their memory was too vague. And the experts would gain too: fewer requests because of better answers the first time around, fewer citizen complaints about poor answers, and fewer direct consultations with citizens, because the front office could take care of more requests by itself.

Mr Helpju brought the issue up at a meeting with the heads of department in the ongoing BPR (business process re-engineering) project (which, by the way, had gone on for a long time without people noticing much happening).

"... so we have a win–win situation here", he ended his long and enthusiastic presentation. "There's something in it for all of us."

As he looked around the room, he noticed that faces were not as happy as he had thought (he truly believed his idea was a good one). Rather, people looked concerned. After a rather long silence, the manager of Social Services spoke.

"I'm sure IT is a good thing in many cases", he said, "but I see more problems than benefits with this. First, my department has the highest number of requests in the city. There is no way we could add a lot of emailing to that. We're already on our knees. Second, if you want us to reduce response time, we need more staff. My people are already working as fast as they can."

"I'm not talking about people working faster. I'm talking about a better system that will reduce lead times, not increase work speed. Citizens will get answers faster because we improve the internal flow, not because we chase people with a burner. That's a quality improvement! We can promise answers within two days or so. And another thing; if you provide written answers we can reuse them at the front office and so reduce the number of consultations. This will save your staff time."

"Well, promising answers means you put a strain on people, whatever you call it. And the reuse of answers is another problem with your plan. There is no way your staff can acquire the same level of expertise as ours. So if you reuse answers you risk a lower quality of service. Your staff may not be completely aware of all the implications of a certain action in a certain situation. They might not realize the subtleties and use an answer given in one particular situation in another one that isn't quite the same, although it may appear so to the unwitting. You at the Citizen Offices must realize your limitations and leave the tricky issues to the experts."

"I'm sure there are limits", Mr Helpju tried to reconcile, "and I don't think we can manage *everything*. But I'm quite convinced we can do much better than we do now. I know this from experience; I have followed up our activities carefully."

"Well, *you* might have a rationalization potential, but I can assure you that *we're* performing as well as we possibly can. And to change things you must have good reasons. I would have a hard time convincing my staff to first spend a lot of time learning IT and then spend a lot of time answering emails on top of their regular activities. And besides – consider the risks. An email is a public document. It must be filed for years. And any fault in it could lead to legal action against us long after the answer was given. People would have to be extremely careful when answering. This will take even longer. So the least you have to do before we can assess your plan seriously is to produce a business plan in which all the costs – and I mean *all*, including education, time spent on emailing and so on – and benefits are estimated."

"So, guys", the chairman of the meeting, the BPR project leader, Ms Benita P. Radcliffe, concluded the meeting, "I believe the best idea is that you, Canay, go home and work out an economic plan for your project."

"It's not the easiest thing in the world, you know", said Mr Helpju. "It all depends on everybody's cooperation. If people resist using email, for instance, we will have to use both email and phone to get in touch. And if they resist giving written answers, we will have the same situation as we have now. So unless people are interested, it will be hard to achieve anything at all. And it's hard to calculate gains when we don't know what things cost *now*. How can I know how much your department will save for each answer to a request when you can't tell me how much it costs today? But because it is a very good idea – sure, I'll crunch some numbers."

# Analysis

## It Takes Courage and Experience

We suggested in the introduction to this chapter that new systems often make people fear negative changes coming their way, including an actual fall in their income, a risk of becoming redundant or losing some of their authority, or extra work coming down the road without a matching increase in benefits. We suggested that this challenge can only be met if a serious discussion of the professionals' role in the new, more technologically equipped, organization is undertaken with those involved.

This advice may sound simple enough, but one major problem is that typically this "serious discussion" cannot be undertaken until some experience has been gained among the staff. As we saw in the Tapville case, there were many obstacles. The Social Service department was not keen on giving away its expertise to the Citizen Offices for free in the form of written answers. They also saw the risk of getting extra work by having to answer more questions, or having to answer them more carefully or with higher quality demands due to the filing requirements for written documents.

This is a well-known ingredient in any systems development project that involves major changes: users are typically reluctant to welcome radical changes for fear that their position will deteriorate in some way. This fear is quite natural, because another typical ingredient of such change projects is that changes are often hard to foresee in detail. As we saw in the Tapville case, it wasn't so easy to foresee exactly what was going to happen.

The following case from Suburbia illustrates this problem.

In 1998, Suburbia established, within the framework of an EU Telematics project, an application aimed at improving the service to citizens of the Citizen Offices established three years earlier. The application was to provide better services (for instance by making email requests from citizens possible), shorter response times and better follow-up of internal procedures by means of some control functions, such as tracking pending works and monitoring response times.

The system was first implemented in a semi-automated way. It was integrated with the Citizen Office, which was also a kind of call centre. All requests passed first through the front office, where there were always two people: one with technical expertise and one with administrative knowledge. Simple questions would be answered immediately by the front-office staff. If neither of them was able to answer a question satisfactorily, the question was passed on to back-office experts. Those experts were not initially used to email, and therefore often answered indirectly by scribbling an answer on a piece of paper which was sent back to the front-office personnel, which in turn delivered the answer to the citizen.

The procedure seemed less than effective; delivering the answer directly to the citizen would seem to be not only faster but also safer. After all, there is a risk that the front-office personnel would misunderstand the answer given by the expert, and thus deliver an imperfect or even faulty answer. And there was the possibility of follow-up questions, which might lead to another round of expert inquiry.

There were at least two reasons for this procedure. One was that the experts initially found that the procedure of writing a detailed and complete answer was too time-consuming. It was easier for them to leave the job of explaining the answer to the front-office personnel. Another reason was that the staff initially saw the system as a policing tool. They felt that the main purpose was to evaluate their performance by making it possible to monitor response times and the number of questions answered. They felt that they ran the risk of being singled out as working too slowly or not providing adequate answers.

However, after some time they noticed that providing good answers led to fewer follow-up inquiries, and thus actually saved them time and effort in the long run.

Two things that were crucial to success in the Suburbia case should be noted. First, there was considerable initial staff resistance. Had the expert community been polled about whether or not it wanted the new system at an early stage, the answer would have been no. Because time was needed to allow people to see the advantages for themselves, it was very important that the implementation had strong managerial support. And it had – the mayor of Suburbia believed strongly in the positive effects of IT use, and made several personal statements to promote his view and to encourage people.

Second, the time until the system begun to win acceptance among the experts was about six months, and those were months of relatively frequent use (the system processes about 2000 requests per month). It was only after solid practical experience that people started to believe in the usefulness of the system.

The conclusion is that it takes both courage and experience to make innovative systems become accepted and thus profitable. And they are needed in that order: courage must typically precede experience, because it is often, as in the Suburbia case, a precondition for allowing the trials that are needed to provide opportunities for any experience at all to be gained.

## What About Quality?

The general thrust of this book is that giving people the opportunity to use appropriate IT may considerably improve productivity, service level and quality, and work satisfaction. But it does not necessarily turn out that way on its own, of course. There are several examples of situations in which IT does not easily align with professionals' expertise and/or roles. One area in which failure is common is the school system. The following example, once again from Suburbia, serves to illustrate the point that IT often forces professionals in other fields to become computer professionals as well – sometimes to a point that makes no sense from the standpoint of their core expertise or their clients' service requests. This not only means a waste of expertise, but it also impoverishes services and nurtures destructive conflicts with a professional society.

> Suburbia wanted to promote Internet use in the public schools. To that end, it provided a server on which all schools were invited to put their home-made "homepages". The city also provided modem connections and some new computers for the schools. All was free of charge for the schools.
>
> The school computers were, however, "misused", as far as the city plans were concerned. Teachers tended to use the new computers, which were newer and more powerful than the ones they already had (which were bought by the national government), for the regular curriculum. They did not connect to the "School Web" as often as they were expected to. Why was this?
>
> Two reasons could be discerned. First, because the Internet is not a compulsory part of the curriculum, they did not have to use it. But this does not explain why there was no use – after all, they got it for free, so why didn't they regard it as an opportunity?
>
> One answer, which can also be seen in schools in many other countries, had to do with maintenance.
>
> In Suburbia, maintenance of the new city-provided computers was initially provided free to the schools by the city's IT department. But after only one year, and with only half of the schools connected, it was realized that Internet use brings many new maintenance problems. Not only is the environment more complicated than the local environment – many different kinds of program, lots of low-quality shareware or freeware, viruses etc. – but the pupils were also prone to download lots of files, which clogged the disks, infected the computers with viruses, and so on.
>
> Because of this, the IT department could not keep up with maintenance. It was therefore decided that the maintenance should be delegated to the headmasters. But there was no computer expertise at the schools, and purchasing such would be at the expense of teaching in maths or something else. The headmasters were told to call the vendors. But they were not eager to take on the task for free. They claimed that it was not a problem of software or hardware failure, but one of misuse, for which they could take on no responsibility.
>
> The IT department assumed responsibility for making one check of all computers at the beginning of the school year, but many things happen in a year.... So the maintenance problem was largely left with the schools. And because there was no expertise, those who used the computers were the only ones who could be charged with the task – the teachers. Needless to say, they were not too eager to do that. Even though the job of cleaning up hard disks, installing and updating antivirus programs and so on cannot be said to be

a task requiring high skill, it certainly requires a lot of time – time that no teacher was eager to spend for free. So they stuck to the compulsory curriculum. Word processing and spreadsheets are much easier from a maintenance point of view.

The choice of the teachers appears quite unreasonable. After all, why should teachers in geography or history spend their working time on cleaning hard disks and downloading new versions of antivirus programs? If the aim was to encourage teachers to use the Internet, it would seem more appropriate to ask them to spend five hours a week on finding and reviewing the material pertinent to their discipline that is available on the Net. Having professionals in fields like geography, mathematics and history spending five hours a week on computer maintenance means losing five hours of professional skill. What computer consultant company would have its consultants spend five hours a week cleaning the floors, cleaning the windows, or emptying the wastepaper baskets?

Apart from these economic considerations, one should consider the change in the role of these professionals' – what does it mean to professional pride, job satisfaction and self esteem to be reduced from a skilled geography teacher to a novice computer technician?

It is not uncommon to spend professionals' working hours ineffectively, or at least seemingly so, for other reasons. There are examples of places where great Internet enthusiasm among teachers has made them turned them into programmers.

At EDUDIST, a school specializing in distance education for adults at college level, a cut in government subsidies for student travel forced the school to consider the use of IT for communication with the students and the Internet for course materials. The idea found fertile ground among a number of teachers. They started to develop Web material on their own, searching the Web to find relevant material, arranging maps of the Internet from their course point of view, installing plugins to provide chat and audio clips, and so on.

For these teachers, maintenance was not the issue, because the school set up an IT department to support the investment in IT-supported tuition. Instead, the issue was that their ambitions grew. Some teachers became skilled in CGI scripting, and spent many hours constructing interactive pages, such as self-correcting tests.

The problem was not one of enthusiasm. Even though some were more enthusiastic than others, morale was relatively good among all of them. Neither was there a problem of compulsory maintenance – the IT department kept up reasonably well, and at least assumed responsibility for the technical feasibility of the system.

But the fact was that many hours of teachers' time were spent on programming. Even though the result was satisfactory, one might question the use of so much of the professionals' time on this.

The words "might question" are carefully chosen. On the one hand, it seems wrong that an English teacher should become a programmer. On the other hand, the new medium created enthusiasm, which in itself is good, and which was a factor in generating not only support for the school's project, but also experience of the new medium, which provided a solid ground for pedagogically innovative use of the new medium. While it seems clear that, in the long run, teachers should teach more and program less, another factor in this case is that the school actually tried to do it differently. Its first move was to hire one of the more established computer consultancies to do the development work, based on the ideas of the teachers. That approach failed completely. The reason was that the teachers did not feel comfortable with the consultants. They felt that educational material should be developed by pedagogues, not by programmers. Communication failed completely, because the two groups did not speak the same language. Even though the consultants' lack of experience of education and teaching was the main reason, it seems that the fact that at that time the teachers were not so familiar with the Internet and its technology also played a role.

The extra spending, and the extra time it took to have the teachers themselves develop electronic material, seems to have been well worth it. Even though the programming time might have been shorter had the system been built by professionals, after just a year the school found itself with a perfectly working system designed in a way that is of at least average Internet standard. And it is a system that the teachers are proud of and like using.

# Conclusions

What can we learn from the examples given in this chapter? In Suburbia, it proved to be hard to launch the Internet because of teacher resistance. At EDUDIST, it worked out well, but it took longer than expected because of teacher enthusiasm and professional pride (in the positive sense of the word). The situations in the different schools are not completely comparable because the economic and social situations were different. Still, the cases show that unless the professionals are on your side, you will get nowhere. In Suburbia, one might say that there was a real problem in that there was insufficient funding for maintenance in the schools. This is the case in schools all over the world. Most have stretched budgets, and the idea of reducing teaching to increase spending on computer maintenance is not easy to sell. However, whether one likes it or not, computers need maintenance, and Internet use leads to more problems in this respect than standalone computers and applications.

This problem of maintenance is generally grossly underestimated. In Sweden, for example, a school teacher is typically paid for 1–2 hours per week to maintain the school's computer equipment, which typically comprises 15–30 computers in one lab plus 5–10 others in classrooms and teachers' workplaces. The users are typically 200–500 pupils. It is easy to imagine what these pupils can download if they use the Internet for only one hour each per week....

Getting the professionals on your side, while necessary, may prove troublesome. It is not uncommon for different professionals, or groups of professionals, to have incompatible interests. So, once again, it is not just about asking them what they want. Looking at our cases, we can see that many things contributed to success as well as to the lack of it. At EDUDIST, there was a fruitful combination of management policy, teacher enthusiasm, no conflicting professional interests, management responsiveness when the clash with the computer consultants occurred, and the establishment of a relatively well-staffed IT department that made for success. In Suburbia it was the unfortunate combination of a curriculum that did not include Internet use, lack of funding for support, and conflicting professional interests (they needed the computers for other things) that stalled development.

In a book on the management of sensitive projects, D'Herbemont and Cesar (1998) analyze the roles of various groups of people within an organization, and their attitude to innovative but controversial projects. They label a project sensitive if its human complexity exceeds its technical complexity. Most electronic services development projects fall into this category. The authors use methods from sociodynamics to explain and predict the behaviour of different groups of people when such a project is launched.

The strong advice of the authors is that people whose work will be affected by the new electronic service model should be listened to and consulted as *individuals*, not as members of a stereotypical group. Most people affected are likely to have many different, and sometimes contradictory, interests with respect to the new service model. This is particularly true if the subconscious feelings of people are given the consideration that they deserve. Such ambiguous feelings sometimes make the attitude of the people involved unpredictable.

It is important to accept and recognize such behaviour, and try to reformulate the development project in a way that makes the interests and emotions that are supportive of the project's goals get the upper hand among most of the people affected. In order to succeed, a project needs allies. In order to persuade allies to stay loyal, they must be listened to, and their views must be used to actually modify the project so as to better correspond to the allies' interests. D'Herbemont and Cesar call such a project a lateral project.

A lateral project keeps modifying its goals while it is being carried out, in order to gain the social acceptance that it needs to succeed. In electronic services development projects, such an approach is particularly valid, since their success depends critically on the support of staff and users. In electronic services, there is also hardly ever a single, infallible "correct path" that alone will lead to success. Sensible modifications can therefore be readily tolerated.

# 8.  Challenge 8: Poor Usability – Let the Users Be Your Guide

Although more and more cities and towns have set up their own Web sites, it is an open secret that many government Web information systems are little used. A closer look at the "hit" figures[1] of systems reveals that it is most often only the front page that is frequently used. Pages deeper in the hierarchy often have few hits, or even none. As the front page is usually a cover page and the more detailed information is typically found deeper in the system, it is not a very daring conclusion to say that many government Web systems are not used in the way they are intended to.

The perception of low system use may discourage you from following the example of other cities. But there is no need to give up immediately. Low system use may be related to many things, some of which you are able to influence. In this chapter, we will assume that the information in your system is actually useful to your prospective users, and we will dwell on the problem of how to make it readily accessible and understandable – that is, usable.

---

1   Web servers log client computers' requests for files. Such a request occurs each time a user clicks on a Web page link pointing at some other object; another page, an image, or a program. Each such request counts as a hit.

Usability – a common term among human–computer interaction (HCI) designers – refers to the ways in which systems are designed to meet the requirements of the interaction with a user. The professionals know that there are many ways for the user interaction capabilities of a system to cause problems. Users might not realize what a Web site contains, might get tired of searching, might not understand the information provided, or might get lost in a badly organized site.

This might sound discouraging, but in fact many such problems are often easily discovered by relatively simple usability tests. However, very few cities have, until they reach this stage, tried this. When they do, they often get a big surprise – not always pleasant.

At this stage (actually long overdue), service providers will have to learn about their users. Who are the people that will use your ESM system? What knowledge do they have, and what do they *not* have? In what situations do they use your system? What do they look for? How do they look? These are examples of the questions that a service provider needs to answer in order to be able to design services properly. For each particular service, there may certainly be special conditions, but there are a few general facts that make a difference in every case. This chapter discusses some usability fundamentals and gives examples from some Web site tests.

## The Tapville Conference Revisited

In Challenge 3, we left the Tapville conference before the university researcher, Mr Boc Worm, had a chance to explain the nature of the problems that users had with finding things in the Tapville Web, and what could be done about those things. Mr Worm mentioned some general usability issues, including the following things to avoid:

- inconsistent terminology
- unclear system cues
- departmentalization of information
- cognitive overload
- unclear or inconsistent mental models

In this chapter we shall explain and discuss these matters. But first a note about users. Clearly "unclear system cues" related not only to the system, but also to the users. A user who is experienced with a particular system may well find the system very clearly explaining its actions, whereas a novice user might find it totally confusing. Therefore it is important to know something about the target users. This insight was one thing that grew out of the Tapville conference.

## *Soap*: Tapville Investigates User Requirements

The Tapville Web system was originally developed as a one-man initiative. But over time, many people had had a hand in it, for different purposes and with different skills and ambitions.

Tapville is a city that is active in European cooperation. It actively strives to win as many contracts for EU Telematics Projects as possible to promote its development. When Tapville won its first contract in that field, the city was obliged to undertake a user requirements study in order to develop "user-friendly electronic services to citizens", in the terminology of the Commission.

The project's objectives were the standard ones. One specifically mentioned "must" was that systems should focus on the elderly and handicapped. The underlying logic seemed to be that the systems were by default so good that "the others" should use the system anyway, and all the cities had to do was to adapt their systems so as to make them easy to use for people with some kind of disability.

The project leader, Mr Goaf Orit of Tapville IT Department, was in a great hurry. The project had been late right from the start. It had taken a huge amount of time to get all the project leaders from the eight participating cities to agree on all the details of the consortium contract, not to mention the time it had taken them to get the contract endorsed at home. Therefore he had had no time to engage people to do the user requirements study. After all, until the contracts were signed, there might not be a project in the first place. Since the first EU money would not arrive until six months into the project, and only after the first deliverable was produced, Tapville would have to foot the bill until then. And his boss was firm: absolutely no spending until contracts are signed with the Commission. So his hands were tied: he couldn't sign up any subcontractors because they would not start work without confirmation; "call us again when you have the money" was the very clear message.

Consequently, Mr Orit had to bide his time as his anxiety grew, unable to plan properly for his project. He did, however, ask Dr Allu Wannanou, a university economics professor who he knew who specialized in market research, for help.

"Well, given the low budget, what I can do is have some students do it under my supervision", said Dr Wannanou. "It will take some time – the course is not due until February, and finishes on 30 March. Perhaps some students will be late. But by 15 April at the latest you should have the report."

"But the first deliverable is due by April 1!", sighed Mr Orit.

"Well, I'm sorry, but this is the way the university works. We have our schedules. Had we known about this a bit earlier, we could have assigned the task to the previous course. But now... well, I'm sorry. You could hire a company to do it."

"Yeah, but do you know what they charge? This is the public sector, we can't possibly pay that kind of money."

So Dr Wannanou agrees to do the job. And Mr Orit starts to figure out how to work out a delay for the first deliverable long enough to get the report into it. He sighs to himself. The report from Wannanou is only the first thing. It has to be integrated into a common report from all eight project cities. "I hope the others are not as late as we are," he wished to himself. But he knew very well that this was only wishful thinking.

"So", said Dr Wannanou, "what do you want us to do for you?"

"We need to know about user requirements", said Mr Orit. "Elderly and handicapped. Electronic services."

"How they use them?", asked Dr Wannanou.

"No, what kind of information and services they need. They don't use any services yet. We're going to build services for them, and we want to know what to build."

"Ah, a market investigation. Well, we often do that for different products. What are the products?"

Mr Orit was a bit stunned. Did the city have any products?

"Well, there is information from different departments. Sports, leisure, housing, transportation, childcare...."

"I think we can skip childcare for the elderly", Dr Wannanou said dryly.

After some discussion, they agreed on 11 City departments that had information and services that might appeal to the elderly.

"The handicapped are more of a problem", said Dr Wannanou "They're not *a* group. They are all kinds of ages and they have all kinds of disabilities and all kinds of interests. A 25-year-old in a wheelchair playing in the National Wheelchair basketball team has little in common with an 80-year-old lady who sits in a wheelchair at the Tapville Garden."[2]

"OK, so can't we just take a few people from each of the groups?"

"Yes, but do you realize how many people that will be? Different ages, ranging from, say, 15 to 80. Different sexes. Different occupations. Different disabilities. Different lifestyles. A few people from each category. We'll end up with hundreds of people to interview. We can't manage that within the scope of the course."

"What *can* we do?"

"Well, to make the results credible, I'd say you skip the handicapped. Go for a subset of the elderly."

"Why a subset?"

"Well, the elderly, too, are not all the same, you know. There are retired professors and retired street cleaners. Some are rich and some are poor. There are healthy and sick people. Disabled ones and ones with perfect physical abilities. You can find the same diversity of interests among pensioners as in any other age segment of the population. They are the same people as the rest of us, just a bit older and with more free time. So, to make the investigation representative for all, you need to make it very big. So my suggestion is: choose a subset."

"Which ones, then?"

"Well, perhaps those who can't get around much. After all, telematics is there to help people to avoid moving around so much, isn't it? Why not go to a home for the elderly and interview the lot there? We'll find people that differ in age, sex, and interests, but who are equal in that they can't move around easily. Plus, it will be easy for my students. I mean, how would you find people who are not in an institution? You would have to use the population register and search. From that, you could take a random sample based on a number of things, such as age, sex and former occupation, but you couldn't find those who can't move around easily."

This was the decision. The students eventually went to Tapville Garden and interviewed the people living there. They divided people into groups by sex and by age: 65–70, 70–75, 75–80 and over 80 (65 was the minimum age to qualify for a room at the Garden).

As Dr Wannanou had warned, some students were late, so it was not until 21 April that Mr Orit had the report on his table. By then, his anxiety had reached an all-time high. This was his first project coordinator job, and he had spent most of the past month making excuses to the Commission Project Officer on the one hand, and soliciting the user requirement reports from the project partner cities on the other. It turned out that all were late. In fact, most had done no investigations at all! "We don't know what to investigate", said one. "We thought you were doing that", said another. "We don't have a budget, you're in charge of the requirements phase", said a third. So, in effect, the only user study actually undertaken was his own.

---

2   Tapville Garden is the newest home for the elderly in Tapville. It was opened last year. Stuffed with technology to aid staff and entertain its inhabitants, and elegantly designed, it is the pride of Tapville social welfare.

And now, as he finally got the report and read it, he almost started to cry. The report went through all the different city services and investigated their attraction to the elderly of different ages and sex. The result was very clear: there was no demand at all for electronic services. Nobody had expressed any wish whatsoever to be served electronically by the city.

Mr Orit picked up the phone and called Dr Wannanou.

"What *is* this?", he exclaimed. "It can't be they don't want any services at all?"

"Well, they live in a very information-rich environment. The staff are very eager to help. When they need something – anything – they just have to ask. The staff call for taxi service when they need it, they look in the paper for sermons, and they read parts of the *Gazette* to them every day, at their request. They've got all the information and service they want. You probably would have found more need with people who live on their own and don't have all the service they have at the Garden."

"But you advised me to investigate people at the Garden!"

"Yes, because the others are very hard to find. It would cost more money than you have, and couldn't be done by our students because of lack of time. It wouldn't have been possible to make a proper investigation methodologically."

Mr Orit was about to say something about where he would put scientific methods if he had a choice, but, with some effort, managed to avoid it. He politely closed the conversation, and sat for quite some time silently at his desk. What now? He could not possibly deliver a report scientifically stating that there was no need for services and then go on building them, or showing off the Tapville Web as the solution. He had a system, but needed some needs. A solution without a problem. And it seemed that the partner cities were not there to help.

It was at that time he happened to visit the Tapville conference. When he listened to Boc Worm talking about usability he saw a straw and desperately reached for it. He talked to Mr Worm afterwards and explained his troubles.

"So, as you can see, I'm in real trouble here. What can I do?", he asked.

"Well", said Boc Worm, "obviously you picked the wrong person to do the job for you. Scientific method is not everything. It seems that Dr Wannanou did a good job on the wrong thing. That's the problem with empirical science. You can only investigate what's there, not what is to come. This is fine when reality is stable, but when major changes are about, like this IT thing, you should watch out for people who tell you how things *are*."

"But we *have* to make predictions. How else can we know what services to develop? The Commission says we must make a user requirement study."

"Well, you can investigate requirements in many ways. Web use will increase over time, and new groups of people will become users. Therefore, the information and services that the city needs to provide will keep changing dramatically for quite some time until there is "typical" Web use. Technology must be given time to find its place before you can do investigations like Wannanou's.

"What you *can* do at an early stage is design your Web services according to sound usability principles. And one more thing: you can examine how people use *current* government services. It's not about the Web, really. It's about when, why and how people need the services government provide. You can investigate that without people being Web users. And then you can design your Web services according to what problems you find in the way things are currently designed. Once you have done that, people will use your Web because it gives them added value. Look at "telephone banking". People do it because it saves them the trouble of going to the bank. And Internet bookshops – people use them not only because they are cheap, but also because they have a more complete supply, and because they deliver much faster than an ordinary bookstore if you want a book that they have to order. There is always a way to make your services better. This is what you should use the Web for: exploit its competitive advantages over other media. Don't blame people for being "technology-hostile" or "ignorant in computer use". Once you have a proper service, people will flock to it."

"So what can I do – I need a report on user requirements as of yesterday!", said Mr Orit.

"Maybe I can help. I can write a report on general usability requirements, which will be anchored in scientific findings. And I can add something about the general nature of the field, which will explain why traditional market research methods are of limited use for you in this situation."

"But the Commission wants to know exactly what services to which group of people."

"I believe they will listen to reason. At least, let's hope so."

And so the deal was closed. Mr Boc Worm was charged with the task of quickly putting together a report. Speaking of charges, he certainly knew how to charge for his services.

# On Users

As we saw from the Tapville Conference, user groups are diverse and grouping them according to common interests is often impossible. So, one might ask, what can we know at all about the people that will use government electronic services? Let us take a look at the considerations from Boc Worm's report. He raised questions such as what knowledge do users have and what do they *not* have? In what situations will they use the system? These are questions that you need to have some answers to in order to be able to design your service properly. For each particular service, there might be special conditions, but for public services in general, there are a few important factors that make a big difference. In two sentences:

● Design for occasional users who *have* knowledge about computer use but *do not have* knowledge about your service (the task domain).

● Using a computer and using the Internet are not the worst problems. Understanding local professional terminology is a skill mastered by professionals only.

Let us now provide some evidence for these statements.

## Design for the Occasional User...

Early users of the Internet and of electronic services were typically well-off, well-educated males aged 25–35, who could not be considered representative of future users in all aspects. Experiences from pilot use could therefore only be used with caution. Further, because people who have never tried electronic services do not know, and often cannot imagine, what they could do for them, it is often meaningless to ask. Investigating hypothetical situations is troublesome. There is a well-known phenomenon in any system's design: users are conservative and tend to compare everything with today's situation. They typically want a little more of everything (a slightly faster system, a slightly larger screen etc.), but they do not suggest radical changes. Only after users have tried new ways of doing things, often for quite some time, are the new ideas accepted and able to be discussed.

Although today there is more experience of the actual use of electronic services, there is still little experience with it in the public sector; most services are private businesses and networks within communities of various kinds. Therefore it is worthwhile asking "how do people in general experience public services, regardless of medium, and what requirements do they place on them?", because most people know something about the services from their own experience, and they have opinions about them. After all, the bottom line of going into the electronic medium is making your service better, so looking at their use today is not a bad starting point.

In Stockwerp, a major investigation was made in late 1996 of people's use of, and attitudes to, the city's services. The investigation clearly identified two very different categories of users:

- Regular users, who had personal contacts within the organizations. These included people who had children in the childcare system, who met with the staff daily and heard about what was going on from them.
- Occasional users, who were new to the service and rapidly wanted to find or do something. These included users who needed to obtain one more form for their annual income tax report, which was due that day, or who needed to apply for a building permit, and so on.

People in the first group reported very few navigation problems, because they already had personal contacts within the organizations and knew where to go. They rated the services relatively highly. The second group was the one that complained most about lack of information and who most frequently stated that they had navigation/finding problems. Because these people were not familiar with the services available, they often did not even know where to find them. It was very clear that an overview of the service supply or search facilities that could somehow understand the problem and guide people to the proper service were missing. Once people arrived at an individual service, the information and service was often considered good, but finding it was considered very hard.

The problem of not knowing where to go to manage business with the government was very significant: In the Stockwerp investigation, only 50% of the citizens said they knew "reasonably well" where to go in a given situation, and as few as 15% knew it "perfectly well".

Only 8% agreed with the statement "it is easy to search the information".

This indicates that electronic systems will have to be designed for occasional users, who are not familiar with the service and thus have to start with navigation, and who are typically in a hurry.

This "group" is not a demographic group. A 30-year-old might or might not have contacts with the childcare system. Professors and clerks, male and female, and unemployed and well-off people all have children at nursery schools. Programmers, hackers, secretaries and pensioners alike use the Internet. The "group" is defined only by having a common relation to the contents and organization of government services – they don't know much about them.

Certainly, earlier experiences have made some people more competent in understanding local government organization. But since details often change, even those people easily run into trouble.

The investigation was made with regard to manual services, but the problems are also valid for the electronic medium. If people do not know in what department a certain service is to be found, they will not easily find the service by clicking around electronic menus that reflect the organizational structure.

However, the electronic medium has some inherent features that provide tools for solving navigation problems and making searching in the electronic medium much easier than in, for instance, a phone book. For example, keyword searching makes it possible to find things without knowing the organization. But these advantages do not come automatically. There is a need for some professional designer's knowledge to provide the terms and names of departments and their relations in electronic menus. In the section on terminology below, we shall provide some evidence for that.

## ...Who Needs Completeness in Coverage

From current experiences with 'manual' service in the public sector, we can conclude that users require a central point providing access to the whole spectrum of government services. One such example can be seen in the generalist front offices serving all government departments in Stockwerp.

> The Municipality 4 "Service Cottages" (the local name for "Citizen Offices") provide a one-stop shop service for the inhabitants of a Stockwerp suburb. The service has been operational for several years. The statistics show use figures for 27 categories of services. Although there are great variations in the number of requests for each category (which corresponds to one department, not one service), typically there are questions for them all. That means the personnel at the Service Cottages need to be knowledgeable in all matters. It is the opinion of the Service Cottages manager that the broad range of services offered is an important key to their success.

There are also a large number of questions. The cottages received 35 531 requests during 1995. From a population of 70 000 people, this means one question for every two people living in the municipality; or, put another way, two questions per family (Botkyrka, 1996).

Clearly people ask about everything, and a government "navigator" will have to handle all kinds of requests concerning all city departments, just as is available at the front office. This navigator function should be provided by an electronic tool.

## ...Who Is Not Surfing

But the fact that completeness is necessary at the "front desk", or "page", is only part of the picture. Another interesting question is whether the visits are evenly distributed among the population, or whether very few people are very regular visitors.

People do not surf municipal services for pleasure. According to an investigation in Stockholm (Stockholm, 1995a), 60% of the citizens said that they were not interested in municipal issues until the day they need something. And when they need something, 80% claimed that "there should be one single place to go when I need information".

There is clearly a great need to facilitate navigation. Since user problems can be of any kind, one access point with complete coverage of the existing information is necessary. Since users are typically new to the services, they cannot be expected to be knowledgeable about local terminology and city organization. This means that the phone book menu style of navigation system is very often not appropriate, and keyword searching must be added.

## ...Who Has a "No Nonsense" Attitude

In the aforementioned Stockholm investigation (Stockholm, 1995a), citizens said that they often found themselves having to talk unnecessarily to "the proper" civil servant. A typical statement was:

> Once we were registered in the queue for childcare, the service was good. But before that it was hard to have them even send an application form. We had to find the proper civil servant first.

Users of public services see the need to find "the proper civil servant" as an unwanted detour. In the early uncomplicated phases of an inquiry – such as when they want to find an application form – they do not want to have to talk to a specific person. They simply want the form. This emphasizes the need for a quick way to the answer, but it also points to the true potential, stated directly by users, for self-service in many cases. This is supported by the fact that 76% say "the best way to find information about the different municipal services is to ask for myself" (p. 42).

On the other hand, the civil servants appreciate their own services more than users do; to the statement "The City should actively see to it that citizens get information", 32% of users but 45% of civil servants agreed strongly. The "green pages" (government information pages in the phone book) were used "very often" by 32%, compared with the civil servants' estimate of only 26% of the users would be frequent users. The answers indicate that users are better at helping themselves than civil servants think they are. The important factor, then, is not the medium, but the information; users will use the medium that is best for finding what they are looking for.

### Conclusions About Your Users

Investigations of the use of government services pointed to some general considerations valid for all information and service delivery in the public sector. Users typically only visit municipal sites when in actual need of a certain piece of information or a certain kind of service. In these cases time is always critical, and as users are normally unfamiliar with the service contents and the forms of delivery, they need a comprehensive navigator, mediating all requests and finding the proper solution in the quickest way.

Current designs of city Web systems typically do not meet these requirements. The way in which Web information is usually provided is defined by the available appearance – hardcopy layout – and it is mostly not reshaped and reorganized in order to (1) be readable on the screen and (2) help in solving some user problems. The requirements are not specific to electronic services; they are general requirements for government services. But because the Web competes with other media, and because it has some inherent features that makes it possible to improve on the above points, things should not be left at that.

Unfortunately, this list of requirements tells us only *what* should be done, not *how* to do it. In the next section we shall therefore investigate the usability issues: what you need to know to make it as easy as possible for users to find their way through a Web.

# On Usability

Producers of traditional media, such as newspaper or broadcasting companies, typically invest a lot of money in interviews and interest studies concerning their readers and listeners. User studies in these traditional media are very common. This is not yet the case in the new medium of the Internet. Even though market research is increasing, public sector Web pages are typically just published and then left without much investigation of their use. One problem is of a technical nature. It is easy to count the number of hits on your Web page, but what do they really tell you? You cannot tell anything about whether or not users found what they were looking for from a high number of hits. You cannot decide whether this means that users didn't find their way through the information and tried several paths without finding what they looked for or whether it means that it was because the particular page was found to be interesting and was therefore visited again and again.

Within the EU Telematics Applications Programme project Infosond[3], considerable effort was made to find out about the usability of the Web information systems of the cities involved, and about users' expectations. In the following sections, we will review some of these findings. They are interesting because they focus on the use of city information. Most usability literature focuses on educational and business systems, and more on technical issues – such as interaction facilities and text layout – than on content. One of the findings we will report below is that in fact the content – its structure and terms used – in public sector Web sites (and activities!) is one of the most problematic issues, and one that cannot be solved by standard Web tools, because it is very much home-made and non-standard.


## Easy to Find Things?

There is currently considerable interest from the public about using electronic services. Although the systems in the Infosond tests were generally found easy to use from a technical point of view – they used standard Web features – by the users, there were some use problems worth discussing here. Ease of use was constrained when people tried to solve specific tasks by means of these systems.

> In Stockwerp, 20 users were assigned 98 tasks in using the main city Web site, 'Stockwerp.se'; in 19% of the cases, the users never made it to a solution. Each user had to go through five tasks. Only 9 of the 20 users, fewer than half of them, found all the information they were looking for. The figures are averages. When we distinguish between tasks of different complexity, we can see that one particularly complex task, which required users to visit two pages to find the information needed, had a failure rate of 40%.
>
> A test of a "business start-up" assistance system in MiddleWhere showed similar results. Out of 48 given tasks (performed by 12 users), only 20 could be solved. On 22 occasions the users gave up without any solution, and on four occasions they thought they had a solution, but it was an incorrect one. Only 14 times were the users satisfied with the results they found.
>
> Solutions and interruptions were widely spread over the whole group, so that there is no evidence that the factors that are often stated to be crucial, such as 'level of education', 'age', 'sex', 'profession' and 'familiarity with computers' have an influence. What did seem to have an influence was familiarity with the Internet and familiarity with the task domain.

These figures seem discouraging, but the Web is in "good" company; we can report that the figures were no better for people's ability to find things in non-electronic information systems; only 8% agreed that "it is easy to find information" in the pre-

---

3   Project number UR 1017.

Internet systems (Stockholm, 1995a). But this doesn't make things easier – rather, the prospect of having an information mess transformed into Web format is not a glorious one. The poor figures give us a reason to look into the nature of the problems that users encounter.

The successes and failures in the above examples were distributed across groups of people. Factors typically associated with differences in proficiency in computer use – level of education, age, sex – could not explain what caused success or failure. We then considered familiarity with the Internet and familiarity with the task domain.

The test group in the Stockwerp usability tests was divided into "tourists" and "inhabitants" (10 of each). The tourists were people who did not live in Stockwerp, while inhabitants were people who lived in Stockwerp or had done so recently and were familiar with the geography and institutions of the city. It turned out the Stockwerpers learned to use the system much quicker. Table 8.1 shows that apart from task domain expertise (the criterion by which the groups were assembled), the amount of Internet use was the only distinguishing factor that might account for the differences in results (unless one assumes that less education is better).

**Table 8.1** Characteristics of "Stockwerpers" and "tourists" in a Stockwerp usability study (Grönlund and Jakobsson, 1997)

|                                | Stockwerpers      | Tourists          |
| ------------------------------ | ----------------- | ----------------- |
| Familiarity with computers     | $M = 2.7$         | $M = 2.4$         |
| Familiarity with task domain   | $M = 4.6$         | $M = 1.2$         |
| Years of university education  | $M = 2.7$         | $M = 5$           |
| Internet use (hours/week)      | $M = 5.6$         | $M = 3.0$         |
| Age                            | $M = 30.9$        | $M = 34.5$        |
| Sex                            | 5 male, 5 female  | 3 male, 7 female  |

What do these results mean? They can mean two things, Firstly, the Stockwerpers had above all a certain amount of task domain knowledge, which gave them – among other things – a certain familiarity with the terminology used. Second, the results can also mean that much of the system's terminology and categorization is home-made, specific to the Web system and not sufficiently general for the public sector or even the local office, and therefore confusing for everyone. As further findings from MiddleWhere show, familiarity with the task domain is certainly an important factor for usability, but users' interpretations of terms vary, and the city's usual terminology and categorization are only one factor influencing this interpretation. Another factor is the general semantic ambiguity of terms, which not even linguistic professionals can avoid. Task domain familiarity may help in this semantic interpretation but is not the only factor for making sense of the information. The inevitable lesson for system design from this finding is that users need alternatives to search by self-produced keywords.

There is another conclusion from the test results. Beside familiarity with the task domain it seems natural that *Internet experience* should have some importance for how quickly you learn to navigate in an unfamiliar information space. People who know the medium well from the start can concentrate on understanding the organization of the information space. This was the only factor distinguishing people who gave up before finishing a task from those who did not. This is a certain kind of media competence, which is not just general familiarity with computers. It is not about pointing and clicking, it is about a feeling for the topology of the Web.

It may seem somewhat surprising that education seemed to have no positive influence, as this is normally of importance for most learning tasks. It may seem odd that the group that showed the smallest (although not significant) learning effect was the most educated. Education does not make up for task domain knowledge.

## On Time and Cues

There is no way that an information system can give answers to complicated user question within seconds. Searching for an answer will take time. One interesting question is "how long can people be expected to go on trying to find a solution to their problem?" The answer to this question would tell us something about the potential of a Web system – how much time will users spend on searching by themselves before they give up and make a telephone call? The answers we have found give some hope to Web designers.

From the MiddleWhere studies it seemed that the reason for people giving up was not related to time, but to hope. The testers were more likely to give up after a certain period of time if they could not figure out any way promising path that would probably lead to a solution. If, however, they had the feeling that they were on the right path, they continued. Table 8.2 shows that the time before people gave up (an average of 8 minutes 17 seconds) was less than the time they spent on working to find solutions (an average of 11 minutes 1 second).

**Table 8.2** The time that users in the MiddleWhere usability study needed to complete their tasks

|         | Norm time | Average time | Average time for solution | Average time until break | Shortest time (solved) | Longest time (solved) | Shortest time (break) | Longest time (break) |
|---------|-----------|--------------|---------------------------|--------------------------|------------------------|-----------------------|-----------------------|----------------------|
| Task 1  | 300       | 729          | 819                       | 458                      | 380                    | 1532                  | 308                   | 642                  |
| Task 2  | 420       | 522          | 709                       | 485                      | 631                    | 786                   | 125                   | 686                  |
| Task 3  | 480       | 566          | 506                       | 578                      | 320                    | 691                   | 239                   | 948                  |
| Task 4  | 240       | 551          | 609                       | 468                      | 408                    | 1039                  | 136                   | 883                  |
| Average | 360       | 592          | 661                       | 497                      | 435                    | 1010                  | 202                   | 790                  |

The MiddleWhere example shows that the time the user needs to find a solution cannot be considered in isolation. Longer search times are accepted if the system is organized in a way that gives users the feeling of being on the right path, that is, if he feels they know where they are and where they are heading within the information space. If this was not the case, users became confused and gave up when they judged that some piece of information or the system's reactions were no longer fitting into their strategy.

On the other hand, time spent waiting is conceived as being longer than time spent actively doing something. Waiting time is therefore crucial for any computer system. When it comes to the Web, there is typically a lot of waiting time, much more than when using traditional office systems like word processors and spreadsheets. An investigation of the Stockwerp Web site provides support to the hypothesis that people will give up very quickly if a system appears slow, and also gives some clues to just where the problems lie.

From watching the users in action it is apparent that people are easily stressed when navigating the WWW. Different people have different thresholds, but the average time for how long some system action can take before it becomes annoying is quite low. It is also important for users to realize that something else will actually happen. In the test system, there were three problem areas that were directly related to the uncertainty of whether or not some kind of work was in progress:

1. The first one was the search engine. A search generally took between 15 and 20 seconds, but the users sometimes aborted the operation in less than one second, believing that something had gone wrong or that the search did not result in any hits. The status bar of the browser is often overlooked.

2. The second one was page load time, which was especially apparent when pages contained large tables. Some pages generated a small amount of text at the top of the page and then began loading the table without even the status bar showing that it was working. Expert users in particular sometimes selected a link from the introductory text before the table was shown. The fastest user in the test group had the most trouble with this. He repeatedly went to a specific page and very quickly chose a link that was supposed to take him to the right section of the table that was going to appear on the page. But by making this selection the loading of the table was silently interrupted, leaving only the faulty message "Page loaded" at the status bar.

3. The third problem occurred when Java applets were used. They took a little longer to appear on the page and were also slower to responding to the users' actions. This repeatedly led to reactions such as "Where did that thing go?" and "Why doesn't anything happen?".

## Complex Questions, Or the Organizational Scheme Meets the User

Although many user problems are simple – "I need this form" – many are not. And you cannot make complex question simple without losing some important aspects of them. The only thing that a system designer can do is to provide a context that facilitates the user finding answers even to the more complicated questions.

The following example task is from the Stockwerp usability tests, where we wanted to provide some complexity – but still very little compared with many of the real-life tasks that users have:

You are considering starting a business in the Stockwerp region, so you want to find a real estate agency. You also want to find out the prices of the local electricity provider, Stockwerp Energy, Inc.

To solve this task, the users had to find two pages: that of the real estate agency and that of Stockwerp Energy Inc. As the two pages were in differently classified categories of the information space, and as there were no cross-references, 40% of the users did not manage to find both. There was a cognitive link (to some businesses the price of power is crucial), but no physical link.

We arranged another task where the difficulty lay in the fact that users had to realize that the term "SiliVille borough administration" was the key to their problem. Thirty per cent of the users did not.

Usability problems like the ones described above arise often, because Web sites are often constructed more from the point of view of the information and service providers and not from the point of view of users trying to solve tasks. They reflect the departmentalization of information in the city's organization, which often does not match the cross-boundary nature of many user problems. However, there are often relatively easy ways to reflect this in system design. Just think of all those brochures with good advice in certain situations that government agencies produce: "If you fall sick...", or "If you're about to travel abroad...". In fact, in many countries special books are produced that deal with problems of this nature. However, solutions from the printed medium are not necessarily adequate in every detail for the Web. The electronic medium could give added value by providing tools to help users translate their problem into the terminology of the government agencies.

The experienced Web user might argue that this problem is already tackled by the search engines that are already available on the Web. But this argument isn't true here, because search engines are useful only when users have a reasonable idea of what they are looking for and can provide the correct name for the object searched for to the search engine. What is needed is a tool to help users manage the process of searching for the proper terminology known by the system, starting with the term in the particular user's mind without the need for any initial knowledge of how the task domain is represented by the information system at hand.

Many problems involve finding objects that are unknown – by existence or by name – to the user. In such cases, a simple synonym list is not enough. The user will have to find out not only the location of some object, but also what objects actually belong to a particular perceived problem.

## Finding the Way

As mentioned above, one aim of our usability tests was to find out where people go wrong and fail to find the shortest or best way from the problem to the solution within the information space of our Web site. The best way route was defined as the way a domain expert user would take; the expert path.

We found that there were several reasons for users' deviations from the expert path, as Fig. 8.1 summarizes. The vertical axis gives the number of occasions. The total number of deviations is 141, which gives an average of 7 per user (20 users), and more than one per task (there were 5 tasks per user, a total of 98).

The test clearly pointed out users' selection of the wrong main category as the main reason for deviations from the expert path. The problem is clearly one of terminology; users could not see the connection between the name of a category and the problem they were about to solve.

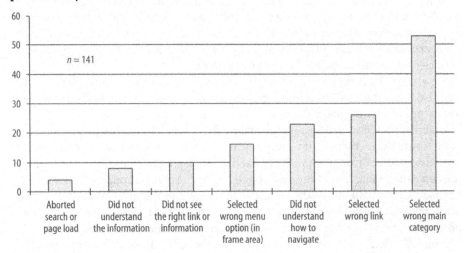

**Fig. 8.1** Reasons for deviations from the expert path through a Web information system (Grönlund and Jakobsson, 1997).

**Table 8.3** "Confusion points" count in the MiddleWhere usability test (Grönlund and Jakobsson, 1997)

|        | Number of users without confusion points. | Number of users with confusion points | Average number of confusion points |
|--------|-------------------------------------------|---------------------------------------|------------------------------------|
| Task 1 | 4                                         | 8                                     | 1                                  |
| Task 2 | 2                                         | 10                                    | 0.9                                |
| Task 3 | 2                                         | 10                                    | 1.2                                |
| Task 4 | 5                                         | 7                                     | 0.6                                |

A usability test in MiddleWhere yielded similar results, as most users got confused by the terminology used (Table 8.3).

The users could not interpret the terms used to convey which information can be found when following the link or keyword. The confusion caused deviations from the optimal path through the information space (the expert path), as shown in Table 8.4.

**Table 8.4** Reasons for deviations from the expert path; 1 = Did not understand how to navigate further; 2 = Did not understand the information on the page; 3 = Took a voluntary detour; 4 = Other. From MiddleWhere usability tests (Grönlund and Jakobsson, 1997)

|        | Reason 1 | Reason 2 | Reason 3 | Reason 4 |
|--------|----------|----------|----------|----------|
| Task 1 | 0        | 10       | 2        | 1        |
| Task 2 | 0        | 12       | 2        | 4        |
| Task 3 | 0        | 14       | 1        | 1        |
| Task 4 | 0        | 10       | 1        | 2        |

Most deviations from the optimal path through the information space were caused by misinterpretation of the category terms and subsequently following the wrong path, not leading to the information needed.

Even if users actually do get to the right place, there may be problems with the use of terms. It sometimes happens that users see the correct answer but do not realize that it is what they need, as the following case illustrates.

> In a Stockwerp usability test, when one user was asked why she did not try the Web guide she answered that she did not know what Web meant in this context, so she did not bother with that category. This came as a surprise to the investigators, who used the term daily, but clearly many of the expected users will have problems with technical terms that are regularly used in connection with the World Wide Web medium, but which have nothing to do with the task domain.
>
> The records from the Stockwerp usability tests showed one more thing: many deviations from the expert path were also due to users' selecting an inappropriate link. This was because the semantics of naming the link were too weak, so that users had to guess what link to choose. This means that users didn't get a proper idea of what they would find when following the link. For instance, a link to "Forms" may not give a good hint if the user dos not realize what kinds of forms there are. Embedded in a clear context of, say, "application for housing allowance", the name will appear clear.

The cases show that technical terms relating to the technology should be avoided as far as possible so as to make the system useful for Web novices. It also shows that categorization of the information in the system must be given more attention. For instance, cross-references could be used to link cognitively related pages contained in different categories. Last, but not least, consistent terminology is an important matter for usability of the Web site. Consistency in terminology means three things.

First, within a system, terms must be used consistently and as sparsely as possible. Second, the links between different parts of the system that for some reason belong together conceptually must be semantically strong. Third, the terminology used should correspond as closely as possible to the users' language. When this cannot be achieved by using that language directly – and this is often the case – translation facilities, such as synonym lists, must be available.

# A Crèche Is Also a Day-care Centre – Some Lessons on Language Use

To convey the meaning of terms to the user is not a trivial thing in the design of Web sites, as we discussed above. This statement is worth further explanation, so we will dwell on professional language use and general semantic obscurity.

## Professional Language Use

There is a lot of professional language around. In the case of government services, and within every city department, there is not only a general vocabulary but also a professional language, sometimes locally defined, sometimes more of a jargon. Special technical terms are created to cover the activities of that department. The occasional service user typically does not know that language. Therefore your system must provide help in translation from the professional language to the lay language of your users.

It is not enough to translate to colloquial language. There may still be synonyms. The following example is from a telephone book.

Suppose you are a visitor in a Swedish city. It is winter, and you want to go swimming, so you want to find an indoor public bath. You look in the telephone book. In Swedish, there are two words for indoor public bath; swimming hall (*simhall*) and bath-house (*badhus*). Both words are commonly used. How to find them in the phone book?

Organizations use different classifications for their services. Let us look at the classification of swimming halls in just one region (see Table 8.5).

There are 15 municipalities, which together use eight different categories – more if we consider the alternative use of "board", "department" and "administration (Table 8.5).

As the table shows, the user facing the problem of finding a public bath, will need to know the following when using the menu model for navigation:

● two different names for public bath (three if we consider the "Vännäs Bath")
● eight different possible classifications (organizational ownership) of a bath

This gives at least 16 possible combinations (24 if we consider the special case). Since there is no way to be sure which city uses which term and which classification, in the worst case the user will have to make 16 (24) searches to find all the swimming halls if using the "menu" method.

Using the traditional keyword method would lead to an average of 1.5 hits when searching at headline level (1 when searching for "bath-house", 2 for "Swimming hall"), and an average of 7 at object level (3 when searching for "bath-house" and 11 when searching for "swimming halls"). A keyword search using parts of strings would also find the Vännäs Bath, thus increasing the average to 7.5.

A thesaurus knowing the two terms "swimming hall" and "bath-house" would yield 2 hits at headline level and 14 at object level if using keywords strictly. In combination with the standard facility for searching on parts of strings, a full score of 15 hits would result.

**Table 8.5** Different terminology and organizational ownership of "Indoor public baths" in the Swedish telephone book of 1995.

| City | Category | Subcategory | Term |
| --- | --- | --- | --- |
| Umeå | Baths–Swimming Halls | | Swimming hall |
| Robertsfors | Culture & Leisure | | |
| Skellefteå | Leisure Office | | |
| Nordmaling | Childcare & Education Administration | | Swimming hall |
| Malå | Service Department | | Swimming hall |
| Lycksele | Swimming Halls | | Swimming hall |
| Dorotea | Culture & Leisure Department | Citzens' Hall | Swimming hall |
| Bjurholm | Leisure | | Swimming hall |
| Sorsele | Leisure | | Bath-house |
| Vilhelmina | Tourism | | Swimming hall |
| Vindeln | Leisure concourses | | Swimming hall |
| Norsjö | Culture & Leisure | | Swimming hall |
| Storuman | Leisure & Culture Department | Swimming hall | Swimming hall |
| Vännäs | Childcare & Education Board | Leisure & Tourism | Vännäs Bath |
| Åsele | Culture/Leisure | Åsele Camping | Swimming hall |

Since a short route from problem to solution is critical, and because problems like the above are common, a thesaurus is necessary. As was shown above, such a tool can be very efficient using only very simple means. In the above case, knowledge of only one synonym increased the hit rate by 100% and reduced the number of searches to 1 at object level. It should be noted that the more words there are for the same thing, the more efficient the thesaurus will be. If there were four words for swimming hall, the keyword method would need four searches while the thesaurus would still need only one (the menu method would need 32).

There are, of course, also limitations to a thesaurus. One is that synonyms are often not equal, only more or less close to each other. This means that having more synonyms means that the quality of hits is reduced and the number increased, two things that can easily cause problems in large data sets.

Many of the universal search engines have taken measures to deal with such problems. But a clear limitation of general search engines for the purpose of finding things locally is that the language used is not general. In the example above, equating terms that are synonyms means adding to the list of irrelevant hits. There is a need for local thesauri (some standardization would help, of course, but this is much more difficult to achieve).

### Semantic Obscurity

The example above showed the need for synonym knowledge when dealing with the public sector in general and with local branches in particular. In our evaluations of pilot implementations of Web systems we could see that the problem of terminology goes beyond the simple use of synonyms.

As our usability tests further showed, one of the main reasons for problems with using the search engine was *semantic obscurity*. This refers to the fact that users did not know how to construct appropriate search terms. In one particular system there was a help function, but only one of the 20 test users found it. This was because it was labelled *Questions* instead of *Help*, which is the standard software term for this kind of problem.

Finding relevant search terms is not just a user problem or a question of interface design. It is also a question of information management. One case from RelaxenBurg demonstrates this, and also gives an idea for a solution.

> A lot of energy was expended on the design of a system to help commuters plan local journeys. With this system, it should be easy to select your location and the desired destination and arrival time. By using that information together with the various timetables for public transport, the system should be able to offer a good suggestion for the journey by train, tram or subway.
>
> When the interface was tested with pilot users a problem arose: users often named the stations by using abbreviations of the official names in the timetables. For instance, when a user asked for "Opern" (the Opera), there was no hit because the official name of the station was "Opernplatz" (Opera Square). A number of such examples made the potentially very useful system not so useful at all. Users did not like having to spend time guessing the official name of a bus stop or subway station. In fact, the response from users was so negative that the system faced closure.
>
> As a possible solution the system was integrated with a database containing the names of all public transport stations with a street database, so now every stop is connected to both the names of the stops and the nearby streets. Preliminary tests after the change have shown that the usability of the system has increased and the managers responsible are optimistic.

The solution is creative in that most people would know at least the name of a street or square in the neighbourhood of the place they want to go. But if they want to go to a particular museum, for instance, and know the name of the street, but the street is not particularly close to a tram station, they still have a problem. They will have to look at the map.

Another problem occurs when people use nicknames for things. For instance, in Stockwerp there is a square named "Stureplan". In this square, there is a special artefact that is both a piece of art and a rain shelter. The thing is shaped like a mushroom, and it is big enough to provide shelter from the rain for tens of people. Because of its shape, the thing is called The Mushroom, and the name is almost official – everybody uses it. Should such a name be included in a navigation system? There are arguments for it (many tourists would know the mushroom, but not the name of the square), but there are certainly also arguments against it: one is the confusion with real mushrooms and the resulting irrelevant hits that might occur.

The problem is one of balancing formal requirements (exclusivity of names), administrative simplicity (only *one* name per thing, please!), and usability (use *my* name for things).

## Mental Models or Mental Muddles?

In interacting with the environment and with artefacts of technology, such as tools or computer systems, people – actually, rather quickly – create an inner picture (called a mental model) of the things they are interacting with. These models provide predictive and explanatory power for a user's understanding of the interaction. The user's mental model reflects his or her beliefs about the system – that is, how the system works, individual explanations of why the system works this way, and how the task domain is represented by the system.

A mental model is very important in the case of interacting with Web sites. As only a small piece of the Web can be seen at the same time, you need some understanding of where the rest is – on top? Below? To the right? Behind? (The last thing, by the way, is one of the most common problems; a new window is opened on top of the previous one. The user does not realize what has happened and gets confused as the Back button no longer seems to work).

When using of Web pages, this means that the first time a user enters a Web site, she creates an internal cognitive model of the structure of the site: how the pages are organized, what information can be found and how the pieces of information are related to each other. This happens relatively quickly (or she leaves because she can't figure it out). Then the user's exploration of the site is governed by that model, at the same time as the user reconstructs her model based on what she finds during the exploration.

A mental model should be simple. Simple models that users easily recognize are *hierarchies*, especially if they are balanced (all branches about the same depth) and not too deep, and *rings* (much like a book: first there is Chapter 1, then a link to Chapter 2, ... and at the end a link to the top), if the order of things appears reasonably clear to users. However, because designers recognize the need for cross-references, many sites instead turn into complicated nets (Fig. 8.2).

There are other models. One is the thread, a coherent line of reasoning embedded in a story. This is a very strong model, but only provided:

- The user understands the thread and can follow the reasoning.
- There are not too many threads using the same material (since this will lead to complicated intersections).
- The thread doesn't split up into too many branches.

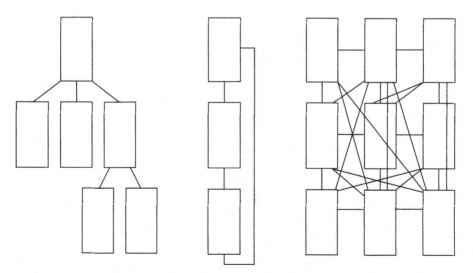

**Fig. 8.2** Web site organization models: hierarchy, ring and mess.

In public sector organizations these criteria often do not apply, or too much work is involved in producing coherent threads for all possible situations. It also does not work well at a high level in vast systems. The method is very good for limited areas, such as "When travelling abroad, don't forget...".

### Navigational Structures

The structure of a Web site should allow clear orientation when navigating through the information space. It should allow users to answer their main questions: where am I, what can I do here, where do I come from, where can I go to and what will I find there? They want clear indications. So it is a good idea to organize the information space around easily recognizable structures, such as hierarchies and rings.

However, these structures have to be constructed carefully, because otherwise 'magic leaps' may appear, which can disturb the user's mental model. This may occur if you follow a conceptual thread through a number of pages and suddenly find that there is no way back to the previous page or to "Start"; you are in a dead end street (Fig. 8.3). You can, for instance, only go to "Start". Unfortunately, you cannot always trust the browser to solve this problem.

It is easy to create a dead end street. One, possibly the most common, is when a new window is opened on top of another. This is often done with external links, which means that the whole environment will be different. This means that the Back button will not work. Worse, all links leading "Home" will lead to another home than on the previous page, as the new page is part of another organization.

Another occasion when "Back" does not work is when frames are involved. In fact, frames are a special problem in Web design, and many would say they are not a good choice at all. This is debatable, but let us take a look at some of their disadvantages.

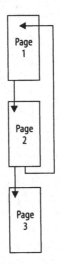

**Fig. 8.3** Dead end street (no way back to previous page).

## Frames May Indeed Suck...

The use of frames is popular, as they enable the display of multiple independently scrollable views on a single screen, each with its own distinct URL. Obviously their benefit is to keep certain information visible, like a table of contents, while other views of the site are scrolled or replaced.

However, from a usability point of view they might cause fundamental problems (Nielsen, 1996). From the point of view of the user's mental model frames break with the unified model of the Web, which is based on having the page as an atomic unit of information. Instead, they introduce a new way of looking at data, where the users' view of the screen is now determined by a sequence of navigation actions rather than a single navigation action. In this case navigation does not work, since the unit of navigation is different from the unit of view. If users create a bookmark in their browser they may not get the same view back when they follow the bookmark at a later date, since the bookmark doesn't include a representation of the state of frames on the page.

There are still other problems with the handling of frames. Older browsers such as Netscape 2.0 had poor usability problems with frames: the Back button in the browser, which is the second most used navigation feature in Web browsers, simply did not work with framed sites. However, the Back feature is an essential safety net that gives users the confidence to navigate freely in the knowledge that they can always get back to safe ground. And some browsers cannot print framed pages appropriately. Furthermore, there is a design problem with frames, as they often don't work as intended due to buggy code, or due to incompatibility problems between different browser manufacturers. And last but not least, search engines have trouble with frames since they don't know what components of a framed page (which may contain several pages) to include as navigation units in their index.

## ...But Not Always

Having said all these negative things about frames, we must recall one thing about mental models. They reside in the mind of the user. This means that a good model is one that users understand. The more frame-based systems are used, the more user get used to them. After some time (which may already have elapsed), the model with table of contents to the left (the most common place) and the actual contents to the right becomes *the* way to design Web sites, and adhering to widely used standards is the best tool to help users create their mental models. Choosing frames or not is a design decision to make. In making that decision, the pros and cons of frame- and non-frame-based designs must be considered. But more important than the choice is to be consistent in design, whichever method is chosen.

## Consistent Page Layout

A further important aspect of helping a user to build up a mental model of the Web site is consistency of page layout. When users move around different parts of a Web site, it is helpful if pages are designed in a similar manner, otherwise users will have to spend too much time orientating themselves within the new page design. Important features of page layout are the placement and design of menus, logos, headlines etc. A poor example is given in Fig. 8.4. The menus on three consecutive

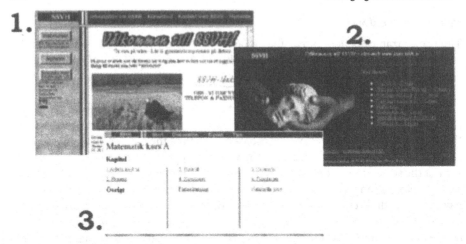

**Fig. 8.4** Inconsistent design of three consecutive pages of a Web system; menu to the left, to the right and bottom, different use of frames (columns), different colouring (Grönlund and Jakobsson, 1998).

pages are placed to the left, to the right and at the bottom. To provide more consistency of page layout to the user, the menu should be placed in one location throughout the Web site. From a cognitive point of view, the left side or the top are recommended.

There are many small little layout details that have already become standard practice on the Web, and which one should therefore follow unless there are good reasons not to. For example, in Fig. 8.5 the buttons are links, whereas the text is not. Most often, the text is also clickable.

Furthermore, the layout of links is crucial for two other reasons. Browsers use standard colours to mark clicked links. Although these settings can be changed by the designer, this should only be done if the standard colours do not go well with the palette of that particular page, because the standards are well known to users and are part of their mental model of what a Web site looks like and how it is likely to work.

Another example is the option to remove borders around pictures that are also links. Doing so increases the risk that users will not realize what are links and what are not. Usability tests with Web sites have often found that people tend to choose verbal links before image links in cases where both exist. And even if there are easy

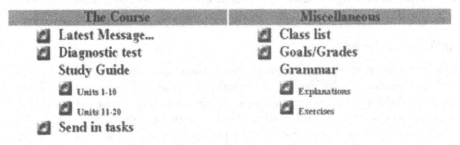

**Fig. 8.5** Non-standard menu design (text is not clickable).

ways to find out, it at least requires extra work; if you don't put a border around link pictures, users have to move the mouse around to find out.

In general, producing good graphical page layout requires as much care and skill as laying out newspapers, magazines, or books. But again, there are different design philosophies on how to appeal certain users and how to support certain tasks. However, it would be too much of a diversion to discuss these issues here.

### Avoid Cognitive Overload

Cognitive overload means that users get so many sensual impressions that they can't cope; there is too much on the screen. This is often seen, and it is very easy to end up in this situation. Because information providers want to provide as much information as possible, and the designers during the design work become familiar with the information, more often than not there is nobody to represent the occasional user – the person who is not familiar with the information or its organization, and therefore needs to learn about it while using the system.

Figure 8.6 is from an earlier version of the Stockholm main entrance, "Stockholm.se". It shows a heavily designed system, where much effort has gone into making it look nice. The result was information overload, as our tests showed; people didn't know where to click, and they didn't see all the information.

What the user sees while using a system is very different from what is actually there. The difference is even greater when the user is new to the particular system or

**Fig. 8.6** An overdesigned menu page, where the same links can be found as text at the bottom, as a partial menu on the right, and as clickable images.

to the information domain. Compared with an automated teller machine, for example, an artefact for service delivery that most people are familiar with, a comprehensive city system like this one is loaded with links, pictures, buttons, text and all kinds of information (even compared with most Web systems, this one is very "designed"). It is simply not possible for the brain to process all of this when the system is first encountered and everything is new to the user. If the user is also new to Web browsing this will further add to this problem of cognitive overload.

This can be studied by watching how the user moves the cursor over the screen before performing an action. Users move the pointer to the area of the screen to which their perception is currently directed. We could see that only parts of what was actually on the screen received attention. Users typically scan the screen from top left to bottom right, but especially salient features, such as the size of text and the colour of images, also have an influence on this process. Things that take longer to load run a greater risk of being overlooked, because users are typically impatient. In our tests, on many occasions when we went back to pages and asked the user why he or she had not performed a certain action, the answer was that he or she had simply not noticed that option.

If there is information overload on the page, the effect is often that things that are important to understand the system go unnoticed. An example from our tests of the Stockwerp site: on the main page, users could chose by categories or by keywords. When arriving at this page, the first action taken was a category search in 42% (17 out of 40) of cases. This was surprising to us, since most users said that what they wanted was the keyword search, but it can be understood by looking at the layout of the page. The area for making keyword searches is near the bottom of the page and in quiet colours. Users simply did not see it, even though they were actually looking for it.

### Provide a Consistent Navigation System

It is very common for Web systems to provide a plethora of navigation tools. From a theoretical point of view this seems appropriate, as different users have different task domain knowledge, different strategies for searching, and different Web experiences for which different search and navigation tools might fit.

*Menus* are easy to use for the novice user because they provide textual cues to what is in the system; the user does not have to think of proper keywords to search for. But menus can be tedious to use, and in fact even misleading, because classification problems will lead to incomplete search paths, redundant information or a complicated system of cross-linking.

*Hypertext links* are clickable hot spots on the screen, embedded in text (an underlined word) or visually indicated by a map or an icon. Our usability tests showed that text links were preferred when images and icons are hard to interpret. Image maps were mostly used when one of the bold print/large font headline items were chosen; that is, the smaller items on the image map were not noticed or understood. Hypertext links are only easy to follow if users can understand their semantics and have an idea about the overall structure. Unfortunately, in a complex system there may be many relevant paths, and implementing them all means that too many links make each individual path hard to discern. One particular problem with hypertext links is that finding the way "back" is hard, because links are unidirectional and because in systems using frames the browser's back button does not work as users typically think it does.

*Keyword searching* is the preferred choice of users when they know enough of the domain into which they are inquiring to find proper keywords. In other cases, users may come up with inappropriate or wrong terms.

*Agents* are pieces of software that can be instructed by either pre-programmed or user-configured profiles. They can also be trained to learn from and adapt to user behaviour, and it may also be possible to educate them as they may learn from previous experiences of user behaviour. Typical examples include shopping agents, which help people to find the cheapest shoes, for instance. However, it is not a trivial task to program such a software tool other than for use in tasks where clear evaluation criteria can be applied.

*"Operator"* (human) contact has the advantage to the user of leaving the translation and searching burden to someone else, and is therefore attractive to users in contact with a vast and often unfamiliar government. Web systems are often hailed because they provide easy "operator" contact by means of email, but the response time is necessarily long. Although the advantage of this is not always clear, there are some indications that people using the Internet are likely to provide feedback and comments on your service. If this is so, this interactivity must be managed. For example, there must be an "Infomaster" (never direct your users to the Webmaster) who answers email and adapts information to user needs, as opposed to the Webmaster's role of managing the technical system.

Although multiple search and navigation facilities may be advisable, it makes a difference how they are implemented. Consider the following example, again from Stockwerp.se.

> In this system, several different strategies for navigation were mixed. Depending on the category chosen, users would have to deal with image maps, frames, traditional links, embedded menus or a combined category/keyword search engine. One problem we found was that the navigation methods clashed.
>
> There was a choice between searching through hierarchically ordered categories and typing keywords, but the same area on the screen was used for both methods, so answers were overwritten; the result from using one method was lost when users tried the other method. ("Back" did not work, since the page was constructed with JavaScripts). The availability of two different methods led many users to think that the two methods could be combined, so that a keyword search only looked within the category that was currently chosen. This was not the case, so users actually searched the same information by the same keyword several times.

## Style Guides for Web Design

You are not the first person to build a Web site. There is plenty of advice available from your predecessors and from people who have tested Web sites with real users.

There are some basic design rules which you can learn about. However, since many problems do not have a single solution, and because not all good principles can be followed at the same time, much is up to the designer. The work can be aided by adhering to Web practice, but it also requires knowledge about the specific users of your site.

The interested reader is referred to some of the many "style guides" that are available on the WWW. The good ones discuss the issues we have mentioned here in more detail, and they also deal with things like use of colours, special effects and page layout.

For our education we use one from Yale University (Yale Web Style Guide: `http://info.med.yale.edu/caim/manual/`). There is also an "official" style guide from the W3 consortium[4] (Style Guide for Online Hypertext (W3C, the World Wide Web Consortium): `http://www.w3.org/Provider/Style/Overview.html`. This material is a little old (1998). It does not take into account the latest technical developments, but is still valid for general principles.

There are many good solutions. The reason we use the Yale style guide is that it gives good examples and explanation, but also because it advocates a strict Web design. We feel this is the way to go for public places such as cities and government agencies, both for reasons of appearance and to minimize maintenance work. The style guides below give somewhat different recommendations, partly because they are directed towards different contexts (business, education etc.) and partly because Web design is still under development and some advice is necessarily a matter of opinion rather than empirical findings. Also, technical developments give designers new tools, making new things possible and things that used to be time-consuming or difficult simple.

To get a good picture of Web design, we suggest consulting at least a couple of the style guides listed below. They all make good points, but no single one necessarily has *the* solution to all your problems.

- Style Sheets Reference Guide: `http://webreview.com/pub/guides/style/style.html`
- The WDVL Style Guide: `http://www.wdvl.com/Style/Style/Guides/WDVL.html`
- HTML Style Guide & Test Suite: `http://www.charm.net/~lejeune/styles.html`
- Composing Good HTML (Carnegie Mellon University): `http://www.ology.org/tilt/cgh/`
- Guide to Good Practices for WWW Authors (University of Manchester): `http://www.man.ac.uk/MVC/SIMA/Isaacs/content.html`
- NCSA TRG Review of Web Style Guides (The National Centre for Supercomputing Applications): `http://www.ncsa.uiuc.edu/General/Internet/WWW/HTMLPrimerAll.html#SG`
- Art and the Zen of Web sites (TLC Systems Corp.): `http://www.tlc-systems.com/webtips.html`

# Conclusions

The following list summarizes in brief the discussions in this chapter:

---

4   World Wide Web Consortium: the official body for technical standards on the Web.

- *Time* is critical. This includes the *time to find a solution*, which means that the time taken to log in, start the computer, etc. is important. It also includes *time spent waiting* for pages to load and for search engines to come up with an answer.
- Design the system to also cater for the more *complicated tasks* that users might have.
- *Terminology* must be consistent, and the *semantic links* in the system must be clear.
- Provide a consistent *mental model*.
- Use a simple *system structure*.
- Avoid *cognitive overload*.
- Provide a consistent *navigation system*.
- Make sure there are proper *system cues*.

Considering these points should make a system easy to use. Clearly some problems may be solved in many ways, but even so, consistent design on these points does improve usability. Above all:

- Use a good Web Style Guide *first* – invent your own solutions only when you know for sure there is no clear answer in the guides.

# 9. *Challenge 9: Where is the Payoff? Some Benefits Come Later*

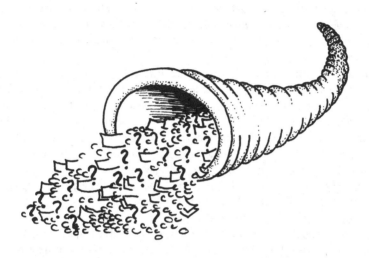

Electronic services can be delivered over many different channels, but the highest hopes and expectations have undoubtedly been placed on the Internet. Business on the Internet is a much hyped phenomenon that often falls short of expectations for private and public service providers alike. "Return on investment" is mostly stated in strategic rather than monetary terms.

There are many potential reasons for failure: that there are not enough users of a given service with access to the Internet; that the users cannot find the service; that you cannot have a service that costs money on the Internet, because the whole concept teaches users to expect all Internet content to be free; and so forth.

But even if services do get used, most potential Internet service providers find the economic assessment of their services a daunting task. The number of uncertain factors involved defies sound financial analysis. It is helpful to look at the problem first from a variety of different angles.

Many different kinds of payoff may be expected: better served citizens, strategic advantages, better market/citizen communication, improved corporate profile, lower costs due to more self-service, and so on. In this chapter we discuss the ways in which different cities look upon the "payback". We also discuss the economic realities of the Internet, as well as the inability of many cities to achieve rationalization gains.

## *Soap*: Return on Investment?

After four years of experience Mr Cal(vin) Culator, the director of City Finances, wrote a report on resources spent on telematic projects, as he was in charge of budgeting the city's finances. It showed that over 10% of the city's spending went on project investment with no hard evidence of any payoff. The report was based on project budget reports from the last four years. The conclusion drawn by Mr Culator, which he had put at the top of his report in bold type, was to stop all telematic project activity at once. This is what he was about to discuss with the mayor and the head of the IT department.

"We cannot go on this way, irresponsibly spending our way into the next budget period", Mr Culator started. "All we have done over the past four years is spend money. We've bought hardware, which is already outdated and needs further investment to cope with today's functional needs. We have spent lavishly on external advisors and consultants. But what has come out of it? Where is the payoff? I will not take responsibility for spending 10% of the city budget without any view of return on investment."

The colour drained from the cheeks of the head of the IT department (Dr I. A. M. Mehrwisser). As hard as he had tried, he had no good reply to this attack. He knew, of course, how much IT had cost the city. Only last week he had asked for more money in order to upgrade all the hardware and software within the city, to provide training programmes for all personnel, and to rewrite all the user instructions and manuals. This would presumably cost another 2% of the city budget the next year. As head of the IT department, he knew all about computers and software and what interesting and advanced possibilities the newer technologies were able to provide. Tapville shouldn't lag behind in development! Demands from all city departments to be given the opportunity to work with the latest versions of hardware and software landed on his desk every week. Most of the time he held them back, but now he couldn't resist these proposals any longer.

The mayor had no ready answer to hand, but he knew (as his background was as a financial manager) that there was more to the issue than the things that Mr Culator had come up with. Of course, he understood Dr Mehrwisser's position. He closed the meeting for external consultations, and promised to come back to the subject in the very near future.

During the next few days, the mayor had several meetings with financial consultants, some with a city background, others with a commercial background. They all advised the mayor to come up with a model that included both expenses and returns on investment, but when the mayor asked what kinds of return on investment they foresaw his advisors stayed quiet as mice.

Then, over the weekend, the mayor had a meeting on the golf course. He met some former football players, with whom he always liked to play. Walking from hole to hole, he saw some similarity with his problems during work. Golf, he said to himself costs a lot. I have bought all this brand new clothing, to keep up with the club colours of the golf association. Also, I have invested in all this material to play golf: many balls (for I lose them a lot), all these different clubs, my own golf kart to drive from hole to hole, not forgetting all the money I have spent on golf lessons, instructional videos and books. And what have I gained? No prize money at all. Playing in competitions costs even more than the subscription fees: travel expenses, hotel bills, and all the money you spend while travelling. The plain truth is I have no return on investment whatsoever.

Is this a reason for me to stop immediately? No, of course not – I like playing golf. It frees my mind from the routines and stress of work. It takes away the stress of all these meetings with Mr Culator and his kind. I get to talk to people I wouldn't talk to if I wasn't here. I get fresh air while I play. And, last but not least, my wife likes having the house to herself all weekend while I play golf, so she can play cards with her friends. I wouldn't want to change my golfing habit at all! In fact, if I had the opportunity I would play more golf. He then decided he would invite Mr Culator to a golf clinic next weekend.

Two weeks later in the city hall an important meeting was held. The meeting was chaired by the mayor. On his right-hand side sat Dr Mehrwisser and on the other side Mr Culator. All the financial managers, IT managers and heads of department were there.

First, the mayor introduced the subject of the meeting. He said that the financial budget of the city had some structural holes in it. He raised his eyebrow to Mr Culator, who smiled almost invisibly. In the meantime, the financial managers' faces flushed, and opposite them the IT managers went pale. The mayor continued: "18 holes I've seen up till now, and Cal says it will become 24 if no real action is taken within the next six months".

Some of the financial managers stood up and almost shouted, pointing at the IT managers, saying that they spent too much and would spend even more in the near future. The IT managers unanimously and replied that the departments demanded this expenditure, and that they couldn't stand in the way of prosperity, that they wouldn't be responsible for stopping this kind of spending and throwing Tapville back to the Middle Ages. The mayor and Mr Calculator looked victorious, but kept quiet during the discussion that followed. Only after coffee did the mayor stand up to make the speech that had he carefully prepared during his golf trip with Mr Culator during the weekend.

"Spending", he started, "meaning investment, is part of the game. We cannot run a city here without investment. So I'm in favour of spending. But of course we need to spend carefully. We have to divide the city budget over all different fields of policy, meeting the needs of our citizens as best we can. Citizens in Tapville are proud of their town. Prosperity in Tapville has grown, starting with Bill Westmark's W3 initiative a couple of years ago. Ever since, I've received invitations every month from throughout the country, yes, even abroad. This has brought new investors to the city, and we earn more from tourists since we launched the Tapville Tourist Web. Young, well-educated people stay in Tapville, while in other cities around us the population is greying. Last month's survey showed us that our citizens feel happy in Tapville. They are eager to use the many possibilities for participating in our city's democracy. They have strong demands for further development of Tapville."

The mayor paused a while to drink some water and look around the table. Everybody was silent, waiting for the mayor to go on.

"Today is an important day", the mayor continued, "Here are your budget plans." He showed a large pile of paper to the financial managers. "They are calculated thoroughly, very precisely, as we have done for the past decades, but from now on this will change!" He tore the pile into pieces and threw them away. Everybody in the room was astonished by the mayor's action.

"From this day on we start from scratch. I will no longer tolerate calculations based solely on IT. IT is not a goal in itself – it is a means to get somewhere, to bring Tapville into the next decade, the Information Age. All spending on IT will from now on be formulated in terms of measurable goals as a means of promoting our city policy areas."

"Secondly" – he looked at Dr Mehrwisser – "I have decided to change the structure of our IT department. It will be divided over all our other departments. Dr Mehrwisser will no longer be head of the IT department; instead he will become my right-hand secretary involved in coordination of affairs related to information policies. Mr Culator and I have decided to start with this now. This afternoon you will meet again, chaired by Dr Mehrwisser, to discuss how to implement the new city structure we just decided on."

The mayor rose and walked out of the room. All stood up and applauded, impressed by the way the mayor had prevented them from running into a financial crisis, but not really able to grasp the consequences of what had been decided that morning.

Outside the city hall sunshine appeared through the clouds. The new spring had begun.

# Return on Investment?

Everybody wants IT to pay off and bring a return on investment, and everybody finds it hard to prove that it does so. But perhaps the very terms "payoff" and "return on investment" are part of the problem. Cities often do not think of IT as an investment, but instead as an ongoing expense.

Setting up an electronic service is an investment. In that sense, it is unreasonable to expect the service to be profitable at the beginning. Investing in a new service pattern implies spending money now on development in the hope of recovering it some years later, the number of years depending on the nature of the investment.

There is also another analogy between setting up electronic services and business activity. This is the analogy with growth. Electronic service provision has an expansive character: electronic services are always new services, and do not initially completely replace any existing service. They therefore represent growth in the scope of activities for a city department.

In a study of Scottish micro-firms, Reid (1995) found a clear negative correlation between growth and profitability. That is, firms that grow are less profitable than those that do not. Setting up electronic services is no different in this respect. The work involved will raise costs without initially generating any corresponding income. But the end result is that more people will be able to use services that are qualitatively better. The city department has grown.

Many have tried to estimate the return on investment in IT; for instance Brynjolfsson and Hitt (1998), who found that business reorganization towards groupwork was a most important factor. But many questions go unanswered. How do you estimate the increased staff skill and satisfaction that come from using company-sponsored PCs at home? And why calculate the "payback" of a word processing system at all when it is a standard piece of equipment in any office? You can't function without it.

In fact, any attempt to assess specific IT investment is problematic, because IT is so intertwined in business procedures. Paul Strassman has researched the links between IT spending and profitability over many years, and found none: "Profitability and spending on computers are unrelated because they are influenced by the way a company is organized and managed and not by the choices of technology. Looking for a 'technology fix' to problems that are fundamentally managerial must end up in failure" (Strassman, 1997).

Hope and Hope (1997) take a radical view of the problem of management in the "third wave". They say that this age requires completely new ways of calculating which focus on the intellectual assets of a company rather then the buildings and machines:

> The third wave economy is dominated by service organizations.... In fact the line between manufacturing and services is now so blurred as to be almost meaningless. Even in manufacturing companies the percentage of production activities and service activities such as design, marketing, and customer support now provide most of the value....] In most service companies the intellect of people is now the primary resource (46 percent are the so-called knowledge workers such as managers and professional staff). But how will this resource be accumulated and deployed in the battle for competitive advantage? Few managers understand the question let alone the answer. (Hope and Hope, 1997, p. 3)

They name ten critical issues as the most important ones in the Information Age:

1. Strategy: pursue renewal, not retrenchment.
2. Customer value: match competencies to customers.
3. Knowledge management: leverage knowledge for competitive advantage.
4. Business organization: organize around networks and processes.
5. Market focus: find and keep strategic, profitable and loyal customers.
6. Management accounting: manage the business, not the numbers. When budgets are cut, organizations typically remain while services deteriorate.
7. Management and control: strike a new balance between control and empowerment.
8. Shareholder value: measure the new source of wealth creation – intellectual assets.
9. Productivity: encourage and reward value-creating work.
10. Transformation: adopt the third wave model.

The Hopes point out that the Information Age requires new ways of managing. They are concerned with businesses, not with cities and the public sector, so of course we should not take their advice without adapting it to the public sector environment. However, many of the points are quite easily transferred to a public sector setting, and they make sense there.

For example, under point 1, when budgets are cut most government organizations *do* shrink rather than trying to reform their operations and find new roles, despite the negative effects this leads to.

Exchange the word "citizen" for "customer" in point 2, and analyze to what extent operations match their requirements.

Under point 4, while cities may not compete with each other directly, different agencies or departments may overlap to some extent. Also, government services sometimes compete with private business, or they hinder healthy competition.

Again, exchange the ideas "citizen" for "customer" in point 5 and "making best use of taxpayers' money" for "profitability", and analyze who to serve, why and how.

And so on.

There is not space here to detail how to transfer the whole of the Hopes' reasoning to a public sector environment (although some issues will pop up later). It is important for cities to note that the transfer to an economy built on services and intellectual capital needs new ways of calculating costs and revenues. In this chapter, we will briefly discuss ways of measuring values and costs in an IT context. But first, let us say something about specific problems that occur along the road. Our point so far is that we consider return on investment alone a poor choice of evaluation criterion for investments in IT in general and in electronic services in particular. We are not alone in holding this view: "IT spending is rarely a discrete investment that can be subjected to financial analysis. It is merely a catalyst for *managing information*, and the real test is thus the *productivity of information*, not some outdated notion of payback or discounted cash flow" (Hope and Hope, 1997, p. 187).

## Investment?

A particular problem in financing new electronic services is the fact that most regionally based organizations do not see changing their service patterns as an investment. This is particularly true for organizations that work in traditional services, such as public services, retail, or publishing.

> In Tapville, the local newspaper had decided to start producing a Web edition. A trial version had been produced by a consultancy. The latter had done it free of charge, in order to get an order in the development process. Suitable editors from among the staff had been identified and had discussed the project, and a suitable system developer had been engaged. In the first meeting of the development project, the CEO of the newspaper surveyed the situation. When it comes to financing the project, he briefly noted: "It seems we need to buy a big Web server for €30 000. Does anybody see any other need for allocating money to this project?"

Managers in classical services are used to seeing investments directed to machinery, hardware or construction. Public services managers, in contrast, never spend on acquisitions. For them, a development project is a frighteningly ill-defined product to buy. For this reason, their investment threshold is lower by one or two orders of magnitude.

> When the financing of the pilot for the teleshopping service for daily grocery in FarawayTown was discussed with the CEO of the retail chain, he gasped at the estimated cost. He invoked the financial analogy that he could hire a shop assistant for an entire year with that amount of money, and that it would be so much easier to calculate the return on investment in that case. The retailer had a lot of money – it had just purchased a local hotel for a hundred times the sum discussed. The problem was the image of vagueness that a development project conveys.

At least two immediate, but unfortunately only partial, solutions can be used to ease the pain of uncertainty on managers. One is to obtain external project funding. This was the one used for FarawayTown teleshopping, and it brought with it the success of launching the first teleshopping service for daily grocery in the country. The other one is to break down the development process into a series of progressively larger subprojects. After each subproject, a decision is made about whether the process has been successful and is worth continuing.

The second approach – splitting the project into subprojects – brings with it an implicit requirement on the nature of the subprojects. In order to give managers a concrete result by which to judge further investment, the intermediate deliverables of the projects must be concrete. One way to achieve this is to invoke prototyping. It is a good idea to start building a prototype version of the new electronic service very early on. Such a prototype will convey a concrete look and feel to the service, and will therefore make it easier for managers to get a hold on the project.

Obviously, no reliable figures on return on investment can be produced during the development project, but as the above FarawayTown case demonstrates, the problem is not really the size of the investment. Rather, it is the associated image of vagueness. A prototype will alleviate this in a very efficient manner.

But the remedy is only partial. A prototype will make a project or a new service more tangible, but it does not answer the question "where is the payback?" in any clear terms. As the Hopes spent a whole book stating, investment in humans – intellectual assets – is far more important (and expensive, and hard to assess the value of) than investment in technology. While it would be too much of a diversion for us to discuss all the problems of the "third wave economy" in this book, we will spend some time looking at some of the efforts that have been made towards that end.

# The Economics of Electronic Services

As we stated eralier, electronic services can be delivered through many different channels, but the greatest hopes and expectations have undoubtedly been placed on the Internet. Business on the Internet is a much-hyped phenomenon that often falls short of expectations for private and public service providers alike. There are many reasons for failure: not enough users of a given service with access to the Internet; users cannot not find the service; you cannot have a service that costs money on the Internet, because the whole concept teaches users to expect all Internet content to be free; and so forth.

Most potential Internet service providers find the economic assessment of their services a daunting task. The number of uncertain factors involved defies sound financial analysis. It is helpful to look at the problem first from a variety of different angles.

The terminology in this chapter is borrowed from the world of business. One of the central objectives of this chapter is making cities, towns and regions ask themselves: *What business are we in?* It is an increasingly relevant question, since many of the services that cities offer their citizens can be obtained by other means as well – particularly in the world of the Internet. And yet a significant part of the answer to this question says: *The business of cities is not business as usual.*

## The Internet as a Global Village

Many early Internet visionaries viewed the Internet as a global, friendly village. Most users followed Netiquette, a set of moral rules closely resembling those of the global academic community. Such values have many elements of democracy: all members of the Internet community are equal, and no one is allowed to bully or pester other members with unsolicited mail. Everything that members produce is freely shared with others. Fairness of judgement and shunning of profit-seeking activities are also some of the moral prerogatives of Netiquette.

The global village worked well for a while, as long as Internauts were few and of a homogeneous cultural background. A comparison with the ancient Greek Polis community of free men is quite appropriate for the early Internet community. But the community did have its dark side, too, from the very early days. It was well on its way to becoming an intense meritocracy, where the significance of a person's contributions to the Common Good of the Community was a measure of the weight of his or her words.

Intensely meritocratic communities are often intensely opinionated and aggressive. And they only function as long as the membership is small and consists only of members actively interested in the functioning of the community. We have had such communities for thousands of years: small religious communities. Such communities deliberately ignore – even reject – economic factors. In its community stage, the Internet was not a business. Nor was there any significant form of business present on it.

The Internet grew past its Community stage in the early 1990s. Most of the newcomers entered after the World Wide Web had fundamentally changed the nature of the Internet. The new settlers saw it as a vast, interesting encyclopaedia. They were not interested in the further development of the Internet, but simply wanted to find out things of personal interest. Many of them also wanted to establish a personal presence on the Web – a homepage.

Once millions of people were using the Web, organizations started to feel the same need to establishing a presence on it. The majority of organizations in the West – public, private and community-based alike – have indeed done so. But the Web as it stands today, in the late 1990s, is not a functioning community. It is like a Platonic mirror image of a true world; just like the shadows of real people in broad daylight, seen cast through a cave entrance onto its back wall. Organizations and individuals tell the world about themselves on their homepages, but the vast majority of them do not carry out significant activities on the Internet, apart from finding out what others say about themselves.

The passivity of the Internet, as it stands today, is a fundamental economic factor that will change relatively slowly. As long as there are no transactions of any economic kind carried out in significant quantities on the Web, there are no economic benefits to be gained from a mere presence on the Internet. As soon as this starts to change in significant measure, the Internet will become a force of economic interest. The change has already started in the USA, and will start in Europe in the early 2000s.

Today, however, economic transactions are not carried out in significant quantities on the Web. E-commerce has still to deliver and become a major economic factor. Therefore there are no economic benefits to be gained from a mere presence on the Internet.

However, the Internet is in a state of constant transition. The current static state will not prevail for even another five years.

## The Economics of Information Management

Sports shoes with a famous European or American brand name are not made in Europe or America. Often they are not even designed there, but they are distributed and sold worldwide. The only thing that gives such global products a local nature is their cultural image – a carefully nurtured asset of the company owning the corresponding trademark.

The globalization of industrial production has raised information to one of the most significant capital assets of any product or service. It is information about production technology, about the availability and cost of appropriately trained labour, about the demographics and preferences of potential consumers, about the suitability of given marketing and distribution channels to a given product or service, and about the current status of any given individual product on its way through the production and distribution chain to a certain customer.

When production and design have become tradable commodities, time is money. The providers that know or guess best which products, sold to which customers and produced when and where, are going to be most in demand, will agglomerate the most attractive business, while slower ones will be left with low-profit market segments. In such a hectic world, information is more important than size or current market share.

The economics of information management are strongly affected by the World Wide Web, even in the passive situation it finds itself in today. After all, most organizations have established their presence on the Web only quite recently, so that what they say on their home pages is still largely true and valid information. Moreover, many organizations have already hit the first embarrassment over outdated information on their Web pages, and have subsequently assigned it to be an explicit responsibility of the marketing department to regularly review the accuracy of the information available on its Web pages.

Search engines make the collection of information fast and cheap. Judicious use of the Web to extract relevant, up-to-date information for business planning is already an attractive option today. But it is not enough just to collect the information. There has to be a sequence of processing steps, in which such information is translated into action. The process of information gathering must also be mechanized into a continuous activity.

Trivial though suggestions such as the ones above may appear, they imply a fundamental change in current business practices. Currently, business value chains are built on a principle of locality. Each link in a value chain is the only site in possession of information relevant to the next link. Since value chains are mostly based on such asymmetric relations between buyers and suppliers – buy cheap and sell at a premium – accurate information is carefully safeguarded.

The Internet allows the information to propagate instantly to those who understand how to use it. Potentially, producers can have customers reach them directly, bypassing all intermediary stages in the value chain. But such an advantage does not come free. It undermines existing business relationships. It may jeopardize significant past investment in distribution channels, such as shops and service points. And initiating such cannibalistic activities will certainly antagonize those falling victim to such change. This may, in turn, result in serious damage to current business before the new business model has managed to establish itself as a stable source of revenue.

Changing business models to take advantage of information management over the Internet is dangerous to current market leaders. The organizations most likely to introduce new electronic service models, based on an information advantage, are start-ups or runners-up. The current market losers are too preoccupied with survival to take notice, and the current market leaders are suspicious – and correctly so – of new, unknown business models.

A city or a region does not have to worry about competition taking over its business. But change will destabilize existing work practices, all the same. Alternative electronic service delivery mechanisms will not replace existing ones for many years to come, but they will nevertheless propagate an atmosphere of uncertainty.

## Measuring the Value of Information Technology

In the early days of computing, when a typical application was a payroll system, costs and benefits were relatively straightforward to assess. The computer replaced so many people who were previously doing the job of compiling the payroll. The costs were the acquisition of hardware, production of software and maintenance of the system. The benefits were the reduction in salaries, less need for office space etc.

Because information technology today is more complex and intrudes into more areas of organizations' activities, evaluation IT is no longer so straightforward. IT support no longer means just automation. Many are the stories of how new computer systems have given companies strategic advantages: the most famous include American Airlines, American Hospital Supply and Bank of America (McKenney *et al.*, 1995). Many stories also tell how companies have redesigned their operations and so achieved radical improvements in efficiency (Hammer and Champy, 1993). Because such things happen, competitors feel compelled to invest in similar systems so as not to lag too far behind.

Other examples show how technology has made new kinds of businesses, or radically new approaches to old businesses, appear (Hedberg *et al.*, 1997). Currently, for example, many banks have abandoned their branch offices altogether and communicate with their customers solely by information technology: by telephone and, increasingly, the Internet.

How much, exactly, are investments like that worth? How much, exactly, is it worth to have a higher level of technology as a competitor? Obviously these things are worth something, but strategic advantages are not easily measured in euros.

Also, costs are not always easy to assess. The price of computer hardware and software can be identified, but the investment in information technology also includes training and cultural change among professionals. Since technology changes rapidly, training tends to be an ongoing activity, not just going on in special courses but also as an integral part of daily work.

Further, the same technology tends to be used in many projects, and benefits often come from several projects, thus making the relationship between investments and benefits less direct.

But the perhaps greatest complication is that many benefits from the use of information technology will come from as-yet unknown applications. Investments in technical infrastructure and staff competence are prerequisites for such future benefits, but just how much it will be worth investing in staff competence and IT infrastructure cannot be assessed with certainty now. Consequently, the question "how much should we invest in information technology and skills now?" does not have a simple answer.

This reasoning applies very much to electronic services. The services currently produced are among the first ones. Use of the electronic medium is not yet widespread. Services are tentative; not only is use new, but the technology changes rapidly, which means that the technical facilities for producing services will be very different in the near future. Security applications, electronic payment systems and broadband connections to homes are among the most obvious examples. This means that future use cannot easily be assessed, if at all. Consequently, many organizational changes that will occur when electronic services become commonplace can only be sketched at this point; they obviously cannot be measured before they have occurred.

The example method we will briefly present here defines "value" as improved business performance, and "cost" as total organizational cost, including explicit consideration of potential risks. This means that values are explored in terms of what the investment in information technology brings to the business.

At one level, the method includes tools for quantifying the benefits and costs of information technology projects. At another level, which typically proves the most important, the method is a process of decision making.

This means that beyond a result in terms of assessment of actual services, the method brings another advantage – arguably the most important – to its users: the result of using the model is a decision-making process that forces a shift in management emphasis away from the information technology to the *effect* that technology has on the business itself.

This shift is not easy to make, and we certainly do not claim that use of such a method alone will do the trick. It requires a view of the organization's operations that is often new, especially for organizations in the public sector, who are often used to monopoly situations and are not used to relating their operations to client needs or to measuring them in economic terms.

One purpose, then, of using the method, which allows us to bring up the method here as a good example, is to bring about a more conscious process in developing electronic services in the cities.

## Values and Risks – Information Economics

We briefly present here the method of "Information Economics" (Parker *et al.*, 1988). We discuss this method because it contains many of the methods of reasoning that we would like to see in the discussions on economic assessment of electronic services. It is not the only appropriate method, and it has its shortcomings, but it is useful for conveying some good ideas.

The method takes two principal perspectives: a *business perspective* and an *information technology perspective*. To support decision making within both these perspectives, data about not only users – usability, usefulness, user attitudes and use – but also pertaining to the provider organizations – business plans, relations between in-house services and services produced by others, IS infrastructure etc. – must be collected. These data come from a number of sources, such as:

- usability studies
- use measurements from log files of different kinds
- interviews and surveys with end users
- interviews with intermediaries
- interviews with local managers and professionals
- written plans on business development and IS infrastructure development

The evaluation model uses 10 evaluation criteria. The first is *return on investment*, and the other nine are divided into two groups: *business domain values and risks* and *technology domain values and risks*. While the first group of factors deals with business goals and strategies, the second deals with the technological possibilities of implementing the strategies.

*Business domain* values and risks are:

1. *Strategic match* ("How does the system support or align with stated business goals?").
2. *Competitive advantage* ("What makes this service unique?").
3. *Management information* ("To what degree does the project provide management information about the core activities of the enterprise or line of business?").
4. *Competitive response* ("To what degree does failure to produce the system cause competitive damage to the enterprise?").
5. *Project or organizational risk* ("To what degree is the organization capable of carrying out the changes required by the project?").

*Technology domain* values and risks are:

1. *Strategic IS infrastructure* ("To what degree is the project aligned with the overall information systems strategies in the organization?").
2. *Definitional uncertainty* ("To what degree are the requirements and specifications known? How great is the complexity of the area and the probability of non-routine changes in the information system?").
3. *Technical uncertainty* ("How great is the readiness of the technology domain to undertake the project regarding skills required, hardware dependencies, software dependencies and application software?").
4. *IS infrastructure risk* ("How much non-project investment is necessary to accommodate the project?").

These values and risks are assessed according to a scoring scheme for each factor. The factors are also weighted by appropriate management. The result can be illustrated in a total score sheet (Table 9.1).

## Model Overview

**Table 9.1** Overview of the model (Parker *et al.*, 1988, p. 45)

| Evaluator | Business domain | | | | | | Technology domain | | | |
|---|---|---|---|---|---|---|---|---|---|---|
| | ROI | SM | CA | MI | CR | OR | SA | DU | TU | IR |
| Factor | + | + | + | + | + | – | + | – | – | – |
| Business domain | | | | | | | – – – | – – – | – – – | – – – |
| Technology domain | – – – | – – – | – – – | – – – | – – – | – – – | | | | |

*Legend*
ROI    Return on investment
SM    Strategic match
CA    Competitive advantage
MI    Management information
CR    Competitive response
OR    Project or organizational risk
SA    Strategic IS architecture
DU    Definitional uncertainty
TU    Technical uncertainty
IR    IS infrastructure
Factor    Some factors are positive (+), because a higher score means a better project. A higher ROI is better. Others are negative (–), because a higher score means a greater risk. A greater technical uncertainty is worse.

## Return on Investment

Return on investment (ROI) is the traditional measurement for investments. There are, however, some problems with this simple measurement:

1.  Traditional cost–benefit and ROI approaches are microeconomic and encourage low-risk investments with small returns.
2.  They are the result of a manufacturing economy where labour is treated as an expense. For the case of spending money on knowledge about use of information technology, this should instead be considered an investment, because future benefits from information technology use cannot be made if there is no infrastructure in terms of human knowledge in place.
3.  The analysis is static and short-term.

For the case of electronic services, it is obvious that ROI would not be enough to describe their value:

1.  People are not used to electronic services, and even if services are good it will take time to change behaviour. A comparison with the automated teller machine may be made; even after more than 10 years of widespread use, not everyone feels comfortable using them. Many older people have never changed their behaviour: they still go into the banks' offices. This is not only because they have never learned to use the machines, but often because they just don't like them.
2.  Access to the Internet is still limited, although in some regions in Western countries users are estimated to be over 50% of the population (Holst *et al.*, 1999, p. 79). With the Internet on digital TV and other broadband connections,

alongside the existing services, the percentage of the population potentially reached will increase further. But technical connection is only the first step. Developing useful services takes time, and it also takes time to change people's habits. Measuring simple ROI *this year* will therefore not give the correct picture. One must look at least a few years ahead.

Measurable costs and revenues may occur in several places. The *costs* of providing electronic services include *investments*, such as personnel training, software and hardware purchase, and programming costs for in-house development or consultants, and *ongoing expenses*, such as the costs of updating information in the electronic system, managing the technical system, staff support, and perhaps more work due to increased demands.

Examples of *revenues* are fees for the use of electronic services, reductions of staff due to the reduced workload following from increased self service, and reduced costs for printed materials. It should be noted, though, as is indicated by the model, that electronic services must not necessarily lead to reduced costs. It may well be that they will lead to *increased* costs, for instance if they make people more aware of what services are available, which may lead to more use, which may lead to an increased workload on staff if services are not of a completely self-service nature or if they need much maintenance and updating due to frequent changes.

In order to calculate costs and revenues for a particular service, obviously not only the costs of the new system, but also the costs of the old system must be known. This means that one must distinguish between investments made specifically for this service and those that also support other services.

Also, which is often most problematic in a city, in order to be able to make a comparison with existing costs, the costs of manual services must be appreciated. This is usually not done at a detailed level in the public sector.

This means that for the purpose of making the ROI calculation, the biggest problem is to distinguish the costs of the service in question from other costs.

## Business Domain Values and Risks

Return on investment means calculating with figures. Although the numbers are estimates, they give some idea of the costs and revenues. The model lists five other values, ones that cannot easily be estimated in money, but rather according to value scales. They are:

1. *Strategic match* ("How does the system support or align with stated business goals?").

2. *Competitive advantage* ("What makes this service unique?").

3. *Management information* ("To what degree does the project provide management information about the core activities of the enterprise or line of business?").

4. *Competitive response* ("To what degree does failure to produce the system cause competitive damage to the enterprise?").

5. *Project or organizational risk* ("To what degree is the organization capable of carrying out the changes required by the project?").

| | |
|---|---|
| 0. | The project has no direct or indirect relationship to the achievement of stated corporate or departmental strategic goals. |
| 1. | The project has no direct or indirect relationship to such goals, but will achieve improved operational efficiencies. |
| 2. | The project has no direct or indirect relationship to such goals, but the project is a prerequisite system (precursor) to another system that achieves a portion of a corporate strategic goal. |
| 3. | The project has no direct or indirect relationship to such goals, but the project is a prerequisite system (precursor) to another system that achieves a corporate strategic goal. |
| 4. | The project directly achieves a portion of a stated corporate strategic goal. |
| 5. | The project directly achieves a stated corporate strategic goal. |

**Fig. 9.1** Strategic match scoresheet.

For each question, the method provides a "scoresheet" which users are required to fill in. The scoresheets require users to give simple answers to complicated questions, as the example scoresheet of Fig. 9.1 shows.

Our experiences show, however, that they usually have no problem in doing so. However, different people have different views, and also different ways of handling figures. Some are careful and tend to use middle of the road figures, while others like to use the extremes. Therefore it is necessary to collect the opinions of many people and to compare their views. The result is obviously not a correct estimate of future events, but a good picture of how people in the organization think about it them and what their expectations and empirical support is.

While it would lead us too far off course to go through the model comprehensively, we shall make a few comments on some of the factors.

### Competitive Advantage

The question here is: *what makes this service unique?* Clearly, electronic services compete with other similar services that are delivered in other media, and they have to be better in some sense to justify the development costs.

In some cases, there may be competition with other providers, but in general the situation would be that government operates the services in a monopoly situation. The question is then not so much how to beat other providers, but whether or not the electronic medium can beat other media.

There are generally two ways in which this can be done, by advantage or innovation:

- *Advantage* means that a service that already exists is delivered in a better way – for example cheaper, faster, accessed more easily, accessible in more places or with longer opening hours. Advantage, then, means saving resources – the organization's or the customer's – by making service delivery more efficient.

- *Innovation* means that the service has changed in quality. It may be completely new, or some value may have been added to it. For example, an electronic list of events may be more searchable than a printed brochure because it adds a keyword searching facility. An electronic form may be provided with a feedback facility, whereas feeding back an opinion on a printed form requires the user to find some other medium in which this can be done. Innovation, then, means service development, enhancing the service level or quality.

This value must of course be estimated by the customers: those who are going to use the new services.

## Management Information

The question here is *the degree to which the project provides management information about the core activities of the enterprise or line of business* (strategic planning; marketing; product planning capacity; facility forecasting; management control – budget, sales, target, service performance, capacity, facility utilization; operation control – customer services, information, claims, capacity, facility scheduling).

An example regarding electronic services might be that the electronic system provides usage statistics. The extent to which these figures are useful for management is a point for discussion here.

Further, Web systems may be complemented by feedback functions that provide such management information. As an example, US politicians report that having email access means that their constituents can – and do – more easily send them complaints, opinions, advice etc. Although they are not always able to answer, this feedback function gives them much more contact and a broader view of the opinions of their constituency, and thus is an important information source for decision making (Bowen, 1996).

From the above it is clear that management information need not only be aggregated data like use statistics, it may also be more statistically uncertain but operationally accurate data, such as the politicians' email. The value of such data must, of course, be estimated by those concerned.

## Competitive Response

The question here is *the degree to which failure to produce the system will cause competitive damage to the enterprise.* Is this system really necessary at this point in time, or can we just wait a while until it gets cheaper and easier to produce it?

In the case of public services, this may mean not only that competitors may show up (which would not always be bad, because government might then avoid some expense), but perhaps rather the risk – in the wake of budget cuts – of providing services so poor that citizens complain and lose *confidence* in the authorities. Another risk is that of image: "government services are slow and out of date compared with the private sector. You can go to your bank and move money from one account to another on the Internet, but you cannot even pick up a simple tax form from the government".

In many cases, government organizations now have to compete with private organizations, or competition is planned. In such cases, the image problem may become urgent. But even when no competition is at hand or planned, government will find a need to argue that taxpayers' money is well spent, and that people get good services for their euros collected by taxation.

### Project or Organizational Risk

The question here is *the degree to which the organization is capable of carrying out the changes required by the project.* The question concerns the user or business domain, *not* the technical organization.

Risks dealt with in the model are:

- Is there a well-formulated business domain plan?
- Is business domain management in place?
- Are contingency plans in place?
- Are processes and procedures in place?
- Is training for users planned?
- Does a management champion exist?
- Is the product well defined?
- Are there well-understood market needs?

From our experience, thorough discussions on these points certainly help to clarify the state of affairs in the organization. The problem is they are rarely held. One reason for this is that many projects come to a city quite unexpectedly from external funding. Because funding is external it is seen as bonus income, and spending on an internal review can only lessen the positive impact on the budget. And the external directives for the projects typically do not require such evaluations, partly because they would have to be done after the project period, which is by definition impossible.

A serious consequence of this is that projects that could have been used as leverage on the road towards a new service infrastructure are instead starved, so as to give the maximum positive net cash flow to the city and not risking it in reorganization, the outcome of which is uncertain. After all, the external project funding is not for *those* costs. And the gains are far away, if they ever come – after all, no one has tried to estimate them. This is a kind of vicious circle caused by external funding, cases of which can be found everywhere within the EU project apparatus.

## Managing the Model

The recommendations for using the model are:

1. Let strategic management assign weights to the evaluation criteria.
2. Let local management assess each service according to the evaluation criteria.
3. Let strategic management assess each service according to the evaluation criteria.
4. Assemble strategic management for a session in which they, under the guidance of an expert in the method, discuss their ratings and come to a shared understanding and mutually agreed assessment.

We have tried using the model without such a comprehensive follow-up. The result is then useful for assessment, but not so good for learning. You get individuals to think carefully about their services, but you do not get the organizational effects that are the most important output of the model.

Table 9.2 provides an example of how weights could be assigned in the final scorecard of the model.

**Table 9.2** Project evaluation criteria weighted (example)

|  | Evaluation range | Weight | Maximum score |
|---|---|---|---|
| *Business domain values and risks* |  |  |  |
| 1. Return on investment | 0–5 | 2 | 10 |
| 2. Strategic match | 0–5 | 5 | 25 |
| 3. Competitive advantage | 0–5 | 2 | 10 |
| 4. Management information | 0–5 | 1 | 5 |
| 5. Competitive response | 0–5 | 2 | 10 |
| 6. Project or organizational risk | 0–5 | –1 | –5 |
| | | | |
| *Technology domain values and risks* |  |  |  |
| 1. Strategic IS architecture | 0–5 | 3 | 15 |
| 2. Definitional uncertainty | 0–5 | –2 | –10 |
| 3. Technical uncertainty | 0–5 | –2 | –10 |
| 4. IS infrastructure risk | 0–5 | –2 | –10 |
| Total values: | | 15 | 75 |
| Total risks and uncertainty: | | –7 | –35 |

## Evaluating the Model

We have presented the above model not as the ultimate solution, but as a good example of a model that brings some advantages to IT development projects:

- It is easy to use.
- The model itself is not very time-consuming (whereas of course making reasonable calculation may be).
- It conveys a clear overview of the situation.
- It leads to a result that is visible and can be followed up as the project runs.
- It stimulates more informed discussions about the project.
- It provides a common language in which to discuss the project.

It shares with any investment calculation (and with crystal-ball inspection), the problem of making correct estimates. But it does bring the estimates into the open, and that is as far as you can get.

# Conclusions

In this chapter, we have discussed some of the characteristics of the Information Age and the problems of information economics in this age, the most important assets of which are intellectual capital rather than machines and buildings. We have presented a candidate model for assessing the values and risks of IT projects in general, which includes simple measures such as return on investment but also many intangible, or hard-to-pinpoint, factors that together give a broad perspective on the venture.

In brief, our advice, as discussed above, is the following:

*Set your goals*
- Decide what would be the ideal composition of an ideal service for your users.
- Decide what would be the ideal role for your organization in delivering it.

*Focus your plans*
- Apply a cost–benefit model that reaches beyond ROI, that encompasses the use domain, and that is measurable. We have suggested one, to convey a picture of what it should be like, but there are certainly others. Find one, or compile one from the advice you get and the situation you are working in.
- Use it! Many projects are started with goals like "better democracy", "getting closer to the citizen" and so on. Be more concrete!
- While there are many models, the important thing is to go beyond ROI, and make sure that the model, whichever you use, is well understood and established within your organization. The model you choose must:
  - be easy to use
  - give understandable results
  - encompass the use domain, not just the technological issues

Our example model, which is only an example, albeit a useful one, included the following factors, which give a broad perspective of the investment:

- *Strategic match* – how does the system support or align with stated business goals?
- *Competitive advantage* – what makes this service unique?
- *Management information* – to what degree does the project provide management information about the core activities of the enterprise or line of business?
- *Competitive response* – to what degree does failure to produce the system cause competitive damage to the enterprise?
- *Project or organizational risk* – to what degree is the organization capable of carrying out the changes required by the project?
- *Strategic IS infrastructure* – to what degree is the project aligned with the overall information systems strategies in the organization?
- *Definitional uncertainty* – to what degree are the requirements and specifications known? How great is the complexity of the area and the probability of non-routine changes in the information system?
- *Technical uncertainty* – how great is the readiness of the technology domain to undertake the project regarding skills required, hardware dependencies, software dependencies and application software?
- *IS infrastructure risk* – how much non-project investment is necessary to accommodate the project?

*Be realistic*
- Do not think you are going to make, or save, money rapidly. Electronic services are investments; they will pay back only over time.

*Compare with what you do today (do you know what you do?)*
- Make an estimate of how much things cost and of what use they are in the way operations are *currently* organized (measure it!) so that you at least have something with which to compare the electronic services.

# 10. Challenge 10: What is Our Role? From Monopoly to Service Provider

Only recently has public administration started to see itself as a service provider to customers: the citizens. Administrations are constantly approaching the status of commercial service providers, in the sense that they must cover their costs, and that users subscribe to the services on a voluntary basis. This transition is still under way, but there are important factors pushing development in this direction. One is competition in the same services from the private sector. This applies to services such as telecommunications and energy, but also health, education and so on. In many countries, private companies or public–private partnerships are introducing competition to services previously considered exclusively public sector business. Electronic services are likely to contribute to accelerating this process. Providing good services requires thinking about what users look for, how they look and so on. This chapter therefore introduces the perspective of users looking for a solution to a problem.

Another factor is the worsening cost challenge of public services. The latter phenomenon enforces public administration to engage private and voluntary sector service providers to complement service chains, especially at the user end. Public administration is becoming increasingly dependent on the wishes of the citizens. Perhaps paradoxically, the reverse is also true: because of urbanization, citizens have become increasingly dependent, in terms of services, benefits and infrastructure, on their public administration. Administration and the citizens it serves have increasingly taken on the appearance of truly becoming a community, not a "service factory".

This challenge has two implications. The first is that the city must find its role in a new environment, technologically and with regard to competition. Different cities work in different environments, and may assume different roles; not every city must provide every possible service. The other implication is that the quality and competitiveness of a service are most important.

What should be private, public or public–private joint endeavours is a political issue, and consequently is not the concern of this book. We focus only on the issue of quality of service delivery in the electronic medium.

## What Is the Role of a City?

The role of cities is undergoing constant evolution. Worldwide, cities started as trading posts. The biggest of them quickly became hubs of central authority. Administration for most of the history of mankind has meant forced collection of taxes and provision of men for military service. The principal return to citizens from giving resources to public administration was for many centuries just the "peace dividend": relative safety from internal and external violence.

The second stage in the development of cities and societies has been one of democratic dictatorship. In democracies, elected representatives have replaced autocratic rulers as the supreme sources of authority, but the top-down, ruling-based structure of public administration has remained intact.

But now, as described above, public administration has started to see itself as a service provider. Before we enter into a discussion about some aspects of this challenge, let us tell a little story.

> NiCity had set up its first city Web server in 1995. The purpose was primarily to inform tourists about the city, events, accommodation etc. Soon, it started to get contacts of many different kinds. Says a project manager in the city: "We were very surprised by the number and nature of the emails we received from all over the world. We were not prepared and not organized to answer all the emails we received. For example, once a lady from Massachusetts sent an email to the city to tell us that a few years ago she had bought a set of four old dessert plates in the Saleya market in NiCity. Unfortunately, she had broken one of them and she wanted to replace with by a new one. Her message included a picture of her plates.
>
> "Some days later, one of my colleagues was on a bargain hunt when by chance he identified the plate. So, one month after sending her email, the American lady received a new plate to recreate her collection."

This is a cute story, but is it really relevant to the discussion of the role of a city? Well, maybe it is. Many people who engaged in early Web service development engaged in this kind of activity. Internet users at that time were very few compared with today, and "the Net" was in many ways a community, a social place to be. So even city officials at times found themselves engaged in this kind of social activity. Even though the Web now is commercial, there is certainly still a strong element of community in many of the activities taking place in cyberspace, and retaining this element is considered most important by many.

How should we look upon the fact that civil servants spend their time on such personal business? Several approaches are possible:

1.  "It is not their role – it is a waste of public money."
2.  "It makes government more personal, and thus improves its image. All business is about personal interaction, and this lady will promote the good image of NiCity. There are many stories in business of winning reputation and customers this way."
3.  "It is the way people use the Web. Cities must adapt to this way of interacting with citizens."
4.  "The effort was spent on a non-taxpayer. Such people are likely to turn up on Web systems because it is easy. The problem is that we don't know whether spending money on them is waste, or if it pays back in terms of reputation and tourism."

In the industrial paradigm, communication is highly regulated. In the Information Society paradigm, also called the "Third Wave", it is abundant, often unstructured and spontaneous. Communication patterns are more like the ones seen in a community, rather than in a factory or in the military. While city staff clearly cannot spend the bulk of their time helping people in odd situations, such as in the NiCity story above, this kind of activity will be part of their day. In fact, for many they have been so for a long time. Most front-office staff spend at least some of their time helping people with things that are not at the core of their business: pointing out the direction to some sight, giving an advice on what shops to visit etc. It is a basic human activity. Only in an extremely streamlined organization with no direct customer contacts can such activities be completely erased. Whether or not Web use in the long run will lead to more such "side activities" remains to be seen. Today there is still a large component of community behaviour on the Web, but as commercial use takes over, the community aspect is likely to be diminished.

It is not likely to go away altogether, though. There is a community aspect to business as well. Local daily newspapers, for instance, find that many of the readers of their Web editions are people from the city or region who have moved abroad and want to keep in touch with their home town. While the Web edition is free and there are no revenues to earn, the newspaper's role as a community tool becomes apparent, and reinforced, which should at least count as an increase in goodwill. Answering emails from emigrants is a part of nourishing this goodwill. We firmly believe that such community aspects are most important ingredients in electronic services. It will arguably be the main competitive advantage of portals and services with a local focus, and possibly the only one, since competing with global firms on a purely economic basis is certain to prove difficult.

## Understanding Your Users

Service is about understanding user requirements – not only what information and services users require, but also how they go about looking for those services. In this section, we shall discuss the problems involved in trying to find out about these things.

## What Are Users Up to When They Visit Your Site?

City information systems are typically designed from a provider point of view: "We have this information and services, now we want to *reach out* to our customers/ citizens". But what if they want something that you do not have? Consider the following case from Seaside City.

> In 1997 the Central Communications Department of the City Hall decided to enter the Web. It made a list of all the information that should be on the Web site. Central to the table of contents was what task the City Hall (as one of several city departments) was responsible for. The table of contents consisted of information on city policy, international collaboration, the members of the city council, the commissions they were in, decisions made in the city council, and so on. There was no information about getting a passport or what procedures to follow in order to get married. They said, "This is not our task; we don't have the budget to provide this kind of information. The Department of Citizen Affairs is responsible for providing it." However, after three months, during which many city council members had asked for it, as had people visiting the Web site, this kind of information was added to the site. An extra page was made with information on opening hours, the procedures for obtaining a new passport etc. This link is offered from the homepage of the City Hall Web site.

People looking for this kind of information are not interested in how the city organizes itself. They just want to have the information, and they know that the city is offering it somewhere. Another example from SiliVille in Stockwerp concerns the process of finding things.

> During a usability test, users in SiliVille were presented with the following task:
>
> "You want to set up a market stall and sell tomatoes on the Main Square, and thus you need to apply for a permit to do so".
>
> People tried the search engine for words like "applications" and "permits" and found nothing. Searching on "market trade" gave the information that such issues were handled by the Market Trade Agency, but there was no address information of any kind. People then went on to search for this agency by means of the search engine, but this yielded no hits. Then people tried the organizational scheme. In that scheme, it was possible to find the right person to send applications to. The different threads in information searching processes were not integrated.

The conclusion from these cases is: organize the information according to how people looking for it expect it to be found. Do not just follow the organizational lines within your city. While those may be very logical and transparent to city employees, citizens are not aware of them. And they do not care much about learning about them.

While the above advice may seem clear enough, the question of how people looking for information and services expect it to be found is not that easy to answer. We will provide some guidelines, but first here is another Seaside City example showing something of the problems of learning about users' requirements.

> The central bureau for information policy of Seaside City made an inquiry about what requirements people had for information and services on the subject of real estate. The study was conducted in order, at a later date, to reorganize the information counters and make them more centralized: one counter would offer all the information. The study of user needs was carried out by an external research bureau. The task was to investigate the requirements of four different user groups: companies, real estate organizations, building companies and citizens. For that purpose, the research bureau made a list of all the information items and services currently offered, asking the interviewees which of the items they needed and which they did not. They did this by showing the existing offer and asking which items on the list were needed and which were not. From the result they drew conclusions about what was needed in the future. What they did not do, and

should have done, was to investigate end users' needs beyond what was already on the list. Only then would the research results have given a proper overview of the overall needs. When asked, the research bureau replied that it did not have well-developed methods for investigating the demand from a demand point of view, so instead they investigated the supply side.

Users' needs can only be understood by truly trying to understand users. Now, how do you do that? The research bureau in Seaside City did the easy thing: it looked under the lamp-post because that was where the light was[1] "Because it's so dark over there, you can't see anything". Looking for users' needs that are not already expressed in an existing service may certainly be harder than looking at what is not necessary in the existing service supply. Still, it is necessary to find ways of doing this. There are several options. Many companies arrange "focus groups": users invited to give their view on services. Another way is to conduct simple texts in laboratory settings. In the following we shall provide some ideas stemming from different user studies.

## Support the Whole Problem-Solving Process

What do people in the process of finding a solution to a problem actually do? A simple model of the process looks like Fig. 10.1.

**Fig. 10.1** Phases in users' investigations of a problem area.

---

1   There is an often told story of a man who was found crawling around on the sidewalk under a lamp-post. A passer-by asks him what he is doing.
   "I'm looking for my car keys."
   The passer-by gets down on his knees to help looking.
   "Can you remember more exactly where you lost them?"
   "Over there" (the man points to a spot about ten meters away in the dark).
   "But why are you looking here if you dropped them over there?"

- *Orientation.* Where should I turn? Which organization(s) provide information or services pertaining to my problem?
- *Investigation.* There may be several ways to solve the problem. Different organizations may provide solutions differing in quality, price, accessibility, terms of delivery or something else. The different opportunities must be found, as must sufficient data to make comparisons.
- *Choice.* Choosing among alternatives may involve many parameters: quality, price, accessibility etc.
- *Implementation.* Once a choice is made, users want to implement their decisions by ordering a product or a service and by specifying parameters such as delivery terms and specific product features (colour, size, amount etc.).

What would an ideal system for supporting this process contain? During the different phases of problem solving, different requirements are placed upon the information/service system:

- *Orientation.* All service providers in the pertinent field must be represented. The system must recognize the user's question, even if it is not formulated correctly according to the professional language in the field.
- *Investigation.* Sufficient data from each provider must be available to make it possible to distinguish between the different alternatives. It is often necessary to transform data to a similar format in order to make comparisons possible. This phase may also involve an element of negotiation, as terms may not be fixed.
- *Choice.* There are many ways to help with comparing products. One way is to provide calculation sheets so that users can fill in data applicable to their situation and view the result, such as when housing allowance is calculated. Another way is to provide results from tests, such as when a consumer organization tests different cars or washing machines.
- *Implementation.* Ordering a service or product involves confirmation and execution. Confirmation can be done by sending in a form, electronically or by physical mail or fax, by a telephone call, or in some other way. It may also involve specification of parameters such as colour, delivery date or hours per week spent in a nursery home. Execution involves making delivery decisions on the producer side, and actually delivering a service, some goods, or just a confirmation that the proper decisions have been made and a database has been updated and so on.

During the problem-solving process, users may have to shift medium. This may be because not all the information is available in one medium, perhaps because at some point one medium is not appropriate for the task at hand. It must be possible to make these media shifts in a smooth way. Consider the following example.

- *Orientation.* A user starts looking for childcare services on the city Web system. All municipal childcare centres are present on the Web, as are the private alternatives, so she gets a good overview.
- *Investigation.* She finds good information about the different childcare centres, concerning education, facilities, staff, opening hours, fees and so on. Still, she wants to "feel the atmosphere", and therefore decides to call a few of them to set

up a couple of visits to look at things in person. That is, she wants to change the medium, because there are things relevant to her choice that she can't figure out from the electronic medium alone.

The telephone numbers of all the nursery homes are available on the Web. She calls the three she was most interested in, and finds that the numbers were still valid. She tells the staff that she saw information on the Web, and she now wants to make a visit to gauge the atmosphere. Meetings are easily arranged. This is an example of a smooth change of medium.

- *Choice.* After visiting the three childcare centres that seemed best, she decided that two of them appeared very home-like, whereas the atmosphere at the third seemed not so pleasant. So she has a choice of two. Because the fees are the same and the distance from home of each of the centres is almost the same, the only problem appears to be availability. Is there a free place at either of the two centres? The staff said there were free places, but they did not know about queues: there might be children waiting who had already been promised a place. So she needs to contact the city administration for childcare.

There is an email address for "administration" on the Web pages, so she tries writing an email, explaining her business. After a week, there is still no answer. She goes back to the Web and tries the telephone number to the administration. After six rings, a voice answers "X-town, how can I help you?"

"My name is Sarah Wagnert. I want to know if there are free places at the Tulip or the Rose."

(After some silence) "What is "The Tulip and the Rose"? A pub?

"Childcare centres."

"Well, in that case you should call the childcare administration."

"That's what I thought I did. I dialled the number I found on the Web!"

(More silence) "What Web?"

"Never mind. Can you connect me to them?"

"Certainly; just a second." (A few seconds pass.) "I'm sorry, no one is answering at the moment. Can you call back?"

"Isn't there someone else you can find there to help me?"

"Let me see... OK, here's Joanna Carlsson."

"Carlsson, how can I help you?"

"My name is Sarah Wagnert. I want to know if there are free places at the Tulip or the Rose."

Have you registered for the queue for childcare?"

"No, not yet. I just want to find out if there are places to apply for."

"Well, those who are in the queue get notified when it's their turn, but if you are not in the queue, it's hard to say... your place in the queue depends on when your application arrives here."

"But can't you give me a hint? What's the situation today, how many are waiting?"

"You should call John Pernicle – he's the one in charge of the queue, he knows the current situation."

Let us stop here. What we have just witnessed was not a smooth transition from one medium to another. Two things failed. First, the person answering the telephone did

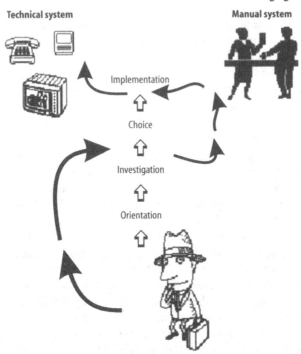

**Technical system**                          **Manual system**

Implementation

Choice

Investigation

Orientation

**Fig. 10.2** It must be possible to switch smoothly between different media during the problem-solving process.

not realize where the customer had come from. This may not seem odd, given our knowledge of the whole situation, but from the point of view of the potential customer it does. She dialled a number she found in a *certain context*. Dialling the number was supposed to take her further in the chain of events leading to a solution to her problem. It didn't – at least not without some confusion; the clerk did not even know about the Web, so she could not understand the customer's situation. The customer and the clerk were not in the same game, so smooth media transitions were not supported (Fig. 10.2).

Second, there was no way to find out about her problem. While this might not be impossible, it should have been possible for at least the hint she asked for to be given without her having to find a particular clerk. This point is not related to the specific medium used: it has only to do with the organization of work pertaining to service production and delivery.

In a good service process, the different media used must be integrated, and this integration must be done from the customer's point of view. As the user works her way along the steps of the problem-solving process, smooth changes between media must be possible.

Users of public utilities do not surf around municipal sites. They use them only when they need to get something done, which is most often when they have an acute problem. This means that they are always in a hurry to find a solution (although a hurry does not always mean seconds). Therefore, systems must be designed with an awareness of the customer's problem-solving process.

## Completeness in Coverage

The system must provide support all the way to a solution (possibly by integration with other media). There must be an answer to every request, even if the actual service is not provided in the electronic medium and the answer is, for example, only a telephone number passing the user on to another channel.

As a tool for searching (the orientation phase in Fig. 10.1) the Web is competing with the telephone book and personal contacts with civil servants at the front desk, which may be a "Citizen Office" or the front desk of a specialist organization. If only a fraction of the available public services can be found in the electronic medium, people will keep on using the traditional information sources, simply because they are more likely to find what they are looking for there. If, on the other hand, the electronic system is complete in its coverage, it may be an improvement over the other media because it can provide more efficient and more personalized search methods, more elaborately structured data, more up-to-date data than the phone book, faster access than a civil servant, 24 hour service, or some other advantage.

## Intermediaries Do Not Always Make the Path From Problem to Solution Shorter

Users have problems, providers (hopefully) have solutions. User problems and provider solutions are often not described in the same way, which will be illustrated in the section on the thesaurus below. The time and effort needed on the part of a user to find a solution to a problem is in most cases crucial for the success of the electronic system.

It is important to remember in this context that computers provide an additional initial threshold for users; it is more complicated to use a computer than to use a telephone. This is true even for experienced users: you have to start it up, log in etc., which can sometimes be time-consuming. Therefore the actual information and services must be so much better than the competing media that it is worth the extra trouble of going through the extra manoeuvres the computer requires.

Existing services are not always designed efficiently from a user point of view. In a Stockholm investigation (Stockholm, 1995a), citizens said that they often found it unnecessary to talk to the "proper" civil servant, something which they were often required to do. A typical statement is:

> Once within the queue for childcare, the service was good. But before that it was hard to have them even send an application form. We had to find the proper civil servant first (p. 1).

The users see the need to find "the proper civil servant" as an unwanted detour. In the early uncomplicated phases of an inquiry – such as when they want to find an application form – they do not want to have to talk to a special person. They simply want the form. This emphasizes the need for a short route to the answer, but it also points to the genuine potential for self-service in many cases, stated directly by users. A convincing 76% said: "the best way to find information about the different municipal services is to ask for myself" (Stockholm, 1995a, p. 42).

In the same investigation, the personnel appreciated their own services more than users did; to the question "The City should actively see to it that citizens get information", 32% of users but 45% of civil servants answered "definitely yes". The green pages in the telephone book (municipal information directory) were used "very often" by 32%, to be compared with the civil servants' belief that only 26% of the users would be frequent users. The answers indicate that users are better at helping themselves, and more willing to do it, than civil servants think they are. The important factor, then, is not the medium, but the information; users will use the medium that is best for finding what they are looking for.

## People Navigate in Different Ways

How do people actually search for municipal information? In Challenge 8, we saw that people typically do not surf around municipal sites to see "what's up". They go there only when in need of something. But we still do not know what they do in those situations; what do they look for, how do they search? A city investigation found that "The atypical is the typical" (Stockholm, 1995a, p. 12). Some want as little information as possible, some as much as possible. Some want information from the whole city, some just about their neighbourhood. Some want it electronically, by teletext or the Internet, some want it in the mailbox, and some would like dedicated telephone numbers.

As for the strategies for finding information, Table 10.1 shows what search methods Stockholmers use.

As can be seen, self-service methods are the most frequently used, with the green pages a clear winner. The green pages, newspapers and contacts with friends can all be considered to be self-service media; those are the top three items on the list. The need for a human intermediary starts at No. 5. There seem to be reasons to claim that self-service is often feasible, and probably often a preferred method.

The "professional human assistance" form of contact can be divided into two categories: information professionals and "agents" – professionals like teachers and childcare staff who pass information on as a side result of their other duties. A comparison shows that information professionals are slightly more popular than

**Table 10.1** Search methods used by Stockholmers (Stockholm, 1995a). The figures indicate the percentage that state they use each item "much" or "some". (The figures for "some use" include "much" use.)

| Search method | Much use | Some use |
|---|---|---|
| Green pages (city directory in the phone book) | 30% | 65% |
| Newspapers | 15 | 20 |
| Friends | 10 | 50 |
| Brochures | 8 | 43 |
| Calling a central city officer | 8 | 30 |
| Local radio/TV | 8 | 35 |
| Staff, e.g. at childcare centres | 5 | 28 |
| Stockholm central information service | 5 | 15 |
| Through membership of some organization | 3 | 15 |
| School teachers | 3 | 13 |

professionals who pass on information as a side task (i.e. staff at childcare centres and school teachers); the differences, however, are not significant. These figures should also be used with care: the popularity of a certain information source probably depends a lot on the information wanted (when people need information about their children's school, they most likely turn to a teacher, not to a central municipal officer).

With regard to how knowledgeable people are with respect to public services, it is clear that their expertise is not great.

This discussion is further elaborated and supported by – among others -Schön (1983) and Dreyfus and Dreyfus (1986). It is often stated that there are "weak groups", such as the elderly, handicapped, youth etc. One finding is that there are no significant differences between different groups (elderly, youth, families etc.) with respect to how much they know about the service supply; 30–40% of each group are "relatively familiar" with it and 5–10% are "very familiar". It is likely that there are great differences within the groups. As we saw in Challenge 8, familiarity with the task domain was the single most important factor for finding things in the electronic service systems we tested. This means that familiarity with the way society works is most important, and differences in this respect are more important than differences in age or physical ability.

In conclusion, we can see that self-service has great potential, but one cannot find a single "best" navigation/search method: all possible methods must be available.

### Navigation in the Electronic Medium

With regard to the electronic medium, there are several methods at hand for navigation and searching. Users can interact with computers in several ways: typed input, touchscreens or speech. Navigation systems can also be differently organized; there may be hierarchies of menus, hypertext networks, keyword searching, "operator" functions (direct contact with another human by means of email or voice), or more or less intelligent software agents. We argue that all methods must be applied, but in such a way that they do not interfere with each other, and so that the user always has a choice of methods.

There will always be different users of the system. They will always differ with respect to their expertise in computer use, their task domain expertise, and their knowledge about the particular service at hand. There are newcomers, using the service for the first time, as well as experts, who have been there several times and know their way around. Where services from the social insurance office are concerned, for example, there are retired professionals who know everything about the services of the social insurance system, and there are people who never have had any contact with the social insurance office before. Those in the former category are likely to be able to perform advanced inquiry by themselves, while those in the latter category might need human assistance or very detailed written guidance, even for simple services.

Novices and experts also navigate differently in the electronic medium. They also typically use different terms because of their different knowledge of the professional language. This was shown by Schön (1983), who investigated the professionals' ways of reflecting upon their work, and Dreyfus and Dreyfus (1986), who investigated the ways in which users of different proficiency approached tasks.

In Challenge 8, we investigated some general search and navigation methods used in the computer medium and their typical advantages and disadvantages:

- *Menus* illustrate the domain well for novices, but a large amount of material leads to many levels of menus, which makes them tedious for the more experienced user.

- *Hypertext nets* make it easy for the user to follow a thread, a line of argument. However, as the number of threads increases, the method very rapidly gets confusing, especially if the user is not very familiar with the task domain. The public sector contains many different services to cope with all aspects of society, so there is an obvious risk of creating complex nets.

- *Keyword searching* is a rapid method for the domain expert. This method is typically not efficient for the novice, because proficiency in the professional language is necessary to find the proper words to search for.

- *"Operator"* connection, a chance to contact a human by mail (most common) or by telephone is important for several reasons: because human contact is important for absolute beginners, because of the personality of the medium, and for complex or special questions that cannot be easily investigated (if at all) by other search methods.

- *"Agents"* can make navigation personalized. Today we can see the beginning of a trend towards greater use of such software, especially on the Internet, where searching is particularly difficult, but also in standard programs. For example, in Microsoft Office, an animated creature pops up to help you under some circumstances ("It looks like you are writing a memo. Let me suggest..."). However, the intelligence of agents is not always impressive and they may be more of a nuisance.

## Conclusions

There is empirical evidence to suggest that self-service is actually requested by users. However, the success of self-service is not automatic: the new services must be better than the existing ones to be competitive – and used.

We have said this before, but it deserves to be repeated: users of municipal sites do not surf; they are under a certain level of time pressure – trying to solve a problem. To help them to do that – which is what you must focus on – there are a number of things to bear in mind:

- *Support the whole problem-solving process*: orientation–investigation–choice–implementation.

- *Integrate media* – do not separate the Web from other ways of service delivery. Users do not care whether they find the solution by telephone or by the Internet. But they *do* get annoyed if they spend time searching on the Internet, get close to a solution, then have to change medium, only to find that they have to start over again by explaining to a switchboard operator what they have spent the past hour looking for. *Smooth transitions between the different media* necessary to solve a problem are required.

- Organize your information to *reflect the way users conceptualize the task* at hand, not the structure of your organization.

- Provide *completeness in coverage*; all services should be reached from one single access point.

- The *path from the problem must be shorter* than in other media (as measured by time, money, effort, convenience or in some other way). Although some users may initially find it fun to use the Internet, this will not last. Ultimately, it is the solution that counts.

- Different users require *different navigation methods*. Providing different methods in a coherent manner may be difficult; navigation methods may clash.

# 11. Challenge 11: Where Are the Users? Users Want Your Service, Not Your System

Many cities have made considerable investments in Web systems, only to find that they are little used. Typically, the front page, which has no information content, has quite a few hits, while pages with information such as political information or City Council minutes have very few visitors. No wonder people begin to ask, "When will the users arrive?".

The answers to this question can be found at two distinct levels: a macro level, concerning business structure, and a micro level, concerning the system's usefulness for users.

*The macro level discussion:* Europe's media chain is missing a couple of crucial links. There needs to be an interesting mix of local content in electronic services, the services have to be bundled in an interesting way by a service provider, and people need to be able to access them easily, rapidly and cheaply. A problem for local services is that cities – especially in rural areas, where they are an important hub – are not concentrating on finding and packaging local content, one of the crucial catalysts for getting people online. So far, there is no equivalent of a book publisher or television or film distributor for the emerging online services.

*The micro level discussion:* A system must be useful for its users. This may seem a truism, but history proves that usefulness is often not considered. Many see it as a great accomplishment to produce a city Web system at all. But what has really been achieved by that? Your Web system may be beautifully designed, interactive, fast and so on, but what *use* does the inhabitant of your city have for it? Your system competes with other media. The interactions between your city's agencies and their clients have so far been managed by use of other media. Users will go on using these media until they find that your new system is more useful to them. It can be made so in a number of ways, most of which do not come about automatically.

# Complete Media Chains for Economic Benefits of Electronic Services: Win–Winning in the Information Society

In an interview in the *Wall Street Journal*, discussing the limited success of EU Web projects, a Philips official says "Europe's media chain is missing a couple of crucial links. There needs to be an interesting mix of local content; the services have to be packaged in an interesting way by a services provider; and people need to be able to access them at high speed, via the Internet. The problem in Europe... is that cities aren't concentrating on finding and packaging local content, one of the crucial catalysts for getting people online. So far, there isn't the equivalent of a book publisher or television or film distributor for emerging online services" (Schenker, 1998, p. 8).

The above quote emphasizes the point that single providers of electronic services will often find it hard to realize economic benefits, either because they are small or because they provide only part of a service bundle that would only make sense as a whole to users. There is need for infrastructural support. This may come from general intermediaries – which in Part 2 we will call Electronic Service Managers – or from partnerships among actors in a value chain.

## Aggressive Intermediaries Can Create a Market

In some places, the need to couple interests so as to provide an interesting service mix has already been achieved. Sometimes, win–win situations can be arranged quite easily. In Seaside City, for instance, it was realized that there was a need for interesting content on the local Web, but for several reasons the SMEs did not immediately join in. One reason was lack of knowledge of the medium. Another reason was the fear of high costs, which when investigated turned out instead to be unknown costs. So there was a problem: without content there will be no users, and without sufficient knowledge of the medium among content providers there will be no content. To resolve this dilemma, a project was set up which marketed the Internet medium in a hands-on fashion.

> In Seaside City, the use of the Internet by SMEs was seen as one way of promoting economic development. The policy of the city was not to sit and wait, but to invest in encouraging use of the Internet by SMEs. One example is the Business Park Seaside project, which was a plan including two steps.
>
> *Step 1*: SMEs were invited by Seaside City (within a project to stimulate innovation) to participate in an information evening about the Internet. Some of the SMEs were already somewhat familiar with the possibilities of the Internet, but most of them were not. Some of them did not even have any experience with computers. The information evenings started with an introduction covering the history of the Internet: The

history of ARPANET, decentralized information delivery for security reasons during the Cold War in the 1960s, the subsequent use by universities, and the introduction of the multimedia facilities of the World Wide Web. Then the concept of providing Internet access was explained: what you need to do to be connected to the Internet; what the costs are.

The most important part of the evening was surfing on the Internet by the SME people themselves. During the evening, people were shown how to navigate: "Use the mouse, click when the arrow becomes a hand" etc. It was all quite basic. Some people started looking for products and companies they knew and were often surprised, for they didn't know that so much was available on the Internet.

At the end of the evening, people were invited to subscribe to a three-evening course (workshop) in order to get their own business onto the Internet.

Since the start of the information evenings at the end of 1995, over 2000 SMEs (about 5% of the total) have joined the scheme.

Step 2: the workshop consisted of learning how to start your own Web site on the Internet, as part of the "Business Park Seaside" Web site. The main goal was not to get as nice as possible a Web site for as little money as possible, but to get an opportunity to gain experience about presenting your business on the Internet. About 10 SMEs at the time participated in the workshop. Not only were Web sites created, but also information about search engines, Web statistics, price structure and marketing was given. For one year, SMEs were subsidised for 50% of their provider costs and Web maintenance hours.

From the start of the workshop scheme in spring 1996 to mid-1998, over 300 SMEs have participated in the workshop, and about 60% of them continued the one-year subsidised experience after the initial three-month period.

The outcomes of being on the Web differ depending on the type of business that the SME is in. For instance, importing and exporting firms use the Internet to get new contacts in Asia and South America, while others are working more regionally and use their Web pages for customer service and support. Some have made real money out of the experience, while others have reduced their costs. All of them get to know the Internet through first-hand experience, learning by trial and error and getting used to using it. In this way, Seaside City is creating a critical mass of users.

The Seaside Business Park project was evaluated by the European project Aesopian, an initiative to set up a database of best and worse practices in the field of telematic applications. Their conclusion was that what made Seaside Business Park into a success was that marketing of services was combined with education. First you educate, then you sell. People do not use something unless they realize why and how to use it.

In the above case, the Seaside Business Park took on one important task of an Electronic Service Manager: it not only published information and services, it also took on the education of providers to increase the service supply sufficiently to make up an attractive site.

## Creative Partnerships Can Add Value to All

In some businesses, there may not be sufficiently many or sufficiently large actors for there to be a need for a general intermediary. The following case is from FarawayTown, and illustrates a partnership solution where the home service joined a local grocery shop to make mutual gains.

North Karelia, in Finland, is an unexceptional Less Favoured Region in Europe. Employment is declining and young people are moving away in search of employment in the booming telecommunications industry in the south of the country. An ageing population and unemployment exercise an increasing strain on the regional public finances. A vicious circle? Certainly not!

FarawayTown provided its home care staff with mobile telephones. Thanks to development projects, partly funded by the European Commission, an Internet-based teleshopping service for grocery was built. The home care staff member – while visiting an elderly client – phones the shopping list to a back office, where another staff member keys it in. The shop delivers the goods a few hours later. This had some immediate positive effects:

● Home care staff members spend more time with each elderly client.
● They can still look after more elderly people than before.
● Some elderly people are greatly helped by just having their shopping brought home – they can receive that part of the home care service, yet it costs a fraction compared with receiving the full-blown service.
● The shop does more business than before, and the new business is more labour-intensive than super-market sales. They employ a few more people.

In the next stage, home care services will be allocated to public or private work teams, who are free to organize their work. The team members coordinate via voicemail and email. They receive technical support from a service centre, as well as 24 hours a day service outside normal working hours.

The system allows many more elderly people to be helped than before, when each social worker called on his or her clients in an uncoordinated fashion, yet it costs much less. The service centre, while looking after its in-house patients, does value-added business by helping work teams help patients to live in their own homes.

We have illustrated above two ways in which to create benefits: by *partnerships* and by introducing *a general intermediary*, an *electronic service manager*. The common denominators are the local context and the local content. There are other ways to create revenues. For instance, America Online is a very successful Internet provider which follows a totally different path. This company gives exclusive rights to service providers, thus eliminating internal competition and leaving small businesses with no chance of taking part in the market. While this is certainly one way of doing good business, it is a way that does not support local business and local culture.

We believe that the successful route to an Information Society for all follows a path where all parties can win. By judicious choice of an organizational reform, coupled to a telematic revolution, everybody wins and nobody loses. Finding such a path may be time-consuming, but it is worth your while. In many places this is an absolute prereq-uisite. Europe, for instance, is a continent of diversity, and preserving some of this diversity is important in a world with a growing global economy and culture. In other places, the importance of local culture and small businesses may not be so great, but it certainly should not be underestimated.

# Usefulness To the Individual; the Everyday Contexts of Electronic Services

Above we discussed different ways of organizing electronic services. Regardless of which is chosen, the services produced must be useful to customers/citizens/users.

## Why Should Users Come to You?

Your system must be useful for your customers, as described at the start of this chapter. It is true that many feel that simply having a Web system is something to be proud of – something that "puts your city on the map". While this may be true internally, for self-esteem, it is not true in general. Poor Web systems today make people laugh – they are bad PR.

Technical artefacts cannot be assessed only by strict measures of utility. A BMW does the same transportation work for you as a Volkswagen, but it has considerably higher status. As for ICT, we have already seen changes. A few years back, it was a high status thing to talk in the mobile on the street or at the airport. Today, it is high status to avoid it. Only recently, it was high status to have a "homepage" on the Web. Today, you should only have one if it is good. Using electronic services may today carry some status in its own right, but this will not last.

There are three distinct types of factors that influence system use. One is usability, which we have already discussed in Challenge 8, one is usefulness, which we shall discuss below, and one has to do with general views of information technology. Let us start with the last.

### System Acceptance Factors

For non-compulsory information systems, it is well known that user acceptance of the system is most important. In investigating the acceptance of hypertext systems, Nielsen (1990) found the following general system acceptance factors:

- Social acceptability: e.g. ethical issues, general feelings about computers
- Practical acceptability:
  - usefulness
  - usability: easy to learn, efficient to use, few errors, subjectively pleasing
  - utility: how easily goals are reached
- Cost
- Compatibility
- Technical reliability

We can see from this list that there are a few factors that cannot easily be changed by providing more efficient services. Social acceptability has to do with a variety of social factors, such as group membership, political views, sex, age and lifestyle. The element "subjectively pleasing" refers to individual preferences and taste, but may not be so different since different groups of people may find certain things pleasing or not.

While not easily changed, it is important to be aware of these factors, and to consider to what extent they pertain to a prospective group of users.

### Usefulness

Usefulness in this context means *relative* usefulness: how does your electronic service perform compared with competing services? In order to be able to measure success or failure, we must be clear about what we are studying. It is not single software modules; nor is it single services only. Rather, it is the *potential of electronic services in the area of government-citizen communication*.

We say *potential* because large-scale electronic services are still very new. The World Wide Web itself is still only a few years old in terms of its use by the wider public. To be sure, services have existed for some years, but they are changing as we speak, in both form and content, because of the rapid pace of technical development. Further such changes are foreseen for the very near future: electronic payment systems will be more widely used, security enhancements will make organizations more confident in providing more advanced services, and broadband connectivity to the home will improve the availability of services and remove the obstacle of high costs for users. Also, familiarity with the electronic medium is rapidly increasing among the general public, and it will continue to increase over the next few years at a pace that will provide a much different context for electronic services relatively soon. Such developments will mean an increase in the number of services, changes in their character and increased use.

The success of each service and each software component is to a large extent dependent on a context that largely does not exist today (extensive service supply, universal access to the medium, universal familiarity with the medium, etc.). Figure 11.1 gives an overview of the area under discussion: the environment of electronic services.

The model should be understood as follows. First of all, there are two perspectives. Above the horizontal line in the middle of the figure are factors pertaining to the individuals' (the end users') perspective. Below the line are factors pertaining to the organization's perspective.

The relationships in the model cannot easily be quantified. First, given the early stage of development and use of electronic services, quantification is an uncertain endeavour. Any figures produced are not likely to be valid for very long, and consequently the risk is that they will merely produce a false sense of exactness. Second, the relative importance of each factor will vary depending on the service and on the user.

*Terminology*

*Usability* (top left) means whether or not the thing you have constructed can be used at all. As already discussed in Challenge 8, this includes questions like "Can people handle the buttons?", "Do they understand the output they get?", "Do they

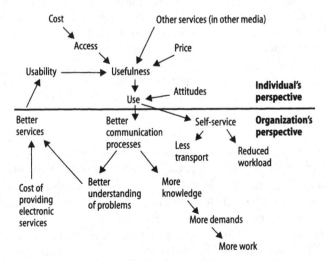

**Fig. 11.1** Factors affecting the use of electronic services.

understand what input they should provide?" and "How do they like using this thing?".

Usability only tells us that a device *can* be used, not whether or not it *will* be. In most cases, the new device has competition from old devices doing more or less the same things.

*Usefulness* (top centre) means the competitive advantage of the new service compared with others that already exist to help the user to achieve the same thing, or – in the case of a new service that enables users to do things they couldn't do before – the value of the new possibility compared with the cost of having it.

Usefulness in the case of electronic services means adding three factors to the study (top centre in the figure): (1) *access* to the medium, which has a *cost* both in money for computers, modems, telephone lines, and in time and effort for learning to master the medium and – more important in the long run – for using it; (2) the existence of competition with *other services* providing the same or similar services in other media; and (3) the *price* of using the electronic service, if there is a charge.

Usefulness is of course best measured in real-life situation, but if this is not possible it can be estimated with some accuracy by asking users after they have learned to use the service in test situations: "What if you had such a system at home – would you use it? For what? In what situations? Would you be prepared to pay a fee for using it? How much?". After having used the system, even a prototype, users have a good idea of what it means to use the system, and they can therefore produce relatively informed opinions of the system's usefulness.

If a service is both usable and useful, there will probably be more *use* (centre). An additional factor, however, which must be taken into account when estimating future use, is the users' *attitudes* towards electronic services. This will appear in different ways among different groups of users. Remember that many people still don't like the automated teller machine, and many would never give up their cheque book for a plastic card. And these people are *not* just less well educated; it is truly a matter of attitudes and not just skill.

Use can be measured, but more interesting – not least from an economic perspective – than mere use are its *consequences*:

- Does it lead to more self-service and a subsequent reduction in use of manual services, printed material, transportation, or other resources?
- Does it lead to *more* use of such resources? This could well be the case for public services: better services may lead to more knowledge among citizens, which may lead to more questions, more complaints or simply more use of services, because people have found services that they didn't know of before.
- Does it lead to civil servants getting a better understanding of citizens' problems, thus leading to more efficient services (because of a better match between problems and services, more efficient workflows, or some other reason)? Or does this better understanding lead to more work, because more problems are detected and dealt with? This is what happens over and over again in medical research and care: new methods of detecting, for example, cancer lead to more cancer cases detected, more treatment and higher costs for medical care.

The above are examples of what might happen; the list is not exhaustive. We have provided the model to show that:

- Many factors influence use of electronic services.
- There is no universal rule to say that greater use of electronic services will lead to savings for the provider organization.

The items in the model must somehow be estimated in advance, before services are brought into regular operation, although they cannot of course be precisely predicted at an early stage.

Whatever the outcome of greater use of electronic services, providers must of course take into account the costs of providing them (bottom left). Such costs include costs for the technical infrastructure, for systems development and maintenance, for providing the information to the system, and for providing help to users, including both technical help and help in understanding the information in the system.

### Beat the Phone

Many cities have set up Web systems to provide information and services to their inhabitants. But this information and these services are also available through other media: brochures, information officers, informal channels etc.

Many of these other channels are readily available without people having to take special measures to obtain them; most people read the daily papers, they meet people at work and at day care centres etc. The most prominent medium that your Web services compete with is the telephone. Many government organizations, banks and other organizations provide information and services by automated telephone systems where users, by choosing from a menu presented by a recorded human voice, can order forms, transfer money from one account to another etc. So let us compare the two.

Picking up the phone to call the city's switchboard and name your problem takes only a few seconds, and you don't have to figure out which person you have to contact: the operator does that for you. When you log on to a Web system, on the other hand, you have to do the following:

1. Start the computer (takes at least 1 minute).
2. Log on to the network (1 minute if you are at home on a modem line – longer if your Internet Service Provider has been too optimistic about bandwidth requirements).
3. Find your city's site (30 seconds on a slow modem line – longer if you don't know the address).
4. Figure out which department you should go to (the time needed depends on how much you know about the city's organization. It often takes several minutes, and quite often fails altogether, according to our tests)
5. Understand the written explanations (which answer several potential questions "just-in-case", as opposed to the "just-in-time" way of having somebody answering only your specific question on the phone).
6. Complete your business (often not possible on the Web: you often find you have to call somebody after all).

So, even if things work well, you will need several minutes and some orientation activities to do what you set out to do. The first two points, and the time taken, will of course not apply if the user has a permanent Internet connection.

There is not much a service provider can do about the boot and login times, so the question then is, how can your Web system beat the phone on the other points? Given that you are already two minutes behind, there is a lot of catching up to do. Point 4, figuring out where to go, is also a point where your Web system is likely to lose out against the switchboard operator. The latter rarely needs more than 30 seconds to find out which department you should be connected to. Fortunately for the Web service enthusiast, there are some properties of the Web that are potentially useful:

- Better search facilities than telephone menus, for instance automatic keyword searching.
- Open 24 hours.
- Asynchronous communication: no need to wait for telephone hours.
- More information can be presented than by a telephone menu or in a telephone call.
- Users can spend as much time as they like reading and thinking; they do not have to keep up with someone at the other end of the telephone line.

But things like these do not automatically do the trick. To understand how to make good use of the medium, you must understand the user's problem-solving methods.

As we saw in Challenge 10, the problem-solving process consists of several parts: orientation, comparison, choice and implementation. Your Web system often cannot support *all* steps the user has to go through. The complexity and the nature of the service may make it more or less suitable for delivery over electronic media. A more complex service probably requires more, and more complex, interaction among the actors, which makes it harder to distribute over electronic media. In such situations, you have to choose what to support. The choice is not always apparent, as the following example shows.

The automated teller machine represents a fairly simple service that is delivered in a fairly simple way: if there is money in your account and you can identify yourself to the system, you may withdraw it. The relation between the nature of the service and the nature of the system is good. Of course, there is more to bank service than withdrawing money, but this activity is very often performed independently.

Other services are very different, even though they *include* such simple operations. Consider the activity "making a flight reservation". This activity seems simple enough, comparable to withdrawing money from an automated teller. It is true that the actual reservation is fairly easy, but the path leading to that point typically includes several complicated choices that are often made in an intertwined manner, such as the following:

1. There is most often more than one carrier available. Price and service often differ among them in ways that are typically not comparable in a straight-forward way.

2. There is often equally feasible alternative transportation: sometimes a train may be a good substitute for a plane.

3. Travel often comes in "packages", including not only transportation but also accommodation, transfers, meals etc. Often charter flights are good alternatives even on business trips, because they typically prove cheaper than regular flights and full price accommodation.

4. Journeys often have more than one purpose; for instance, travelling for your job might be combined with family weekends. A typical feature of many airlines' price policies today is to offer cheap APEX tickets if you stay away over the weekend. The price of such a ticket is often only 1/3 of the full price, which means that staying away longer is cheaper. This makes the times of departure and return a matter of discussion, placing points 1–3 in a different light.

5. The problem situation may change suddenly, for instance when you discover during discussions with the travel agent that bringing your wife or husband along will cost you virtually nothing extra. You might then decide to turn the trip into a combined business and pleasure trip.

Where these more complicated activities are concerned, it seems that computerizing only the reservation doesn't make much sense. The "reservation problem", as described above, turns out not to be a reservation problem at all. Whether or not I can order a ticket from my home computer is not important if the real problem is *finding the best transportation*. If the Web system does not include support for this activity, I will have to call the travel agency anyway, and once I have done so, why not let them order the ticket? The problem of delivering services like this is not primarily a complexity problem, but a problem regarding the *nature* of the service. But since conferring is more complex than information delivery, it also evolves into being a *complexity* problem.

If the problem is *finding* rather than *buying*, systems must be designed in other ways than the automated teller. The travel agent may serve as a model: systems for "finding" must be designed for inquiry and communication rather than just information delivery because they must deal with activities like the "flight reservation problem", activities that often change during the course of events.

### Outservice Your Competitors

The role of cities is undergoing constant evolution. Only recently have public administrations started to see themselves as service providers to customers: the citizens.

As service providers, and as communities, cities have competitors. There are private service providers, for instance in areas of tourist information, home services, commuting services and health care. There are other communities, such as professional communities in different fields. The reasons for engaging in such affairs, where other organizations, national, professional, private, non-profit or other are already engaged, require analysis. Why should your city be there at all? Is there a niche for you? There may certainly be, but the answer is not yes by default.

If you decide to enter – or stay – you must provide a better service than your competitors in the particular arena you choose. You are typically only able to do so if there is a local touch to the content you plan to provide. And even if you can, you must ask yourself: do we really want to provide this?

The question is not so far-fetched as it may seem to many who have grown used to the welfare state providing virtually all the services pertaining to the convenience of its citizens. While cities have services in many fields, neither the number of services nor the number of fields are automatically determined. Perhaps some of the services should be provided by others. There are public sector agencies at other levels (regional, national), there are voluntary organizations, and there are private companies that can do some things that do not have to do with exerting the authority delegated to a city. One example is tourist information; another is health care, where national rules always apply, at least to some degree. Before you decide that this is in fact *your* arena, identify what your goals are for entering, or staying in, this business. The following checklist may guide your considerations:

- What would be the ideal composition of an ideal service for your users?
- What would be the ideal role of your organization in delivering it?
- Who would the other content providers be, and what would their roles be, in your ideal electronic service?
- What would the ideal workflow and interaction structure look like?

### Design for the Context

In Challenge 8 we gave general advice on design from a usability viewpoint. There are additional matters to consider. One is to design for the context of your material. Who is going to use it, and in what situations? It is important to distinguish between surfers and "bread-and-butter users", goal-oriented people in search of a solution to an everyday problem.

Different design ideals apply if you are looking for vacation leisure activities or you are looking for building permits or day care fees. In the former case there is often an element of surfing around and taking a look, while in the latter case users are typically very goal-oriented. It is very easy to design the material in a way that does not appeal to, or have an effect on, the prospected users.

> The Swedish government designed a Web site intended to keep young people informed about, and as much as possible away from, drugs. The page included written information, but also a game, the thrust of which was for the player to "survive" a Saturday night on the town. The young people who tested the game saw not just the fun of it, as intended. They also saw a teacher or a parent telling them what to do, and consequently said there was "nothing new" in it (Aktuellt, 1998). While the game form clearly appealed to them, it seemed that no new information was conveyed. They recognized the message, and the content, from school and from home.

What added value did this system bring? An alternative would have been to build a system providing more and/or new information in a simpler design to make discussions in class or at home better informed. This would certainly have been much cheaper, and perhaps it would also have added some really new impact for the target group. While there is no simple solution to the problem of adding value, there are some points to consider before providing a service:

- Identify your main user groups (and we don't mean your most important constituents!); who are they, how many, what characteristics do they have?; age, sex, socio-economic status, preferences, lifestyles etc.
- Identify *when* your user groups want to use the service; every day, weekly, once a year....

- Identify *in what situation* your user groups will use your services (while working, from home, on the street etc.).
- Identify *what gains* (in time, money, reduced difficulty, ability to make better choices) your users are able to make in comparison with alternative services (telephone, magazines etc.).

In the drug game example, only the answer to the first question is obvious. As for the second and third questions, there are several options. Are young people intended to use it in class as a general information system? Or just as a pastime? Or should they use it on Friday night just before going out, so as to remind them of what they learned in class? Or is it intended for students who don't bother to attend class, or who don't listen to what the teachers say, don't read the books and don't participate in group work?

The answer to the last question depends on your answers to the previous two questions. If the system is a pastime, it may bring the gain of having a laugh during class. If it is intended to bring new information, the value in this case was null, according to the students' reactions. If it is intended for students who for some reason do not digest the traditional material provided, it is beyond our knowledge of the actual system to assess the potential for success (although an educated guess would be that it takes more than a computer game to help in such a situation). If it is a reminder before going out, our guess is that it won't be used significantly at all in that situation.

### Select Your Audience

Not all people use electronic services now; the penetration of Web technology in the home varies from 1% to well over 30% in Western countries, depending on which country you live in (Holst *et al.*, 1999, p. 245). Connectivity from the workplace reaches 50% in some countries. Design services for people who use computers *now* and those who will become users *in the near future*. This means those who have easy and affordable access, are regular Internet users, and for whom you can provide useful services. Here, one consideration is again boot and login time – people who have their computers up and running and connected to a network all day (at work, mostly) are more likely to be regular service users than those who sit at home and have to boot and login each time. Some figures from Sweden illustrate this (Table 11.1).

*Do not let political correctness obscure reason.* Build services based only on user requirements and economic reason. The above-mentioned people may certainly be "haves" rather than "have-nots", but they are still the only audience you have at your

**Table 11.1** Percentage of Swedes using the Internet from work and from home in 1998 (adapted from Holst *et al.*, 1999, p. 214)

| Use | From work | From home |
|---|---|---|
| Daily | 43% | 26% |
| A couple of times per week | 24% | 31% |
| Once per week | 19% | 24% |
| More rarely | 14% | 19% |

disposal. Do not produce systems for the "elderly" or "handicapped" for political reasons only, without analyzing the need for the service. If there is such a need, you should of course respond to it, but not otherwise. If you do decide to implement a service for political reasons, be honest about your choice. Do not expect users to flock to it, or for you to make any economic gains from it.

We can see that self-service has great potential, but it is important to choose the right context. What you need to think about most of all is the usefulness of your services:

- How many of your users will access your electronic service over time? Is this an existing group, or a group that you hope will come to you? Is it an expanding group?

- What would be the ideal service your users could get? In the case of public services, it is necessary to consider the option of letting others provide a service.

- How will they come to it? Directly – by starting at your homepage – or indirectly, following a link from some other place? That is, do they follow the logic of your site or of someone else's? The answer is important for how independent of information given elsewhere in your site you will have to make each service or page.

- Why do they use the Web in general and your service in particular – are there synergies? Can you, for instance, make use of communities of some kind? Consider the way newspapers have users come to their site by providing interactive discussions on the Letters to the Editor page, chat or other methods.

- What kind of value-added services would be helpful for your electronic service? A simple example would include having a currency exchange calculator at a shopping site (very few have that). Value-added services to providers might include user polls, format conversion, publishing templates etc.

## Conclusions

The bottom line of this chapter has been that it is important to make sure that users gain benefits from using your system *now*. You can only win users by giving them a better alternative to current services.

*Build services on added user value.* Give users a genuine improvement of service. Make sure your users gain or save something by using your service. If the electronic version of a service does not save any of the user's effort or money, she will not use it.

*Do not let political correctness obscure reason.* Build services based only on user requirements and economic reason. Do not produce systems for some underprivileged group for political reasons without analyzing the need for the service. What you need to think about most of all is the usefulness of your services:

- How many of your users will access your electronic service over time?
- How will they come to it?
- Why do they use the Web in general and your service – are there synergies?

- What kind of value-added services would be helpful for your electronic service?
- What would be the ideal service your users could get? In the case of public services, it is necessary to consider the option of letting others provide a service.

*What you need to know:*

- Identify your main user groups (who are they, how many, what characteristics do they have?; age, sex, socio-economic status etc.).
- Identify *when* your user groups want to use the service (every day, weekly, once a year...).
- Identify *in what situation* your user groups will use your services (while working, from home, on the street).
- Identify what gains (in time, money and difficulty) your users are able to make, in comparison with alternative services (telephone, magazines etc.).

*Do you really want to provide this?*

While cities have services in many fields, neither the number of services nor the number of fields are determined automatically. Perhaps some of the services should be provided by others. There are public sector agencies at other levels (regional, national), and there are private companies that can do some of the things that you currently do (basically anything that does not have to do with the exertion of authority). Before you decide that this is *your* area, identify what your goals would be for entering, or staying in, this business.

*Set your goals*

- What would be the ideal composition of an ideal service for your users?
- What would be the ideal role of your organization in delivering it?
- Who would the other content providers be, and what would their roles be, in your ideal electronic service?
- What would the ideal workflow and interaction structure look like?

# 12. Challenge 12: Managing Administrative Tribes – Projects Don't Fail Because of Too Many Enemies, But Because of Too Few Friends

As human beings, we have only recently emerged from a tribal existence. Loyalty to your clan was the leading guarantee of human survival for thousands of years. This legacy sits deep within our subconscious, and is the source of much of the excitement, but also antagonism, at work.

One of the principal problems of modern society is the difficulty of identifying a tribe to belong to. We feel many sympathies and loyalties, and thereby identify ourselves with many different "tribes" of like-minded people. However, it is not uncommon that our various tribes end up in conflict among themselves. In such a situation, our loyalties are torn and we are forced to take sides, often against our will. Any significant perturbation in the working environment is likely to provoke a tribal challenge – and there are few other perturbations as potentially controversial as the process of replacing manual service patterns by electronic ones.

The stated goals and business practices of many professional organizations are widely disparate. As professionals, cardiologists do their best to help seriously ill people to attain an acceptable quality of life. More cardiologists should therefore imply better care for the ill. As a professional community, they try to protect the uniqueness and appreciation of their expert skills, which are both connected to the level of compensation that the community's members receive, by limiting access to the cardiology community.

Municipalities may openly wish to serve their members efficiently and well, always seeking ways of improving their service and cutting unnecessary costs. As a professional community, however, city officials do not want to rationalize away city jobs. Cities are reluctant to shed jobs because that would decrease state subsidy to the city, as well as its relative economic importance in a region. Shedding jobs might also aggravate a city's financial position by pushing former employees into the ranks of the unemployed.

In both of the above situations, members of the corresponding "professional clans" are torn between their loyalties to their explicit professional mission and to their professional community.

Introducing electronic services amounts to changing established service patterns. The professional staff influenced by such a perturbation will be divided by their tribal loyalty. If the tribal chief or council concludes that such services will do more harm than benefit to the tribal community, the electronic service will prove to be very cumbersome and awkward to use, and definitely too immature to be seriously considered for operational adoption.

## *Soap*: Broadband Telemedical Trials in Tapville

Tapville hosts the regional university hospital. With its broad base of medical specialists, the Tapville university hospital serves many a regional hospital and surgery in the surrounding towns and municipalities. This service is rather costly for one of the towns, Moulineux, because it is located two hours' drive away from Tapville. A radiologist from Tapville arrives at the town hospital of Moulineux once a week to produce reports on that week's X-rays. Because of the distance, he has to stay overnight in a hotel, and obviously spends up to five hours every time driving between Tapville and Moulineux.

One bright spring day, the Tapville head of the big national teleoperator suggests to the Tapville hospital director a trial application of broadband image transmission. He believes that their new digital broadband link, just built to connect Moulineux to the national data network, would be a very good vehicle for demonstrating the usefulness of broadband data transmission, possibly attracting industrial customers to subscribe to the service, too. The teleoperator is willing to offer the link for a telemedical trial at a very moderate price for a period of six months.

The hospital director catches on to the idea immediately. He is constantly under fire because the university hospital always ends up exceeding the costs budgeted for its services at Moulineux. This is, of course, only because there are more and more elderly and sick people in Moulineux, which is being hit by emigration of young people and immigration of elderly people from the surrounding countryside. For some reason, however, the fiercely infighting Moulineux politicians never seem to be realistic when budgeting for university hospital contract services.

A broadband telemedical trial at such a low cost would decrease the cost of the university hospital's services to Moulineux quite a bit. It would also demonstrate the hospital's special commitment to Moulineux, and not just Tapville. Since the trial will be the very first of its kind between a regional hospital and a university hospital in the country, it will also gather favourable public attention and portray the Tapville university hospital in a very innovative light.

After a couple of months' technical and contractual preparation, briefing the town mayor of Moulineux as well as the head of the health care office, a connection between the two hospitals is established. X-ray images are transmitted within an hour of being taken, in a digital format, to Tapville university hospital. The same radiologist that used to travel to Moulineux copies the images onto his workstation, writes a digital document and sends it back to Moulineux within 24 hours of receiving the image. He no longer has to travel to Moulineux, and also has the convenience of viewing the images at any suitable time.

The images are successfully copied from hard disk to hard disk, and the trial commences in an optimistic atmosphere, with quite a lot of press attention. After just a week, however, problems suddenly crop up. The image analysis software used to store the images at either end of the link is different. It appears that some images have been subtly distorted because of the conversion. The radiologist feels he cannot give a firm diagnosis in the case of a rare but fatal condition, involving metastatic activity of just such a scale of absorptive variation that is distorted in the image conversion process.

Also, the radiologist does not feel he can fulfil his sworn duty of signing the diagnosis statements. Without the signature, the statement is not strictly valid. Who will assume responsibility if there is a false diagnosis that he has not signed? Image transmission is fast, but the analysis workstations cannot cope with the conversion process, and it takes many minutes of waiting at the workstation for each image to be converted with the necessary degree of precision.

The radiologist insists that he should visit Moulineux at least once a fortnight anyway, in order to sign the statements printed there. During his visits, he will also inspect the original images for the possible appearance of the aforementioned dangerous metastatic condition.

On the other hand, since he will have to travel at least once a fortnight in any case, he could just as easily inspect all the images at the same time. The broadband transmission does not really provide any advantage over the old practice. The radiologist feels that after two months of rather unsuccessful attempts, the telemedical trial is really not worth pursuing any further, and should be discontinued.

The mayor of Moulineux and the head of the health care office are quite disappointed, although they must trust the special medical expertise of a seasoned and well-known radiologist. Instead of saving a monthly sum of €3000 in compensating the visiting radiologist for his travel time, hotel costs and extra hours spent staying overnight in Moulineux, they have simply incurred useless extra costs in time and money in the process.

# Tribal Wars in the City Office – of Clans and Electronic Services

It is not only individual interests that may distort the assessment of new electronic services. There is an even bigger issue of continuity and change. Continuous operational activities are managed by the hierarchical city administration. Development projects involving electronic services bring with them dynamic, young project managers who visit staff and users alike, making them modify well-established practices without first asking for management's permission. *Ad hoc* groups are formed to improve the prototype service. In such groups, spontaneous work teams agree on new working practices without consulting their management. There are many secondary activities, such as proper reporting, that are endangered by such spontaneous change.

Clashes do not have to be over major professional issues in order to arouse intense controversy. Very often, the fiercest opposition faces minuscule changes to work practices that touch everybody. Such battles take on a symbolic dimension, and may result in successful service development trials getting buried in the debris.

It is advisable for electronic services trials to move cautiously over uncharted organizational terrain. There is bound to be an office tribe watching over the land somewhere. Smelling suspicion before it is expressed openly is a critical project management skill for any innovative project manager. Such managers should defuse any such organizational landmines by open discussion before open confrontation. At the very least, project managers should safeguard themselves by asking for support from the management one layer above. In the end, however, the grassroots level is the decisive one. If the new service makes its users and providers happy, organizational strife can normally only delay its adoption, not block it completely.

"Tribes", as we have called them, are not necessarily groups of people of the same profession, a work team, a department, a task force, or any other formally authorized group. Although all these groups certainly form subcultures of some strength beyond their formal appointments, there are more invisible forms of informal organization. The concept of "communities of practice" refers to "a group of people who are informally bound to one another by exposure to a common class of problems" (Stewart, 1996). They can be found in a single organization, but a community may also be formed by people from different organizations that have a lot to do with each other. They are typically small groups (around 50 people seems to be the maximum), and they know each other well from having worked together for a long time. Such communities play a great role in the organization's operations. Sharing values and having mutual respect and a feeling of interdependence, they form communities for learning, but also for resisting change initiated elsewhere in the organization:

> It is likely that one of the reasons why many laudable initiatives fail is because they hit these invisible barriers. Take for example, a new reporting system (such as activity-based costing) or a new quality program. It is unlikely that either the finance or quality people will share the same community of practice as divisional mangers or frontline operators. Salespeople or engineers, for example, instead of seeing such initiatives as improvements to operating capability, may well see another "flavour of the month", with more work for no extra reward (in their eyes any benefits will accrue to someone else). The battle is not with the design of new ideas and initiatives, but with cross-cultural commitment (Hope and Hope 1997, p. 80).

Experiences from telework in other sectors indicate that mostly only highly productive employees seek to do part of their working hours at home. Mostly this is because it is difficult for active and busy employees to get down to written work assignments in the office, with a lot of meetings and phone calls interrupting their concentration. So the reason for formally defining teleworking rights is really not primarily a concern for an even distribution of workload. Rather, it is the impact of the void left by a missing employee at the office.

Uncertainty is a phenomenon generally abhorred by organizations built upon a presupposition of stability, such as city administrations. If there is lingering doubt about a lack of rules concerning any work practice, employees feel like trapeze artists without a safety net. Rules, to the majority of employees, are like a backbone that guarantees the stability of the entire working environment. Basically this is a consequence of the Western principle of Rule by Law, applied by public administrations.

The "Legal tribe" of employees is increasingly being sidestepped by the "Market tribe". The latter sees rules only as the means to an end of efficient, high-quality service to the customers: the citizens. The latter tribe prevails in a competitive situation, where several service providers compete for the same customers. The former establishes the rights of customers in a monopoly situation. Both therefore have a justification, but the balance between the two tribes varies as the role of city administrations evolves.

The following example of home shopping and IT management is an example of such a conflict.

> When the first Internet shop for daily grocery was opened in FarawayTown, staff from the retail chain's central IT office in Helsinki visited the pilot shop. After a long, detailed technical discussion, they concluded with the remark that "the pilot is very interesting and well organized – but it, of course, was not the proper way of building such systems". This remark was honest, since the central IT office was carrying out its own internal study on the possibility of implementing a teleshopping service within the structure of the central IT system of the retail chain.
>
> The study dragged on, however, because the central IT structure was very complex, and it proved very difficult to give definite answers on the feasibility of such a cross-application service that needed to integrate the products database with the central financial transaction system.
>
> The retail chain was owned and operated by regional cooperative companies. The regional companies grew increasingly impatient with the delays, especially when the competing retail chain also started setting up teleshops in the capital region. So the Helsinki regional cooperative company eventually ordered a FarawayTown style teleshop, against the wishes of the central IT office.

## Conclusion

A quote from Hope and Hope (1997) captures the essence of the tribal problem well: "The battle is not with the design of new ideas and initiatives, but with cross-cultural commitment" (p. 80).

There are in your organization tribes, or communities of practice as they are typically more politely called, that have their own interests, and form strong communities. These communities do not necessarily follow any organizational or professional borders: they are informal and arise among people who share problems and experiences. They are hard to discover, but since any change initiatives will have to be accepted by the tribes who will be affected by them, it is essential to recognize them and move cautiously on their territory. You cannot beat them; you can only win them over to your side.

One important tool in trying to do so is the insight that people do not resist change so much as they resist *being changed*. How, then to proceed? How to take tribal battlefields?

## How to Take Tribal Battlefields?

The first – quite striking – principle in tribal battles is that there are no conquests, just conversions. Beating the other tribe will gain nothing – converting it, even partially, to one's own tribe is the ultimate victory. There can therefore never be real battles either. In the end, most members of both tribes will still occupy the positions within the city administration that they held before. Any change in the *status quo* will have taken place in the minds of the staff members.

A second fundamental observation is that people mostly do not oppose change. They are simply afraid of it. Therefore the goal in taking a tribal battlefield must be to alleviate the fear of the enemy – not to enhance it. These two fundamental observations lead to a strategy that D'Herbemont and Cesar (1998) call the strategy of the Lateral Project.

A Lateral Project is appropriate in a situation where a project is sensitive, rather than technically challenging. Electronic services projects often fall into this category. In a sensitive project, the reactions and attitudes of the people involved are critical to the success of the project. Unlike in technically demanding projects, the appropriate method for managing sensitive projects is not careful planning and monitoring. It is flexibility. In a sensitive project, the management must be ready to constantly redefine the project's goals and approach if the feedback to the current plan is negative. The project moves its goalposts laterally, hence the name.

Some of the guidelines laid out by D'Herbemont and Cesar for managing lateral projects, which are very appropriate for projects developing electronic services, are the following:

- When the original project faces a slowdown or outright opposition – take a break. Stop forging ahead with the previous plan and allow the situation to settle down for a while.

- Listen to the opinions of the people affected by your project – both your allies and your opponents, as well as people that have an independent standpoint.

- Think how you could modify your project so as to make it appealing to a set of potential allies that are not dependent on you.

- Take the modified project to such potential allies for their discussion.

- If your plan meets with a favourable response, try to have these new potential allies take the "moral responsibility" for the success of the new project agenda, so that they will do their part when this is called for. They should be persuaded to do this voluntarily, without being pushed by you.

- Try again to get the project moving. If the attempt fails again, return to the first point and proceed down the steps yet another time.

Sensitive tribal battlefields are taken only by listening, adapting and sharing. Most sensitive projects do not fail because of staunch opposition. They fail if there are not enough allies for the project.

In the case of most projects, most of the people involved do not wish to be actively engaged, yet will have an opinion on them. These people form the passive majority. We are all passive with respect to issues that are not on our personal agenda, yet will normally have an opinion on them. The passive majority among the people involved ultimately decides the fate of any sensitive project.

The passive majority is most effectively convinced by people who have an active but independent interest in the issues that a project manager proposes. Such people are seen as independent judges, but they can become the best salespeople of a project manager if he is able to prove to them that they, too, will benefit if the project succeeds. If the original project plan does not convince them of this, it must be modified so as to correspond to the interests of such independent actors. This is possibly the single most important piece of guidance that can be given to a project manager in charge of a telematic development project.

# 13. Conclusions From the Dozen Challenges

In the first part of this book, we have outlined a series of challenges based on experiences from cities and other organizations that have spent several years on the road towards implementing electronic services. As we look at the challenges, we can see that each has a particular focus.

1. The *"Start-up... of what?"* challenge. Here, the problem was a lack of sufficiently common goals to form a city-wide policy for the forthcoming years of development. This is a strategy issue, but one that does not appear clear at first. The crux, and the need, is to find some common, realistic and reasonably well-defined goal for the electronic services. The Web *is* a cuckoo in the nest; you had better realize that it will grow.

2. The *"Thousands of pages"* challenge. Here, the problem was how to organize Web maintenance rationally – again a management issue. Although it concerns how to organize procedures effectively, it includes strategic elements. We saw that this challenge could not be met in a durable way if there was not a reasonably good solution to Challenge 1.

3. The *"Messy appearance"* challenge. As systems grow big and there are multiple information providers, responsibility for information provision and updating is delegated, which tends to result in the different departments all wanting to do things their way. This is a problem of understanding the users – what design works best? What ways of interacting with the organization are preferred? – but also one of organization; common standards – at a reasonable level of detail – must be employed everywhere. This is to some degree a management issue, in that a learning process concerning these matters will have to be implemented.

4. The *"Parallel systems"* challenge. Because electronic services typically expand as projects, detached from the ordinary business, the development typically does not lead to a decrease in the resources spent on delivering services manually. Rather, as new activities are started, people are committed to their development, so they tend to prevail. Old systems also prevail because of the argument that "not everyone has access...". The trick is to see to it that the new activities complement or replace the old ones instead of just copying them. Again, this is an organizational issue, and one dependent on the solution of Challenge 1.

5. The *"Future technical platform"* challenge. The obvious problem is one of choosing the technology: Web platforms, distribution channels, required functionality, competence requirements etc. But behind this conspicuous

problem lies one that is more subtle, yet crucial, since it greatly influences the choices. This is the problem of choosing metaphors: what *is* this thing we want to build – a magazine, a database, a catalogue, a forum, a pipeline or what?

6. The "*Cross-departmental integration*" challenge. Here, the problem was to organize in such a way that resources could be smoothly shared among different city departments. Obstacles are typically departmental reforms, rules for internal charges etc. Again, this is an organizational issue, and one dependent on the solution of Challenge 1.

7. The "*Staff motivation*" challenge. When genuine operational Web services come to be suggested, the staff involved realize that this will affect their roles. This challenge is an organizational one, which can only be met by undertaking a serious discussion of the professionals' role in the new organization with those involved. Many of these issues can be solved at lower managerial levels, but if a major organizational overhaul is due, the issue is definitely strategic. Starting too late is dangerous, but so is starting too early and exaggerating the changes.

8. The "*Poor usability*" challenge. This problem is one of understanding the service's users. Who are the people that will use your electronic services? What knowledge do they have and what do they *not* have? In what situations do they use your system? What do they look for? How do they look? These are examples of the questions that a service provider needs to answer in order to be able to design services properly. This is most of all an issue for the professionals and management at the operational and tactical levels. But here, too, if major changes are initiated, the issue becomes one of strategic interest.

9. The "*Where is the payoff?*" challenge. Most potential Internet service providers find the economic assessment of their services a daunting task. Measuring results in a reasonable way is very hard, and the risk of applying simplistic measurements and measuring the wrong things is apparent. Clarity is necessary; you must dare to say what you want to achieve, and you must be able to show that you have done so in concrete terms. The issue here is to incorporate the values of electronic services into the economic thinking of the organization – definitely a task for top management.

10. The "*What is our role?*" challenge. This is an issue of understanding the needs of service users. Many cities do not realize that they act in a competitive environment. City organizations, and staff, are used to working in a monopoly environment. They are not used to thinking about what users look for, how they look, and so on. This challenge is only met when the city finds its role, its market niche. Different cities may assume different roles; not every city needs to provide every possible service.

11. The "*Where are the users?*" challenge. In many cities, people ask themselves about their Web systems: "There is not much use yet – when will it come?". This is, again, an organizational issue pertaining to strategy; one problem is that cities aren't concentrating on finding and packaging local content, one of the crucial catalysts for getting people online. Related to this is the problem of understanding what is useful for users. A Web system competes with other media: magazines, TV, radio and others. Users will go on using these media until they find that your new system is more useful to them than the other available

media. Public–private partnerships have often proved useful. This issue is definitely a strategic one.

12. The "*Managing administrative tribes*" challenge. Introducing electronic services amounts to changing established service patterns, which will impinge on the tribal territories of the professional staff. Having a nose for upcoming tribal wars before they break out is a crucial issue, especially for local/operative management – one of understanding people.

Summarizing the nature of the challenges, we can see that they fall into four areas (Table 13.1).

In looking at the classification of challenges into the four main topics (users, organization, economy and technology), a striking observation can be made:

Of the challenges identified, 10 out of 12 belong to the area of users and usability of electronic services and the ensuing organizational problems that arise when trying to serve users. It is therefor fair to say that the challenges of use and usability are the most prominent and the organizational ones come second, because they follow from the former. Third place is occupied by economic challenges. Technological problems rank as the least prominent source of problems. The two latter types cause one challenge each, but the one about economic assessment is harder to resolve.

Against this observation, it is curious to notice that most often electronic services are developed under the leadership of the city IT department, whose main expertise is technology. Indeed, a crucial conclusion that summarizes most of the lessons learned by the authors of this book from developing electronic services is that, in order to succeed, an organization is needed that looks first and foremost at issues of:

**Table 13.1** Classification of the 12 challenges

| Challenge No./issue | Users | Organization | Economy | Technology |
|---|---|---|---|---|
| 1  Finding a strategy | | X | | |
| 2  Organization of procedures | | X | | |
| 3  Understanding what design suits users best<br>Organizing a common design | X | X | | |
| 4  Cutting down on old services as electronic ones expand | | X | | |
| 5  Choosing future technical platform | | | | X |
| 6  Organize for smooth sharing of resources among departments | | X | | |
| 7  Staff motivation | | X | | |
| 8  Usability | X | | | |
| 9  Developing and applying models for assessment of electronic services | | | X | |
| 10  Finding the appropriate role for the organization | X | | | |
| 11  Usefulness – creating added value | X | | | |
| 12  Managing tribes | | X | | |

1.  How to get users to use services.
2.  How to organize their production successfully.

We will call such an organization an *Electronic Service Manager*.

This is a point that we have encountered in many projects; it is very common for people to set out on "IT projects" or "system development projects", only to find that most problems have nothing to do with IT, but are to do with people and with organization. Electronic services projects are organizational projects.

An organization that embarks on the road towards offering comprehensive electronic services will have to prepare to overcome all of the 12 challenges. This means that there are four areas that must be addressed simultaneously, and in a way that makes developments in all areas go well together. This is of course a problem in any city. Typically, neither expertise in, nor responsibility for, all these areas can be found in a single city department; all topics must be dealt with in an organization-wide manner, starting at the top managerial level.

However, the novelty of the medium makes it hard to introduce all these issues directly into the standard procedures of management. Therefore, in many, if not most, cases, there is a need for a special entity specializing in "Electronic Service Management" (Fig. 13.1). This is our name for the whole process of not only bundling services from different service providers and publishing them in a coherent fashion, but also providing support to service providers during the process of inventing, refining and evaluating services and improving operations. In short, Electronic Service Management means being aware of the dozen challenges and making strategies and solving problems that come up in ways that do not just aim at overcoming

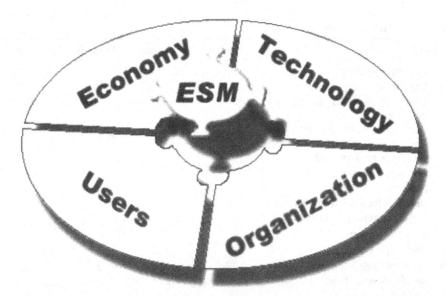

**Fig. 13.1** An Electronic Service Manager, ESM, is an organization linking service providers to their users by providing expertise in four important areas: users and usability, organization, economy and technology. One major conclusion from our line-up of cases is that the different areas are in fact very differently sized, with Organization and Users being biggest (where the size is determined both by the number of challenges pertaining to a certain area and the complexity involved in resolving the challenges).

one challenge at a time, but which focus on overcoming them all without too many backward steps having to be taken.

Part 2 of this book examines the role and activities of an Electronic Services Manager.

## Do We Really Have to Deal with All These Challenges?

We have introduced a large number of challenges, some of them relatively complicated to meet. Does every organization really have to take all these steps? The simple answer is no: you may settle for a system that is less invasive in organizational matters, but this system is probably also less useful, both for you and for your users.

As we discussed in Challenge 5, there are different levels of services (basically the following four), which are characterized by increasing complexity and cost:

1. *Static Web content*, "pages". These are used for advertising products and announcing news.
2. *Dynamic Web content.* When the content of a site gets too vast, too complex to get an overview of, or changes so frequently that updating the Web becomes a problem, data must be collected from databases, already existing or specifically designed for the new Web service, based on queries from a search engine.
3. *Interactive electronic services.* Many organizations would save a lot of work if users themselves could provide input to the system. Examples include requests for product information, government forms and applications for standard items such as birth certificates.
4. *Integrated electronic service processes.* When services of type 3 above become integrated in office routines in an automatic way (integration with workflow systems and decision-making processes) we may talk about integrated services. Simple examples include telephone voice menus by which you can order a birth certificate, which is printed and placed in an envelope automatically (but which today is typically mailed manually for security reasons – to make sure it reaches the person whose personal identification number was given even if the request was in fact made by someone else).

As we see in Table 13.2 – not surprisingly! – the more ambitious the plans for the service system, the more challenges there are to deal with. We must also recall that the complexity of the challenges generally increases with their number. The first three are fairly simple to solve. Numbers 4, 6, 7 and 9 are very problematic, but still rather easy to understand because they deal with tangible things like internal costs for using information from another department, deciding how to economically assess systems, deciding if, when, and on what conditions a new system should replace an old one etc. Challenges 5 and 8 should not be too complex, but if system construction has gone on for a long time, changes may be very costly and cause controversy among individuals and departments.

Challenges 10 and 12 are different. In the first case, it is about changing an organizational culture. This is hard, and it takes time. In the case of Challenge 12, it is even

**Table 13.2** The 12 challenges mapped onto the different kinds of system. Note that "Yes" means that the challenge must be met, but just once (if well managed). If a "Yes" appears in more than one cell on the same row, it does not mean the challenge reappears. For instance, challenges 1, 2 and 3 will appear whatever type of system you go for. However, a later change from static Web content to dynamic Web content should not cause the startup challenge to reappear

| Challenge | Type of system | | | | Comments on the "no's" |
|---|---|---|---|---|---|
| | 1. Static Web content | 2. Dynamic Web content | 3. Interactive electronic services | 4. Integrated electronic service processes | |
| 1. Start-up | Yes | Yes | Yes | Yes | |
| 2. 1000 pages | Yes | Yes | Yes | Yes | |
| 3. Messy appearance | Yes | Yes | Yes | Yes | |
| 4. Parallel systems | Not likely | Yes | Yes | Yes | Type 1 systems typically cost little, unless very big, and if costs are wisely distributed, the parallelism which will no doubt be there will not be seen as a problem |
| 5. Future technical platform | Not likely | Yes | Yes | Yes | Only with big systems, where many people are involved in updating, and things like change of editors may be problematic. A wise organization should easily avoid this challenge for type 1 systems, although especially early starters sometimes have had problems. |
| 6. Data integration | No | Yes | Yes | Yes | As long as the Web is seen as a tool for the individual to use at will, and data can be co-used without technical integration or cost. |
| 7. Staff motivation | No | Yes | Yes | Yes | As long as the Web is seen as a tool for the individual to use at will, staff will be happy as they typically see the new tool as an asset that increases their capability. |
| 8. Poor usability | Yes but no | Yes | Yes | Yes | Usability applies to all types of systems, but because the investment is low in the first case, and systems really don't replace anything, nobody will bother much to investigate usability. This challenge thus does apply to type 1 systems, but will typically not be detected. |

| | | | | | |
|---|---|---|---|---|---|
| 9. Where is the payoff? | No | Not likely | Yes | Yes | Asking for payoff requires some significant amount of investment, and in the first case, often also in the second, costs are so small they are typically handled within a single department. Increase in the investment, as well as a change of manager, will change the situation. |
| 10. From monopoly to service provider | No | No | Yes | Yes | A change in attitude may certainly occur also in the two first cases, but because the change typically does not concern changes at the organizational level, but rather is something each individual can handle herself, the problem does not necessarily appear as a challenge. |
| 11. Where are the users? | No | Possibly | Yes | Yes | The eagerness to see much use – which means asking for less use of similar services in some other medium – increases with the size of the investment, and in the first case, often also in the second, costs are so small they are typically handled within a single department. |
| 12. Administrative tribes | No | No | No | Yes | Though disputes may occur in connection with all types of systems, it is only when organizational routines are dramatically changed that the stakes get so high tribal wars are worth fighting. |
| Number of challenges having to be overcome: | 4 | 8–9 | 11 | 12 | |

worse. This is about changing the culture of a group, the existence of which you may not even be aware of (but certainly will be as soon as you try to do something that intrudes on what they perceive as their territory).

# Part 2

*Electronic Service Management*

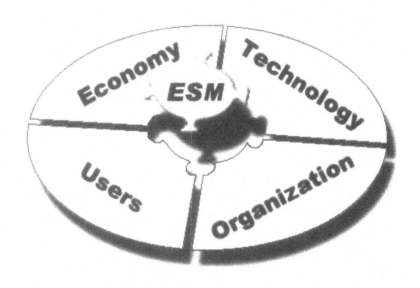

# 14. Introduction to Part 2

*To make it possible to read Part 2 independently of Part 1, the first section of this part summarizes some of the conclusions we made at the end of Part 1.*

As we have seen in Part 1 of this book, a number of challenges occur on the road towards offering electronic services. We do not claim that in every organization each of them escalates to the level of what people perceive as a crisis. Neither do we claim that the challenges necessarily appear in this order (although generally they seem to). As an example, late starters may be better off than those who started in 1994, because there are now better tools available for the construction and administration of Web sites, and some of the challenges may therefore be more easily avoided, for instance, the "thousand pages" one. On the other hand, late starters will not be able to benefit from the bonanza of the early Internet years, and will have to show results more quickly; that is, tackle the latter challenges, such as "Where are the users?" and "Where is the payoff?".

Still, the issues we brought up are such that any organization attempting electronic service delivery must consider them and make judicious choices based on adapting the emerging technology and experiences from use elsewhere to the local situation. In this part of the book, we will discuss Electronic Service Management, by which we mean a dedicated "publishing" function that we have found is necessary to be able to take an organization through the dozen challenges.

Summarizing the nature of the challenges, we saw in Part 1 that they fall into four areas:

- *Users*: No. 3 (understanding what design suits users best), No. 8 (usability), No. 10 (understanding the needs of service users), No. 11 (where are the users?)
- *Organization*: No. 1 (strategy), No. 2 (organization of procedures), No. 3, partly (organizing a common design), No. 4 (cutting down on old services as electronic ones expand), No. 6 (organize smooth sharing of resources among departments), No. 7 (staff motivation), No. 12 (tribes)
- *Economy*: No. 9 (developing models for assessment of electronic services)
- *Technology*: No. 5 (future technical platform)

Looking at the classification of challenges into the four main topics (users, organization, economy and technology), we made the observation that:

> Of the challenges identified, 10 out of 12 belong to the area of users and usability of electronic services and the ensuing organizational problems that arise when trying to serve users. It is therefor fair to say that the challenges of use and usability are the most prominent and the organizational ones come second, because they follow from the former. Third place is occupied by economic challenges. Technological problems rank

as the least prominent source of problems. The two latter types cause one challenge each, but the one about economic assessment is harder to resolve.

Based on our findings that:

Technical matters do not pose the biggest problems. The most important are user issues and organizational issues, in that order, because organization must be done according to users' requirements, behaviour and preferences

we drew the conclusion that:

In order to succeed in developing public electronic services, an organization is needed that looks first and foremost at issues of how to get users to use services, and how to organize their production successfully.

As we saw, most issues pertain to organizational matters, concerning either strategy or implementation. The second highest number of challenges concerns understanding users, what they require and how the services and system design meet those requirements. The organization that embarks on the road towards offering comprehensive electronic services will have to prepare to overcome all of the 12 challenges. This means that there are four areas that must be addressed simultaneously, and in a way that makes developments in all areas go well together. This is a problem in any city. Typically, neither expertise in, nor responsibility for, all these areas can be found in a single city department; all the topics must be dealt with in an organization-wide manner, starting at the top managerial level.

However, the novelty of the medium typically makes it hard to introduce all these issues directly into the standard procedures of management (yes, even today!). Therefore, we claimed that there is a need for a special entity specializing in "Electronic Service Management" (ESM). This was our name for the whole process of not only bundling services from different service providers and publishing them in a coherent fashion, but also of providing value-added services and support to service providers during the process of inventing, refining and evaluating services, and improving operations. In short, ESM means being aware of the dozen challenges and making strategies and solving problems that come up in ways that aim not only at overcoming one challenge at a time, but which focus on overcoming them all without too many backward steps having to be taken.

Before elaborating on the ESM concept, let us look at recent developments on the Internet, where we will find more that supports our arguments.


# Digital Communities and Local Communities

Recent developments on the Internet have emphasized the role of *portals*. Portals are gateways to Web-based services that people use. Most of us start our Web roamings by first logging on to some homepage that is common to many people, before moving on to searching for something else. Both our first homepage and the search engine homepage act as portals. Many advertisers are already using this opportunity to try to sell us some new products or services. Browsers today come with a prepro-grammed start page, the manufacturer's own portal.

Portals appear at many levels, though. Any Web site that contains a collection of information, such as news or links that interest some group of people, is a portal. People use many portals, depending on their interests. Local interest is central to people's daily lives, and any Web site that links to many local services can be a very powerful portal. An organization that hosts such a Web site is a *Local Electronic Service Publisher*.

The business of a local electronic service publisher is to collect so many interesting services onto its Web site that many people will come and search for these from its homepage. After attaining such a position – and only then – it is also possible to charge service providers, and possibly even users, for a presence on the homepage. Portals channel the routes that users take to services. If there is no portal to lead users to a service, the service may never find the road to its users.

A portal can also be much more than just a mall. It may be a virtual meeting point of a *community* of people. A meeting point must facilitate collective discussion, as well as the exchange of private messages. It must contain archives and interactive services for its members, independent of whether or not the latter are formally identified.

In the case of local communities, local interest provides a good defining structure for a community. However, since the content providers for such a local portal are organizations that target the same group of individual users with very different kinds of approaches and attitudes, a local electronic service provider must fulfil a range of roles outside the Web site. Examples of such roles are:

- Achieving good public–private partnerships in setting up and providing content to a local portal.
- Setting an example to local businesses on how to put services on the Internet, thereby helping them modernize their business models.
- Attracting individual users and potential content providers to the portal by offering them concrete financial incentives when doing so.

A city, as a dominant public authority in its area, is often in a good position to adopt a leading role in creating a local digital community around a local portal.

Services where a broad range of local activities are needed are, for example, cross-organizational telematic care and education processes. In both cases, many different local and sometimes non-local actors need to agree on a common information exchange and transmission process. A good agreement will result in both savings in cost and improvements in service quality to users. A city may be the unique local organization in a position to create a platform for such negotiations.

Another advantage that public portals may have is an emphasis on universal access, covering all social classes of people. A good portal should be very easy and intuitive to use. It may include free email and messaging services, picture archival and other services, implemented in such a way that users do not need to own a computer to use them.

It may well be that for various reasons, such as availability of interest, investment resources or technical skills and equipment, a city may end up yielding the role of a local Electronic Service Manager to another organization. Suitable candidates may be local newspapers with a Web edition, Internet service providers, or sometimes even national or international portals. The city should, however, see to it that a local electronic service provider does emerge from somewhere in the reasonably near future, in order to get its own electronic services used by the citizens.

## The ESM Concept

An ESM, Electronic Service Manager, is an entity that provides a general framework for publishing electronic services that are produced by others: service providers. An ESM is a well-defined role, but organizational implementations may vary; the ESM may be a company, an organizational unit or a responsibility within some existing organizational unit.

An ESM is necessary because individual service providers are often not big enough to carry on the whole way through all the challenges. Earlier we invented the term "the iceberg syndrome" for this. The concept refers to what we have seen in many projects: organizations who want to develop electronic services often – typically – set out on "a systems development project", or "an IT project", only to find – they all do – that in fact they have embarked on an advanced project of organizational change. From the start, all the organizational and human problems to come are concealed from them; they see only the technical gadgets necessary. They talk about fibre optics, megabits of transfer speed, homepages, applets and firewalls, and not too often about use, users and quality of services. When it is realized that these problems are in fact the hardest, the project period is over. And anyway, seriously digging into the user issues was not at the top of the agenda from the beginning.

As we saw in Part 1, there are in fact a lot of tricky issues that will have to be dealt with. Many of those issues need an organization of some scale for them to be dealt with properly. This is the reason we suggest the concept of ESM. There are a number of things an ESM must be competent about in order to increase the quality, reach and profitability of services under its roof, including the following:

- It must have, and constantly update, a clear view of customers and users.
- It must serve as a value-adding link between service providers and their customers, for instance by providing general value-added services (such that they can be used across services: search tools, user studies, market surveys, format conversion for different media etc.).
- It must understand how to make work processes more efficient and assist its service providers in doing so.
- It must have technical, organizational and marketing expertise.
- It must contribute to achieving advantages of scale by bundling several services together using a common concept for service delivery.
- In contrast to global electronic service publishers, such as America Online, it should be a local and/or regional concept, publishing services in a way that promotes local/regional competitiveness as well as small and medium enterprises and cooperation and creative partnerships, whether public–private partnerships or some other type.
- It must be able to cope with the rapid technological changes on the Internet.

- It must engage in more than just actions in the electronic medium alone, for instance promotion in other media.

- It must take into account, in marketing as well as in services, that the different ways of doing this stem from the multicultural societies of Europe.

- It must concentrate on effective publishing and strive to reshape any underlying processes when necessary.

- It can promote services in a more powerful way than information providers can do themselves, because of economies of scale.

- Because of scale, it can invest in software tools, statistical analyses, design issues, user studies and other things necessary for the business.

- It must have direct contact with the end users in order to get a clear overview of what is still missing in offering a bouquet of services and help devices.

- It should be a speaking partner with providers of hardware, software and infrastructure.

- It must not have the overheads that information providers have, so as to be able to offer services at competitive prices.

An ESM, then, is not just a concept for a city to produce Web systems. It is a more general business concept aimed at helping the many, many small (mostly) service providers in cities and small businesses into the Information Age. In the next chapter we shall dwell on this aspect of it for a while.

# 15. Cities and the Local Information Society

Electronic service management is not just a matter for the individual city or region involved. There is a wider political issue pertaining to the problem of how to organize the trade as a whole: how the many small companies that work mainly locally or regionally can find ways into the Information Society. Here, we briefly discuss this issue.

## Cities and Electronic Service Processes

Cities are a focal point in people's lives as well as a public sector organization. Cities are responsible for a large share of the most important services needed by citizens, such as education, health care and social services. Although the roles of cities differ in different countries, their importance is significant everywhere. The cities also play an important economic role in their regions.

Information and telecommunication technologies are changing the conditions for many services and business activities. Such changes produce both threats and opportunities to national and regional economies, as well as public services. Some important examples of such changes are the following:

- With the advent of the Internet, cities have a new way of accessing a rapidly growing percentage of their citizens. Cities can both improve their services to citizens and make them economically more efficient by using Internet technologies, but adopting an electronic service model is by no means simple. Stable telematic working patterns are difficult to find for any city department, and yet many departments are solving the same technical and organizational problems each at the same time. Not only is this wasteful, but it also results in divergent Web practices in different city departments. It is very difficult for citizens to navigate through the Web of different web sites of even a single city. Moreover, the best electronic services are often cross-departmental in city administration.

- Sales of non-perishable goods on the Internet are quickly becoming a transnational business. Many online service providers get their revenue from granting exclusive sales rights for goods and services to a single company. Examples of such agreements are those granted by America Online to a single bookstore or to a single music shop worldwide. There are, in fact, arguments to say that the Internet is one of the most centralizing technologies ever. The current "portal" struggle is one example. Over the past years we have seen Web search engines becoming ever more overloaded with commercial advertisements. Currently, many have stepped up the struggle by providing "portals", which go far beyond company information and an effective search engine. The companies engaging in this business are not only the browser manufacturers, Netscape and Microsoft, and the companies specializing in searching on the Net, Excite and Yahoo, but also the magazine group Ziff-Davis, dedicated companies such as Intuit and CMPnet, and the security company Network Associates. The portals are intended as starting points for visiting the Net. Competition leads portal managers to provide bonuses to users, such as the option to create personal homepages and free email addresses. Portals have different focuses: branch focus (like Intuit's SME portal or Telia's Swedish School Net), special interest (like ZDNet's focus on computers and the Internet) or local focuses. Competition is tough, often leading to active promotion activities; one example is Netscape's lottery, where users can win TVs or DVD players – if they go there regularly and check.

If most online communities that people spend time in are global, local businesses will be effectively excluded from doing business on the Internet. Advertising revenue on the Internet is already more concentrated on only a few sites than in any other medium. Such virtual communities have no local identity, and cities have no role in them.

- In many Western countries the population is getting older. An increasing number of old people means an increasing need for social and health care. Yet the basis of tax revenue, from which public health and social services are funded, keeps diminishing. We must find more efficient ways of looking after the elderly than keeping them in hospitals. Electronic technology will help in this, allowing for information, emergency procedures and communication to proceed efficiently, even from home.

Developments such as the ones described above deserve the serious attention of cities in countries where the electronic medium is by now quickly becoming a standard service delivery channel.


## ESM Development Issues

As we have seen in Part 1 this book, the creation of electronic services can be both costly and tricky. We have seen that most of the problems in running electronic services are not technical, but rather organizational, social and economic. We also saw that the problems are quite similar everywhere.

All cities have basically the same tasks (serving an ageing population while not being able to increase budgets; promoting local business and culture). They don't compete directly with each other, therefore they can easily join networks to cooperate on ESM matters. Cooperation might include benchmarking, pooling of resources for endurance etc.

There is therefore both a need and fertile ground for an entity able to bring together organizations with an interest in electronic service provision for citizens in a city or a region and jointly walk the road through the "dozen challenges". Such organizations would be cities, teleoperators, newspapers, cable TV companies, universities, consultants, Internet service providers and Internet software providers. While it is clear that the composition of partners may look different in different cities and regions, the basic need remains the same.

The Electronic Service Manager was described in the previous chapter as a business concept. But it is more than that. It is also a concept that is necessary for creating the necessary cooperation among cities on issues that are crucial for the local societies. Individual ESMs are not enough for this task; there is a strong case for cooperation among ESMs through ESM development networking.

We saw in Part 1 that an ESM needs to focus on social, technical, economic and organizational questions related to restructuring city activities for the Information Age. Beyond being good business, the "Association of ESMs" should focus on the improvement of services from a societal perspective. Beyond developing services, such an association should engage in studies of services and service improvement processes. Studies should be devoted to concrete technical and service themes, such as:

- How to revise health and social care for home patients, with electronic service processes coupled to service restructuring.
- How to make electronic services pay back the investment needed in setting them up.
- How to process electronic forms in city administration – legal and organizational issues.
- What technical paradigm to adopt in restructuring service processes to take advantage of telematic technology.
- How to use Web communities to reach the citizens. Community building has hitherto been a largely private matter, and cities have not been prominent participants. But if local political professional societies want to stay in business, they will have to engage somehow in bringing their business to the Web, because that is where their constituencies are to an ever larger extent.
- A special European challenge: how to ease the path of Central and Eastern European countries into the European Union by helping them improve their deficient public service structure with telematic technology.
- How to carry out the integration of cross-departmental electronic service processes without causing inter-departmental strife that stops the process.
- How to make EU-funded and national development projects have a lasting impact in cities, using them as a catalyst for a service paradigm shift?

Compared with going it alone, cities, but also individual ESMs, will receive concrete benefits when tackling issues such as those above because several necessary activities can be carried out jointly, for example:

- Focus Study Groups, arranged jointly with technology providers. The findings of such study groups should be edited into state-of-the-art reports, featuring recommendations to cities.
- Training seminars for city staff on planning and implementing electronic services.

- Fund-raising for electronic services trials.
- Evaluation studies on the feasibility and usability of electronic services in a given field.
- Consultation on implementation strategies for electronic services.
- Planning, organizing and implementing electronic service pilots for cities.

Many of these activities are such that they can hardly be undertaken by a small service provider, or a small ESM, alone. On the other hand, results from user studies and pilot implementations can often be used across many services and many organizations.

In summary, ESM activities have a technical and a local focus. The technical component includes activities ranging from computer applications to user studies and can be undertaken in cooperation with other ESMs, while the local component, focusing on the promotion of local communities, business partnerships and value chains, must be developed within the local context (Fig. 15.1).

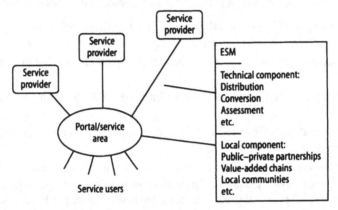

**Fig. 15.1**  A local ESM provides technical support to service providers and promotes local business partnerships and local communities.

# ESM Activities

Looking at the four activity areas of ESM activities – users, technology, organization and economy – we can see that there is a need for activities on several levels (summarized in Table 15.1). Some of these are appropriate for single ESMs, while a few may only apply to big ones or to ESMs in association.

One thing that is clear is that most organizations today focus on just a small part of the table, in particular the production level and the technology focus. Very few EU projects, for instance, deal with organizational change, usefulness studies, or even usability issues. The way to get funding is to propose the development of a new technical tool, not to study users or experiment with service designs. Success is often measured by simplistic "hit" counts without much analysis of who the users are, what they actually used the site for, or even how they used it (for instance by studying the "click track" they made).

**Table 15.1** ESM activities.

| | Activity areas | | | |
| --- | --- | --- | --- | --- |
| | Users | Technology | Organization | Economy |
| Policy level | Promoting the idea of usability and usefulness studies | Software development partnerships<br><br>Usability championship | Promoting a common service model | Promoting the idea of building economic models for assessing investments in TS |
| Production level | Support in realizing improvements based on the below studies | Advice and support concerning software modules | Assisting in implementing ESM strategy<br><br>Assisting in setting up ESM strategy<br><br>Organising a user community and facilities | Assisting in setting up assessment model |
| Analysis level | Usefulness studies<br>Usability studies | Assessing technical infrastructure | Assessing organizational infrastructure | Assessing ESM system |

Let us now take a look at the contents of the above table. What needs to be done in each activity area at each level, how and why?

*Note*: in the following, the logic of the narrative is the typical order in which things have to be done in real life. This means that the order of things is a little different from that in the perfectly hierarchical order of the table.

## Users

Clearly, so far not many cities have seriously engaged in user studies. This is unlike many businesses, who often spend considerable resources on usability testing and "focus groups", inviting users to air their opinions on services and site design. This is most often because cities have not yet come to that stage in their Web development projects. Typically, cities would be found having passed Challenges 1–3, with many by now engaged in overcoming Challenge 4, keeping an eye on Challenge 5, and possibly entering Challenge 6. Certainly very few have spent much effort on overcoming Challenges 8–12. Challenges 8 (usability), 10 (understanding needs of service users), and 11 (where are the users?) belong to the "users" field, and so should be the natural upcoming focus of interest for most of the cities who have already spent some time in the electronic information and services business.

One problem here is that cities often have problems engaging in user studies and user requirements analyses because they, unlike business, most often don't see their relationship to citizens as one of service, but rather one of exertion of authority. Although service is certainly not the only aspect of citizen–authority interaction, it is definitely an underdeveloped one. An important task for an ESM is therefore to introduce and promote a service attitude, paying attention to users' requirements and activities. This includes a number of activities at the *policy level*, such as by means of seminars, discussions, good examples and service quality development programmes promoting the idea of users and services. But policy level activities often need material backing to be taken seriously by a sceptical audience. One way of getting such backing is actually to do some user studies (*analysis level*). Because user studies elsewhere tend not to have too much credibility because people tend to feel "we have a special situation here", it is important to do studies at home.

User studies need not be very expensive or require lots of work. Often even limited studies can provide useful input to seminars and quality development programmes. It is important to go beyond the log files' hit counts, which typically provide very little information on users. Two examples of activities that do provide useful information are usability studies and usefulness studies.

### Usability Studies

Usability refers to the ability of a Web (or other system) to be easily understood and used by users (of the target group). Very few organizations have made studies of the usability of their systems, although it is a standard procedure in product development. Usability studies need not be complicated or expensive. They can be made at three distinct levels, each of which can be most useful depending on the ambition and the situation at hand.

1.  *Expert assessment.* The system is tested by an expert on usability. The result is that the system is "benchmarked" against the state of the art in the field, best practices and findings in human–computer interaction. Typically, such a test provides new ideas for service providers.

2.  *Pilot tests*, in which a few users, selected from the target user group, use the system under observation. They are given prearranged tasks that test critical features of the system. The result is the above plus a fair knowledge of how the prospected users will use the system. Although such a test does not provide figures on how many users do this or that, they often give good indications of where and why users get lost, what they see and what they don't see, why they go to one place and not another etc.

3.  *Complete tests*, in which there are a relatively large number of users, representing at least the most relevant target groups. Factors such as age, sex, education, economic status, frequency of use etc., are typical variables. The result is the above plus metrics: "25% of users under 40 use this service", "80% of users never observe this service", "90% of the users need more than 12 minutes to fill in this form, and typically never fill it in completely" etc.

Experience shows that the first two levels are most often enough. They are relatively cheap and produce enough results to improve services and system design. The third level is typically not (yet) so interesting to cities, because their systems are not stable, and both use and technical solutions on the Web change rapidly. It may not seem a good idea to spend much money on evaluating something that changes so rapidly and significantly. Because a large number of users are necessary, the cost increases a lot, and the results are not worth the extra effort unless there is a well-defined product. In such situations, on the other hand, it makes good sense.

## Usefulness Studies

Usefulness refers to the competitive advantage, from a user point of view, of a service compared with other similar services. Here we are not only concerned with the usability of a service. Although this plays a part, the focus here is on the user situation. Consider a user having to take care of a particular task. What options does she have? Suppose there is a choice between using the telephone and using the Internet. Why would that user prefer the Internet over the phone? Reasonable criteria for the choice include those that pertain to the medium, the service and the user:

- *The medium*: cost in money and time, accessibility, ease of finding the correct source to information, reliability (that the medium will work technically)
- *The service*: quality of information and service encountered, credibility (the degree of trust the service enjoys in the user community)
- *The user*: familiarity with the medium, habits, attitudes and personal preferences

New media typically lose out on criteria like habits and familiarity with the medium, so they have to compensate by being better on other criteria. To be very frank, there are currently very few government Webs that can beat the telephone on either of the above criteria where typical activities are concerned. Obtaining forms, for example, is done much more quickly by automatic telephone systems with voice menus. Slow sites and non-trivial navigation makes the city's operator a much quicker way to find the correct services in most cases. Use of computer communication is still typically much more expensive than a telephone call for everyone except those who have free access at work.

The situation is somewhat different when it comes to unusual activities. An example includes the Swede who, in the early days of deregulation, wanted to find the cheapest electricity supplier, and found that NUTEK (a government agency for industrial development) had a complete list, including prices, on the Web. Or the people in the Stockwerp tests who discovered the huge amount of tourist information on the Web and realized that there was in fact a new tool for planning their vacation available right under their noses.

Even rather simple ESM activities at the analysis level more often than not create new insights among users as well as among Webmasters (and the like). It is not uncommon for Webmasters to be almost shocked to hear that, for instance, only 80% of users find what they are looking for, and in some cases only 60% succeed. Or that students do not use the "Web course material" online as the producers intended, but print it out and read it as a book, and – which is typically the worst shock – say they would prefer to have it delivered in print in the first place so they wouldn't have to bother with looking it up on the Web and taking the time to print it out.

At the *production level*, ESM activities have to do with providing support in realizing improvements. Analyses of systems may lead to finding that there is a need to improve them. Usability studies give some advice on just what to do, but implementing that advice is a different matter. Usability studies can often clearly tell what is not good, but getting things right can be done in many ways, and one necessary condition is mastering the art of adapting systems to local conditions. However, the whole point of an ESM is to facilitate service delivery by applying a common business model to them all. This may include producing everything for the customers, but it may also include setting up a number of requirements, from a usability and usefulness point of view, which service providers can use as guidelines for their own production, arranging seminars or other educational and – don't forget – community-fostering activities. The ESM role at this level can be one of managing production, but it can just as easily be one of licensing service producers (not necessarily in a formal way) as a means of fostering common ideals, and in this way contributing over time to the convergence of different service providers' systems.

Realistically, both these ways of working will have to be applied by most ESMs.


## Technology

*Analysis level.* An ESM will attract service providers with different backgrounds. Some will be new to electronic services, some will have already invested considerably. One purpose of an ESM is to reduce the risks involved in using new and developing technology by using a common technical infrastructure.

One first step is therefore to assess the customer's technical setup in order to find out how efficient it is and how, if at all, it can be integrated in the common infrastructure. This may not be possible immediately, so many different kinds of solution are foreseen.

Many cities have a working technical infrastructure – networks, servers, service organization etc. – but not one adapted for cross-departmental information production, user self-service or market communication; all those things that pertain to efficient electronic services. Or they have different organizations for the different functions. In any case, the time until a city's electronic services can be technically aligned with those of other providers under an ESM umbrella can be considerable. This means that an ESM must be open to temporary solutions of many kinds. Because cities typically need a long time to make decisions about infrastructure, it is often not feasible to push hard for immediate compliance, even if that would be economically correct.

In any case, the ESM's task at the analysis level is to make clear to a provider the feasibility of its current technical infrastructure, as well as outlining a road towards compliance with the common ESM infrastructure. The ESM needs both good arguments – which can come only from having enough competence in the area – and endurance to bridge the (possibly long) period of tentative solutions until the necessary decisions are made by the public sector service providers.

At the *production level,* the role of an ESM is to provide advice and support concerning software modules to service providers. As we discussed in Challenge 5, the Internet area is technically volatile, and any advice can only be more or less informed assumptions about the future. However, being better informed rather than less is one of the advantages that an ESM can achieve by the nature of its role. The ESM task in this area is to invest in expertise in the area and promote a common technological standard among service providers. Since this is best done on a large scale, it would be an advantage if many ESMs cooperate. The best development would be to see an "ESM advisory board" being established as a cooperative effort among several ESMs, but a local or regional ESM of some size and high level of competence in the area should be able to do plenty of good on its own.

At the *policy level*, we want to see ESMs engage in what we would like to call *usability championship*. Much of the product development on the Internet today is done to support the development of global businesses. Although certainly some of these efforts will result in tools that are also useful for individuals, small businesses and government, there will be areas that are not covered. The ESM role here should be to solicit product ideas among the user community and organize product development in joint efforts with software producers. By drawing on usability standards and a large organized user community, an ESM could reach a position as a valuable contact between users and producers.

Cities should not become software producers, and neither should ESMs. One general problem in government-funded use projects, such as the European Union Information Society Technologies programme as well as similar ones at national level, is that it is very hard to follow up projects. During many projects, some good ideas for products will arise, but a major problem is to take care of such ideas after the project period. The organization is gone, there is no budget and good ideas will typically be rapidly forgotten. Product development is not a part of a city's usual business, and business partners in EU projects are typically there to market the products they already have rather than producing new ones

In fact, good ideas are not just forgotten. They are forgotten over and over again. We have looked at many IT use projects, and we find that typically they all find similar problems, but do not manage to make much change during the project period, and are not able to pursue the ideas after the project period. This means that the wheel is reinvented over and over again. Or rather, the idea for a wheel is born over and over again, but no wheel gets beyond the prototype stage, if it even gets that far. There are millions of euros spent on cities producing home pages with no innovative touch whatsoever. Pages that teenagers could build for next to nothing cost millions when several cities in several countries have to decide on matters. "Style guides" are produced again and again by different projects, none of them adding anything of importance to those that are already available for free on the Internet (see Challenge 8 for a sample). In fact, many, if not most, of them are incomplete, created *ad hoc* from a local situation with the only purpose being to meet project delivery deadlines and minimum requirements, without taking in existing knowledge in the field.

This is a pity, because the findings from projects where cities or others have tried to use IT are desperately needed in product development. An ESM, or ESMs in concert, have a role to play here. Because ESMs organize many services, and must invest in gaining market knowledge, they will be sources of valuable information about users and the use of services. An ESM could even formalize user communication by setting up a network of user organizations (see "Organization" below). In this way, the ESMs will be interesting as partners for software houses. ESMs could serve as test beds for new products, and as development partners in a way that is completely impossible under the project-by-project user–business cooperation that is current practice.

Let us provide an example to illustrate the above.

> The "Infosond Eyescool" navigator was developed within the Infosond project. It was implemented as a prototype version in SiliVille, a Stockwerp suburb. It works well, and it fills a gap: there is no product available that does what it does, and there should be one, because it gives obvious advantages to users. It complements existing products and builds on them. It has received positive independent evaluation. However, in order to become a product, development resources need to be found on a long-term basis. For example, advances within the field of linguistic techniques are being made, for instance, by the companies constructing search engines, and these advances must be incorporated into the tool. Such knowledge is rare and expensive, which means it can only be acquired by big companies. Also, a potent production and sales organization is needed to motivate investment in product development, which can only be found within the industry. On the other hand, experiences from use (such as how to handle interactivity and local adaptation) rest with the project staff and management alone; software companies do not have it. In this situation, a joint effort would be necessary to progress any further. For businesses, the purpose would be to integrate their products into a subtler tool, at the same time reaching a growing user community of (partly new) customers. For the ESM that would be the partner in the endeavour, the purpose would be to refine the prototype into a better tool, which not only functions better but is also sellable to others, thus generating revenue.

As things are, this nice product idea is likely to be forgotten. Had it been invented in a network of service providers coordinated by a strong ESM, the situation could have been much different. An ESM, if big enough itself, or else in cooperation with other ESMs, could gain a key position between software producers and users. It would be able to organize users, soliciting and defining new product ideas on the one hand and engaging in industry contacts and providing tests and user access on the other. ESMs in cooperation would be able to disseminate good examples all across the European continent.

## Organization

It is very hard to change organizational procedures. It is clear that adding more IT to existing procedures is not effective; what are needed are more effective procedures. IT can help, but it is not in itself a solution. Paul Strassman has researched into any links between IT spending and profitability over many years, and found none: "Profitability and spending on computers are unrelated because they are influenced by the way a company is organized and managed and not by the choices of technology. Looking for a 'technology fix' to problems that are fundamentally managerial must end up in failure" (Strassman, 1997).

There are certainly many managerial issues involved in creating effective electronic services. We have shown in Part 1 of this book that electronic services are often cross-departmental in that they require information from more than one department. They are also disruptive in that they require professional or departmental monopolies or territories to shrink.

Although many projects funded by the EU set out to use IT to achieve more effective procedures, most fail because they can never operate with the necessary time horizon. First, two or three years is not long enough to achieve credibility and support for the actions envisioned. Second, the purpose for cities engaging in telematic projects is not to achieve change. It is rather to get some funding for projects they have started or are going to start anyway. So "IT projects" are interesting because a city may get a million or two to invest in their fibre network, or to pump into their IT department, or for some other project. Project leaders wanting to achieve changes beyond that have a hard time gaining credibility. Because most cities have not yet reached the latter half of the challenges, issues of organizational change in connection with electronic services still rank low on the agenda. To gain credibility for such issues, such as those concerning usability and usefulness, there is a need for a strong, competent actor with local anchorage: an ESM.

The ESM's task in the field of organization is at the *policy level* to promote the idea that organizational change is necessary if IT investments are to be rewarded tangibly. Trivial as it may seem, it is not. In 1998 there was a worldwide TV commercial by one of the largest computer consultant companies, the message of which was: "it is not an IT issue, it is a management issue". The fact that not even this very big and renowned company can get the message across without spending hours and hours in each project explaining it says something about the magnitude of the problem.

As in the case of usability, this idea cannot be promoted without substantial backing from the local arena. Therefore, at the *analysis level*, the ESM must be competent to assess the service providers' organization for delivery of electronic services. Such analysis will show inefficiencies such as work being duplicated because the activities of many departments overlap, and because there are strong-willed entrepreneurs in many places (recall the "Clashing Conquistadors" story in Challenge 6). It will also show services being produced which have no customer base or no economic or service meaning, as well as user requirements which are not detected and not met by any service provider.

It will also show different city departments having very different visions about how things should be arranged. Therefore, at the *production level*, the role of the ESM is assisting in setting up and implementing a strategy for electronic services.

One part of this strategy is most likely organizing a user community and facilities. Communities must be created to promote issues where cooperation is necessary. Examples include the "Services to the citizens" group in Stockwerp (see Challenge 6) dealing with coordination and mediation among the 24 districts, which each have service delivery points which have some degree of independence and need some level of coordination and common standards. Another example is the Nordic Network of Citizen Offices, in which over several years enthusiasts from cities in countries in northern Europe engaging in the idea of "Citizen Offices" or "One-stop shops to the public sector", have met to discuss issues and strategies for the future (Ministry of the Interior, 1993).

It would be very useful for an ESM to be a hub in several such networks of users. In this way, the different groups could be cross-fed, thus gaining in interest and enlightenment. This is of course most important, because the other – and the main – ESM task is to design and implement a common business model for electronic services. The different user communities are only one part of this work, but an important one in that they serve both as sources of ideas and as forums for disseminating and gaining understanding and acceptance for ideas.

## Economy

Assessing investments in IT is hard. Assessing investments in Internet technology is harder. There is a story that aptly illustrates this, about a famous professor who suggested that in order to tell the good MBA students from the others, they should be given the task of evaluating IT investment in some companies. They should have all the relevant data on investments, production, and other aspects. The ones who come up with an answer should be fired.

While all agree that simple return on investment measures are not enough, several models have been developed to measure the intangible benefits and costs in order to be able to assess investments beforehand or evaluate them afterwards. Intangibles typically involve estimates of strategic values, intellectual assets, risks etc. We have found in our work that all cities motivate their systems for electronic services by strategic value only. This may be wise in a situation where most of the variables are uncertain. Still, it seems that most would need a more structured approach – and many indeed ask for such. In the long run, it sticks in people's minds that rather large investments are made without clear follow-up on what they have cost and what they have delivered.

Although the area is complex, one important task for an ESM is to help service providers assess the costs and benefits of their investment. Although there are no agreed-upon standards for measurement, there are candidate methods that can at least be used as a start. And given the lack of a universal standard, at least cooperation within a city or a region would be greatly facilitated if there were clear common standards and views.

At the *analysis level*, then, the task of an ESM would be to assess the customer's service provision system according to some model, either the one we have used as an example here or some other model. This would be for the main reason of raising awareness and firing discussions on how things should be measured.

At the *production level*, the ESM should assist cities in setting up their own assessment model. This work should be based on some of the existing models, but be very open to local conditions and ambitions. This is a very tricky task in the public sector, in which people are not used to thinking in such terms at all. Investments are typically made according to a budget, and a larger budget is most often gained by reference to "citizen needs", "equality", "neglected area for many years" etc. – in other words, for political reasons rather than economic reasons or those related to measurements of service quality.

At the *policy level*, the obvious task is to promote the view of following up investments on a clear and sound basis. "Clear" means explicit and well defined. "Sound" means a locally decided mix of economic measures and social and political values, and this is the biggest trick, of course. However, in many countries, the idea of also measuring performance in the public sector is gaining some ground, although measures are typically simplistic. The work of a proficient ESM will provide a long-awaited contribution to the improvement of this process.

# 16. Conclusions

To conclude this book, let us briefly summarize our advice to cities wanting to start their own electronic services, or wanting to improve those already existing. The advice is organized according to the four-leafed clover of the ESM model: users, organization, economy and technology, in that order. This order is determined by the relative importance of each leaf of the clover.

The advice is necessarily in the form of "things to consider" rather than exact specifications of how to do it. There are many ways to go about doing things, and in any organization making things happen is always something of an art. Each piece of advice has a reference to a corresponding chapter in Part 1, where more explanations and illustrations are provided. But even so, we are not talking about straightforward things like finding out what Web server to buy. We are talking about *initiating and maintaining a process of changing to a new concept of doing business, or serving citizens*. This change calls for considerable expertise and skill. Reading a list of good advice is not enough: it has to be combined with great skill in a number of fields. Neither is it possible to detail every action that has to be taken to succeed. The art of implementing the advice is a skill that the professional ESM must develop.

## The User Perspective

*Users of municipal sites do not surf.* They are acutely trying to solve a problem, often under pressure of time (Challenge 8). To help them in doing that, you must:

- *support the whole problem-solving chain* (orientation–investigation–choice–implementation; Challenge 11). To be able to do that, you must...
- integrate media – do not separate the Web from other methods of service delivery, such as telephone and manual services (Challenge 10). To be able to do that, you must...
- organize your information to *reflect the way that users conceptualize the task* at hand rather than the organizational structure of your organization (Challenge 8).

Some factors that characterize users of the kind of service sites that cities have are the following:

- Users are typically unfamiliar with the service contents and forms of delivery. Therefore you must *design your site for the occasional user*, and provide translation from the user's problem to the organization's solution (problem/task translator). Do not leave this burden to the users; they will then call you instead of using your site. Or call someone else (Challenge 8).

- Users typically visit municipal sites only when in acute trouble. *The time needed to find a solution is therefore critical.* This includes time to start the computer and log in, but also *time spent waiting,* which means waiting for pages to load and for search engines to come up with an answer (Challenges 8 and 9).
- Provide *completeness in coverage:* While "portal" is the in-word today, what you need is a "navigator": a single place to go from where all services can be found, and where you provide the best possible help in finding things (Challenges 8 and 9).
- There must be as *short a way from problem to solution* as possible (Challenge 10).
- Make sure that users find added value in using your system *now* (Challenge 11). Value comes first, use later, not the other way around (this is not equally true for hobby sites). And it is the users who decide what is added value.

*Your system competes with other systems* for service delivery, for instance the telephone. It may also compete with others' systems, in the case of tourist information, for instance. Therefore, you must either leave the job to others (an attractive solution in many cases) or make your system give the users added value compared with other systems:

- Figure out why users come to your system, in what situations they do so, and who they are (characteristics, not identity).
- Design the system also for the more *complicated tasks,* for instance when users explore alternative solutions or when a solution requires more than one contact and action (Challenge 8).

*Terminology* must be consistent (Challenge 8).

- Terminology must be in accordance with *users' ways of naming things.* When this can't be achieved directly, *translation from the users' language to the professional* one – the official as well as the local – must be provided, for instance in search engines (Challenge 8).
- The *semantic links* in the system must be clear. This means that users must be able to tell what is behind a link (Challenge 8).
- The site must be built on a consistent and simple *mental model,* for instance a pyramid or a ring (Challenge 8).
- Use a simple *system structure* (Challenge 8).
- Avoid *cognitive overload* (Challenge 8). Do not put too much on the screen: your system is a tool, not an action movie.
- Provide a consistent *navigation system* (Challenge 8). Different users prefer different navigation methods depending for the most part on their *expertise in the task domain* (*note:* not so much their technical expertise); novices click, the more experienced use the search engine. Offer both methods, but in a consistent way.
- There must be proper and understandable *system cues.* Menu text must be intelligible for other than domain experts and search engines must indicate whether they are finished or still working, and the same goes for page loading etc.

- Design your systems according to *Web standards* whenever possible (which is typically more often than the enthusiastic do-it-yourself Web designer thinks and enough for any city system). Do not attempt to reinvent the wheel; use the style guides that are available.

*Evaluate* your system. Before you spend a lot of time designing your own wheel, test what you have:

- What is *really* a mess can be relatively easily decided by a test against Web usability design standards (benchmarking). Do that.
- If the system is not a total mess, but simply has an inconsistent appearance, do a usability test with real users to see to what extent the diverse appearance is a problem for them. Other candidates for poor usability are inconsistent terminology, cognitive overload, poor organization of information, wrong information in relation to user problems etc. Spend your resources first on the problems that cause the worst problems for the users (Challenge 3).

*Organize the service improvement process* (Challenge 6). You cannot build the perfect Web site on your first attempt. Technology develops and demands increase with increasing use; your understanding of these demands will also increase, provided you keep your eyes open. How do you do that? The usefulness and usability of a Web site have to do not only with appearance, but also – and most of all – with content. Some kind of *editorial board* must be set up to address the issues pertaining to service content, methods of delivery (for instance use of different media), system appearance on behalf of the organization as a whole, usage patterns, usage problems etc. The editorial board must keep updated on all activities of the city within the field of the Internet, as well as best practices in the trade. Tasks include:

- Deciding what "corporate profile"/attitude towards clients you want, and specifying this at a guiding but not too creativity-restricting level of detail.
- Deciding on standards and guidelines for content, again at a reasonable level of detail.
- Deciding on update frequency, when necessary, and other quality-of-service matters.
- Making evaluations of use of services and *using them* to improve quality.
- Keeping informed on the new possibilities of the Internet, in order to implement them within the city.
- Trying to understand users' requirements, demands and wishes, not just as a reaction to direct complaints, but to spot the directions that use is likely to take in the future.
- Encouraging local Web champions who want to try to experiment with more advanced systems or new kinds of services.
- Propagating results of such experiments within the organization.

This list could be continued, but perhaps the most important advice is: *do not let political correctness obscure reason.* Build services based only on user requirements and economic reason. Do not produce systems for the "elderly" or "handicapped" for political reasons without analyzing the need for the service. *If* a certain service would be of benefit to middle-aged men and *if* providing this service would mean savings for your organization, do build it instead of another one that is directed towards the elderly or the handicapped but which would not be used. The experiences you gain from this will be useful the day you find a reasonable service directed towards the elderly. Self-service has great potential, but it is important to choose the right context. What you most of all need to think about is the usefulness of your services:

- How many of your users will access your electronic service over time?
- How will they come to it?
- Why do they use (a) the Web in general and (b) your service – are there synergies?
- What kind of value-added services would be helpful for your electronic service?
- How can you follow the usage of your service?
- What would be the ideal service your users could get? In the case of public services, it is necessary to consider the option of letting others provide a service. The public sector is not obliged to produce everything itself. Neither must you do everything yourself. Small companies and small cities, for instance, often have a lot to gain by doing things together, especially when they are done in similar ways in both places anyway, for instance sharing a system for booking and information.

Now here is some more detailed advice on what you need to know, how you can find out, and how to proceed when good ideas show up.

### What You Need to Know

- Find out what users ask for, instead of pushing out what you have (Challenges 8 and 9).
- Test your system against users' tasks. Use real users, use services that are in demand and frame them in situations that make sense – are the problems real? Does the system really support users in their efforts to solve their problems? (Challenges 8 and 9).
- Identify your main user groups – who are they, how many, what characteristics do they have; age, sex, socio-economic status etc.? It is a sure bet that the user groups do *not* include everyone. And we do not mean your most important constituents or your most important customers, but precisely those who are in fact going to use your system (Challenge 11).
- Look at the access possibilities – technical and practical – that your user groups have now and in the near future (Challenge 9).
- Identify what your user groups require – what information, what services, what navigation/search methods, what the preferred way(s) of being addressed are (Challenges 8 and 9).
- Identify when your user groups want to use the service – every day, weekly, once a year?
- Identify in what situations your user groups will use your services – from work during daytime, from home at night or at weekends, from a kiosk on the street on their way home from work, at the post office while waiting in a line (Challenge 5).

- Identify what gains – in time, money, convenience etc. – your users are able to make by using your service instead of the alternatives. (Challenges 4 and 11).
- Make sure that use of the system is well measured to improve your service when possible. The number of hits on your home page usually does not mean anything (Challenge 2).
- And once you have an electronic system, be serious about interaction; answer emails politely, promptly, correctly and to the point (Challenge 10).

### How to Find Out?

- Prototype, involving users in tests. It is not enough to ask them, you must show and test things. Start with a really necessary service (Challenge 6).
- Develop methods for following user behaviour/requirements. There are several methods, but you need one that works in your organization and realistically will be used (Challenge 6).
- Offer a service that is as understandable, comprehensive, easy to use and well-structured according to user ergonomics as possible. This is the only way to make use grow so as to make the above points at all relevant (Challenge 8).

### Do You Really Want to Provide This?

- Some organizations have well-defined client interactions, and large volumes of them. For others, not least cities, it is the other way around: there are numerous types of contact, each with low frequency, and many different kinds of clients. The first question to ask yourself is which of these you really need to maintain. While cities have services in many fields, neither the number of services nor the number of fields are determined automatically. Perhaps some services can be provided better by others? There are public sector agencies at other levels (regional, national), and there are private companies that can do some things that do not have to do with the exertion of authority (an example is tourist information). Perhaps several small cities could join forces.
- Identify your main goals, what client interactions you want to have, and what possibilities you have to maintain these in a good way (Challenge 10).
- Decide what functionality you want to offer to your end users, and what you can leave to others (Challenge 11).

# The Organizational Perspective

*Build services on added user value* (Challenge 4):

- Select a popular service (one that is popular elsewhere, or has a good chance of becoming popular through you).
- Give users a genuine improvement of service. Make sure your users gain or save something by using your service. If the electronic version of a service does not save any of the user's effort, he or she will not use it.

- Use electronic services in the first place to eliminate simple, tedious service processes. Choose services where people currently merely investigate documents, fill in a form, choose something from a list, make calculations by fixed rules etc. – not ones where it is necessary to communicate with other people (note that even filling in forms may require this).
- Insert the electronic component of a service seamlessly into current operational practice, with minimal change to established working patterns (unless the advantages of new routines are apparent to people involved).
- Once you have a service that is used, find a way to achieve savings.
- Monetary savings are not the only way to realize benefits. Could you get income by expanding, selling or exporting your service? Or perhaps you can avoid complaints, returns of purchased goods etc.?
- What kind of economies of scale can be achieved?
- Can outsourcing be economic?

*Make sure you have the support of* (Challenge 6):

- Top *managers* – endurance is necessary, as engaging in electronic services means a long-term commitment, and endurance cannot be achieved without the support of the strategic management (Challenge 6).
- *Change agents*, those people who make things happen (Challenge 7).
- The professionals – enrol them in your team. Do not rush into implementation. Make sure that they too get advantages, not just more work (Challenge 7).

*Project success factors* (Challenge 4):

- Positive publicity, internally and externally.
- A joint venture is often a good idea. At least you have a partner to help you push the wheelbarrow.
- Script attractive roles for partners. No one should have to stand in the shadow of some other partner, no one should have to take the role of subcontractor to someone else involuntarily etc.
- Bring along a prominent partner; this is good for durability, visibility and reputation.
- Perhaps the single most important piece of advice in this category is *do not let organizational domains come before usage requirements (market needs)* (Challenge 6).
- Set up a managerial "editorial board"/mediation group which operates across departments and which has a strong mandate. This is needed as an arena for handling the negotiation and learning processes, and for discussing how to relate to issues of content, organizational change and technology. The trick is to create space for the development of new competence and to give it a platform within the organization, at the same time as it has to support the transformation of old static IT solutions into a Web-based – which means more integrated – context.
- The work of bringing cross-departmental data and legacy data onto a Web site is also genuinely complex and time-consuming. The editorial board is required to keep a steady course.

- In order to make this work effective a strong mandate from top managers is necessary.
- The need for information, education and discussion around this new development cannot be underestimated, *but* this must be done in the context of development and concrete challenges, not separately as isolated courses on this or that technology or management concept. This task can be named *vision management*.
- EU projects can be an important trigger for the development of such needed integration competence, *provided* they are not seen just as an increased cash flow.

*Integrate media – do not separate the Web from other methods of service delivery* (Challenge 11):

- Identify what services you want to offer. Begin with the most used or most asked for services (Challenge 10).
- Identify your data sources: start by using data that are already contained in the database and which are part of the core processes within your city (Challenge 6).
- Identify which departments are responsible for, and own, the underlying data.
- Involve the people who are offering existing services, as they are the most immediate source of knowledge about users and services as they currently are (Challenge 7).
- Make a clear division of responsibilities between the Infomaster (the one who knows the task domain and how this is presented on the Web), the Webmaster (technical responsibility) and help desk functionality. The user who has a problem using a service does not want to talk to a Webmaster (Challenges 2 and 6).
- Make shifts in people's tasks; do not ask them to work *more*, ask them to work *differently* (Challenge 7).
- Make sure that there are opportunities for people to learn what they have to know. This does not necessarily mean formal courses, but assigning new tasks without offering the opportunity to update or change a person's skill when necessary will prove devastating for service quality and people's confidence in, and support for, the change process.
- Involve management in using new information technology. Their importance as role models is not to be underestimated (Challenge 6).
- Do not organize everything as a project (a temporary undertaking), but make sure that positive things that come out of projects are made into lasting changes – new processes – within your organization (Challenge 2).

## The Economic Perspective

*Set your goals*:

- What would be the ideal composition of an ideal service for your users? (Challenges 4 and 11)

- What would be the ideal role of your organization in delivering such services in that way?
- Who would the complementary content providers be, and what would their roles be, in your ideal electronic service?
- What would the ideal workflow and interaction structure behind such services look like? (Challenge 11)
- Who can you realistically get to join you in building the ideal service? (Challenge 4)

*Focus your plans*:

- *Create a cost/benefit model that reaches beyond ROI*, that *encompasses the use domain* and that is *measurable*.
- *Use it!* Many projects are started with goals like "better democracy", "getting closer to the citizen". Be more concrete! (Challenge 9)

While there are many models, the important thing is to go beyond ROI, and make sure the model, whichever you use, is well understood and established within your organization. The model you choose must:

- be easy to use
- give understandable results
- encompass the use domain, not only the technological domain

Our example model – which is just an example, not the only possible one – includes the following factors, which together give a broad perspective on the investment:

- *Strategic match* (how does the system support or align with stated business goals?)
- *Competitive advantage* (what makes this service unique?)
- *Management information* (to what degree does the project provide management information on the core activities of the enterprise or line of business?)
- *Competitive response* (to what degree does failure to produce the system cause competitive damage to the enterprise?)
- *Project or organizational risk* (to what degree is the organization capable of carrying out the changes required by the project?)
- *Strategic IS infrastructure* (to what degree is the project aligned with the overall information systems strategies in the organization?)
- *Definitional uncertainty* (to what degree are requirements and specifications known? How great is the complexity of the area and the probability of non-routine changes in the information system?)
- *Technical uncertainty* (how great is the readiness of the technology domain to undertake the project regarding skills required, hardware dependencies, software dependencies and application software?)
- *IS infrastructure risk* (how much non-project investment is necessary to accommodate the project?)

*Be realistic*:

- Do not think you are going to make money or change working patterns quickly. Prepare for a long-term commitment (Challenge 9).
- Make sure you take yearly costs into account, not only for updating services, but also for training personnel, updating hardware and software, promotional budget, evaluations etc.

*Compare with what you do today (do you know what you do?)*:

- Make an estimate of how much things cost the way they are organized now (measure it) so that you can see what impact your forthcoming changes will make (Challenge 9).
- Offer services at reasonable prices. People have already spent money for their Internet subscriptions and telephone use. Do not try to recoup your investment in a too short a time.
- Reserve a marketing and promotion budget to make sure you can help people find your new services.

*Replace, don't just add*:

- Reduce your spending on old services as soon as the new ones become available (Challenge 4).
- Give your staff new tasks, not just more work.
- Use European and national funding to make your services and organizational changes permanent.
- Employ a long-term perspective.

*Do not go chasing new technology*:

- Do not spent too much money on buying techniques and hiring consultants; use your own intuition and your own personnel whenever possible (Challenge 5).

*Integrate your operations*:

- Look for economies of scale when purchasing hardware and software.
- Look for economies of scale in reorganizing your production. Don't forget to look for partners – you don't always have to do everything yourself.

# The Technical Perspective

*Define your role (Challenge 10)*:

- This is particularly important for public sector organizations. Cities should normally not be at the forefront of technical innovation. A little bit behind – not too far – the water is calmer, and both the level of investment and the level of risk are lower.
- Build upon off-the-shelf technology.
- Be innovative in service processes rather than in technology.

- Define your role with respect to other players, public or private. An appropriate role for a big city (where many big players, private companies, also are) is often relatively smaller than that for a small town in a rural area (where the city is often the biggest player with a role in, for example, supporting local SMEs).

*Use open technology only (Challenge5):*

- Use Web-compatible technology only.
- Stick to state-of-the-art hardware and software which has already been proven to work (Challenge 5).
- Cities are not software houses. Do not try to write the software yourself (as a city): buy it.
- Make systems scalable, upgradeable and compatible rather than standardized (Challenge 5). You will never achieve "the" database structure. Use what you have (databases etc.) with a data warehouse approach in mind (which includes clear concepts, data dictionaries etc.).
- Beware of proprietary kiosk technology. It may have fancy editing tools, but if it is not Web-compatible it is a dead-end street.
- Do not delay development for fear of the Internet ("will it really reach everybody?"). It has already proved its usability for all kinds of sensitive services. The market will solve security and payment-related issues in due course, and governments will eventually endorse them (but this will take longer). Until then, build trials upon existing solutions.
- For communication with citizens and between city staff, push for wide adoption of email. This medium is already the mainstream way of communicating for millions of people.
- Don't go chasing new technology! It is very easy to become overwhelmed by the rapid technical developments on the Net, such as cameras and sound files. These are nice things, but users want services, not gadgets (this is different at leisure sites, but you are not building one of those).
- Pool resources (Challenge 5).
- Do not leave important decisions about technical development to each department, but to the ESM (Challenge 5).
- Document what you do. Personnel will change rapidly and knowledge about how things work will be lost. The dependence upon a few enthusiasts is a big problem in many organizations.

*Manage your consultants:*

- Both external consultants and city departments tend to see city services from a predefined viewpoint that fits nicely with their own business mission. Be aware of this bias when judging different technical metaphors to adopt, but do not let such a concern delay decisions. Do not let your consultants define your business (Challenge 5).
- Find out the basic facts about a number of relevant technical metaphors yourself.
- Try to start planning from a blank piece of paper, with the goal of providing good service to citizens with minimum trouble from the point of view of information access and storage.

- After formulating a vision (at least to yourself), see if you can find a metaphor that supports that vision. The metaphor should capture the service you want to create, not just the technology you use. This metaphor will be your most important tool in the contacts with your consultants. Without it you will get lost in their technical jargon.

- Be prepared to use external advice more than before: rapidly changing technologies force organizations to outsource an increasing portion of their planning.

# References

Abrahamsson, K. (1994) *Den lilla samhällsdialogen*. Stockholm: Fritzes.

Aktuellt (1998) *Aktuellt*. Swedish Television News, Channel 1, 31 August 1998.

Bevan, N. (1997) Usability issues in Web site design, in *Proceedings of HCI International '97*, San Francisco, 24–30 August, Elsevier.

Botkyrka (1996) *Botkyrka Service Cottages; use statistics 1987–1995*. Botkyrka: the Information Office.

Bowen, D. (1996) Presentation during the Electronic Democracy Panel at *2nd Annual Summit on Service to the Citizen*, Denver, Colorado, 28–29 February.

Brynjolfsson, E. and Hitt, L. (1998) Beyond computation: information technology, organizational transformation and business performance, in *Proceedings of ICIS*, Helsinki, Finland, 14–16 December.

Caudle, S., Gorr, W. and Newcomer, K. (1991) Key information systems management issues for the public sector. *MIS Quarterly*, 15/1991.

Dennis, A. R. (1998) Lessons from Three Years of Web Development. *Communications of the ACM*, 41(7).

D'Herbemont, O. and Cesar, B. (1998) *Managing Sensitive Projects – A Lateral Approach*. Basingstoke: Macmillan.

Dreyfus, H. L. and Dreyfus, S. E. (1986) *Mind over Machine. The Power of Human Intuition and Expertise in the Era of the Computer*. Oxford: Basil Blackwell.

Fletcher, P. and Otis Foy, D. (1994) Managing information systems in state and local government. *Annual Review of Information Science and Technology*, 29/1994.

Goldkuhl, G., Röstlinger, A., Hedström, K. and Hagdahl, A. (1998) Organization & utveckling av IT i kommuner. En översikt. (Organization and development of IT in municipalities. An overview). In *IT och kommunerna*. Svenska Kommunförbundet, Stockholm.

GP (1997). Kommunal IT-feber (Municipal IT fever). *Göteborgs-Posten*, 17 February 1997.

Grönlund, Å. (1998a) *Deliverable D7. Report on usability and prospected use*. Informatik Centrum Antwerp.

Grönlund, Å. (1998b) The Infosond "facilitator" – an interactive tool for tracking users' questions. *Proceedings of WebNet '98*, Association for the Advancement of Computing in Education, Charlottesville, PA, USA.

Grönlund, Å. and Jakobsson, M. (1997). *Infosond Project deliverable D7, Verification of demonstrator. Report on usability, user satisfaction, estimated usefulness and prospected use*. Informatik Centrum Antwerp.

Grönlund, Å. and Jakobsson, M. (1998) Användbarhetsstudie av SSVHs Webkursmaterial (*Usability study of the Web Course materials of SSVH*). Project report. Härnösand: SSVH, National Institute for Distance Education.

Hammer, M. and Champy, J. (1993) *Reengineering the Corporation: A Manifesto for Business*. New York: HarperCollins.

Hedberg, B., Dahlgren, G., Hansson, J. and Olve, N.-G. (1997) *Virtual Organizations and Beyond. Discover Imaginary Systems*. Chichester: John Wiley & Sons.

Holst, G.-M., Jörgensen, J., Thorngren, B., Vedin, B.-A., Viklund, B. (1999) *TELDOKs årsbok 2000 (TELDOK Yearbook 2000)*. TELDOK report 130. Stockholm: TELDOK.

Hope, J. and Hope, T. (1997) *Competing in the Third Wave. The Ten Key Management Issues of the Information Age*. Boston, MA: Harvard Business School Press.

Lutze, R., Albinson, L., DeBeukelaer, R. and Grönlund, Å. (1996) *Deliverable D3. Report on User Requirements, Functional Specification, and System Architecture.* Informatik Centrum Antwerp.

Johanson, R. and Mascanzoni, D. (1996) *Medborgarnätverk – IT i ett lokalt perspektiv (Citizen networks – IT in a local perspective).* Stockholm: Sveriges Tekniska Attachéer, Utlandsrapport Italien 9601.

Ministry of the Interior (1993) *Medborgarkontor – redovisning av pågående utvecklingsarbete (Citizen Offices – an account of ongoing development work).* Ds 1993:67, Stockholm: Ministry of the Interior.

Ministry of the Interior (1996) *Samhällsguiden (Guide to society).* Stockholm: Ministry of the Interior.

McKenney, J. L., Copeland, D. J. and Mason, R. O. (1995) *Waves of Change. Business Evolution through Information Technology.* Boston, MA: Harvard Business School Press.

Nielsen, J. (1990). Evaluating hypertext usability, in *Designing Hypermedia for Learning* (eds. D. H. Jonassen and H. Mandl). Berlin: Springer-Verlag, pp. 147–168.

Nielsen, J. (1996) *Why Frames Suck (Most of the Time).* http://www.useit.com/alertbox/9612.html.

Parker, M., Benson, R. and Trainor, H. E. (1988) *Information Economics: Linking Business Performance to Information Technology.* Englewood Cliffs, NJ: Prentice Hall.

Reid, G. (1995) Early life-cycle behaviour of micro-firms in Scotland. *Small Business Economics,* No. 7, pp. 89–95.

Rheingold, H. (1994) *The Virtual Community. Homesteading on the Electronic Frontier.* New York: HarperPerennial.

Schenker, J. L. (1998) Drawing fire: EU spends big on high-tech cities, but some ask, where's the payback. *Wall Street Journal,* Interactive Edition, 16 March.

Schivenaars, T. (1998) *Deliverable D8. Report on validation, revised functional design, cost/benefits and ergonomics.* Informatik Centrum Antwerp.

Schön, D. (1983). *The Reflective Practitioner.* New York: Basic Books.

Stewart, T. A. (1996) The invisible key to success. *Fortune,* 5 August, p. 125.

Stockholm (1995a) *Info '97; Report on the communication between the City of Stockholm and its citizens.* City of Stockholm: Social Services Department.

Stockholm (1995b) *Mellanlandning Skarpnäcksfältet (Landing at Skarpnäck); Report on the service in the district of Skarpnäck.* Stockholm: Utrednings- och statistikkontoret.

Strassman, P. (1997) *The Value of Computers, Information, and Knowledge.* http://www.strassman.com/pubs/cik/cik-value.html.

Svenska Kommunförbundet (1998) *IT och kommunerna. En översikt (IT and the municipalities. A survey).* Stockholm: Svenska kommunförbundet.

SUNET (1998) *Swedish University Network Directory Services,* http://www.sunet.se/.

Tsagarousianou, R., Tambini, D. and Bryan, C. (1998) *Cyberdemocracy – Technology, Cities and Civic Networks.* London: Routledge.

Da Villa, F. and Panizzolo, R. (1996) An empirical study of the adoption and implementation of advanced technologies in the Italian public sector. *International Journal of Technology Management,* 12(2).

Winnberg, H. (1995) *Datorisering till varje pris! En studie av informationsteknologi i kommuner (Computerization at any cost! A study of IT in municipalities).* Konferensen Kvalitet 95, Göteborg.

Österman, T. and Timander, J. (1997) *Internetanvändningen i Sveriges befolkning (Internet use in the Swedish population).* Stockholm: Teldok Report 115.

Öhrling, Coopers & Lybrand (1998) *Internetmarknaden i Sverige (The Internet Market in Sweden).* Stockholm.

# Index

# The Unified Proces
## for Practiti
### Object Ori

# PRACTITIONER SERIES

Series Editor: *Ray Paul*
Editorial Board: *Frank Bott, Nic Holt,*
*Kay Hughes, Elizabeth Hull,*
*Richard Nance, Russel Winder*

# These books are written
# by practitioners for practitioners.

They offer thoroughly practical hands-on advice on how to tackle specific
problems. So, if you are already a practitioner in the development,
exploitation or management of IS/IT systems, or you need to acquire an
awareness and knowledge of principles and current practice in an IT/IS topic
fast then these are the books for you.

All books in this series will be clear, concise and problem solving and will
cover a wide range of areas including:

- systems design techniques
- performance modelling
- cost and estimation control
- software maintenance
- quality assurance
- database design and administration
- HCI
- safety critical systems
- distributed computer systems
- internet and web applications
- communications, networks and security
- multimedia, hypermedia and digital libraries
- object technology
- client-server
- formal methods
- design approaches
- IT management

All books are, of course, available from all good booksellers (who can order
them even if they are not in stock), but if you have difficulties you can
contact the publishers direct, by telephoning +44 (0) 1483 418822 (in the UK
& Europe), +1/212/4 60/15 00 (in the USA), or by emailing orders@svl.co.uk

**www.springer.co.uk    www.springer.de**
**www.springer-ny.com**

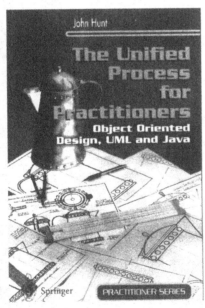